INTRO 7

EDITORIAL BOARD

INTRO 7

ALL OF US AND NONE OF YOU
and other original fiction and poetry
with a symposium on
Book Reviews in America

EDITED WITH AN INTRODUCTION BY GEORGE GARRETT

Assistant Editors—
James Whitehead and Miller Williams

ANCHOR BOOKS
Anchor Press/Doubleday
GARDEN CITY, NEW YORK

1975

The Anchor Books edition is the first publication of *Intro 7*.
Anchor Books edition: 1975

Library of Congress Cataloging in Publication Data

Intro 7
All of us and none of you

    1. College stories, American. 2. College verse, American. I. Garrett,
George P., 1929–   II. Whitehead, James. III. Williams, Miller.
IV. Series: Intro (New York, 1968–   ); 7.
PS508.C6I63   no. 7   811'.5'408
ISBN 0-385-07158-2
Library of Congress Catalog Card Number 74-33607

CONTENTS

II SYMPOSIUM

III POETRY

CONTENTS   *ix*

INTRODUCTION

By this time, the seventh year of the *Intro* series, there is no need for a long-winded introduction. Let these writers speak for themselves in their own voices. They do that very well and can do without gestures of editorial protection or puffery.

Still, there are a few things to be said.

There were a great many more submissions, more than ever this time, coming from all across the country. Which means, on the one hand, that we have a larger and more various gathering of fiction and poetry than we have had before. On the other hand, because this volume has to be at once selective and representative, many manuscripts of high quality could not be included within the limited boundaries of a single book. And that may mean a number of things. On the credit side, it is good evidence that in spite of the state of the economy and the thousand and one discouraging details of our times, there remains a growing number of gifted and working new writers out there, almost everywhere, who are so far undaunted. We have a surplus, an affluence of talent, lean years or no. But, of course, that also means that most of their work exists and circulates only in manuscript form and will continue to do so until, and if, occasion and blind chance combine to let some of them have a life in cold print. This volume of *Intro,* like its antecedents, will introduce some good writers, but there are many more who are worthy of introduction and worth your time and interest. I can wish that they may thrive and prosper in the exercise of their lonesome craft. And, more practically, I can hope for them, hope that they will prove tough enough and lucky enough to persevere.

All of the manuscripts were read, examined, and evaluated by

George Garrett   *xi*

people, writers themselves, who gave freely of time and energy to make this book happen. The final choices and selections, right and wrong, are all my own, my own burden of responsibility. But that burden was eased by the aid of the seventy-five or so writers and teachers who did the original scouting and reading. I received really invaluable help from my co-editors, James Whitehead and Miller Williams, outstanding writers and teachers, who read through reams of material and offered advice and counsel. I went my own way, but I wouldn't have gone very far without them.

The fiction, both the short stories and the excerpts from novels-in-progress, is varied in subject matter and treatment. The range is wide, from the modern *fabliau*, like David Reich's "Jocko's Tree" and Gary Gay's "Trombone Holiday," to Stan Lippman's Barthian fantasy "Still Life." We are offered a picture of the family life of Mexican-Americans in Rafael Zepeda's "The Cyclone Racer," and Sarah B. Davenport's "All of Us and None of You" (from which we take the title of the book) brilliantly dramatizes the conflicts and joys of a black family trying to survive in contemporary Richmond, Virginia. Real work, the hard labor in America that is so much of our experience yet so often absent in our fiction, is celebrated in the excerpts by Charles Minyard and Charles R. Richison and satirized in Austin Wilson's "La Cucaracha, La Cucaracha." These are good stories, and I find a couple (you may find others) which could hold their own in any anthology—Joanne Meschery's "Why Do Things Die in the Country?" and Tom Turner's "Tapering Off." For those who are looking for hints and clues to the imaginable future—and who isn't?—there is more of what is being called "the new realism." "Straight" stories, as distinguished from the fables and fantasies so prevalent in recent years, seem to be in the ascendant; though, labels and name tags aside, the range of technique, like the range of experience dealt with, is wide and inclusive.

The poetry—for which Miller Williams has written an introduction, saying the important things—has variety in form and content, too, although there seem to be, at the moment, more *habits*, both good and bad, among the new poets. If you look, you will see at least some indications of subtle changes in direction. My guess, for what it may be worth, is that there is a new kind of "formalism" in the future, not just around the corner, but at least within walking distance. But never mind my guesswork. Read and enjoy these poets for what they are doing and doing well.

The "Symposium" section of this volume, written especially for *Intro*, deals with the present condition of book reviewing in America.

Finally, it seems to me only fair, since the alphabetical order of the writers has always been arbitrary, to do it backward this time, if only to prove that even in the inequitable world of letters sometimes the last can be first.

George Garrett

INTRO 7

I FICTION

*Make it a journal of thoughts and impressions, she said,
not a diary of events. Nobody else can think like
you, not another soul can have the same
impressions.*

from "Cold She Moves Amid the Lambent Blaze"
by W. H. BATTERSHELL

Rafael Zepeda

THE CYCLONE RACER

A neon sign of a clown laughing hung over the entrance to the amusement park. Manuel was on Tío Salvador's shoulders, and he read the spaghetti-written letters that said, "Nu Pike of Long Beach."

Manuel's mother had left Mexico during the revolt, after her husband had been stopped and robbed by the guerrillas and was brought back to Ocotlán dead with his teeth kicked out for the gold. She had taken Manuel and boarded the train for Mexicali and then taken a bus to Los Angeles. She was afraid that her rich father-in-law would take Manuel away from her. Her mother and her brother had come to Los Angeles a year later.

"Míra," Mother said. "La luz; muy bonita."

"Míra alla," Tío Salvador said, and he pointed at the lights of the double ferris wheel that turned like a bicycle on a stick while both wheels turned.

Manuel, Tío Salvador, Mother, and Grandmother were there on a Sunday night. Mother wore a dress of spangled black fringe that she wore at other times to go dancing. Grandmother wore a flowered dress of light yellow and blue and she had a white mantilla draped around her neck. It was warm and there was no need to have it around her neck, but it was her habit to wear the mantilla.

Tío Salvador had been to the pike before, but none of the others had. He had come with two girls he had met at a dance in the colony. Driving over they had shared a bottle of tequila and two limes that were under the seat of the pickup truck. Salvador didn't remember their names, but he remembered that they were friendly and that they were fun that night, and he wondered if they were married by now. They went to confession too often—when he saw them again they had told him of confession—but there was nothing to confess, he thought, because tequila led where it led.

Past the tattoo parlor with the eagles and flags in the window, Manuel was like hod on Salvador's shoulders. Sal puffed his cigar, and when Manuel tipped his hat forward, he shouted, "Mi sombrero, cabrón, cuidado!"

Mother walked ahead, as if she were alone, and Grandmother walked alongside of Salvador. Mother turned and looked back to make sure they were coming, then went toward a mirror that was bent like an S from the side. She touched her hair lightly as she had seen Harlow do, to look like a movie star—like Harlow for someone to notice, at least to look.

Manuel's eyes were full of light. There was the music of the calliope coming through the park from the merry-go-round; coming boop-boop-ump—boop-boop-ump. "Where . . . what do we go on first?"

There were red and blue and yellow and black and green cars bumping red into yellow and black into blue. Couples in the cars held each other as the cars swerved and bounced. Women screeched. Men gritted their teeth. A red car hit a blue. Grandmother watched and laughed at the cars, and Tío Salvador laughed belly laughs that shook the boy so he had to grab onto Salvador's greasy hair.

"¡Cuidado! Manuel," Tío Salvador said. "Do you want to see the fish swimming?" he asked Grandmother.

"How can we see fish swimming?" she asked.

"The diving bell; I was there before."

Mother watched the couples bumping as if the others weren't there, but she heard Tío Sal and followed like Harlow.

"You should go, Mother. You owe it to him."

"I can't go. I'm afraid when I go. I can't."

"You owe it to him. He's your brother. He'd go for you."

"I didn't go to Mother's rosary. I never go. I'll go to church and say a rosary instead. I'll put on my black dress and hat and go to early mass in the morning. That would be enough."

"He's your brother."

"You go for me."

Sal put Manuel down on the ground and walked toward the diving bell, past the red and yellow double ferris wheel where he stopped for a moment and stood puffing his cigar and looked up at a descending white skirt, then a face that was laughing and surrounded by smooth yellow hair. The dress filled like a parachute when the wheel descended.

And when they walked on there were porcelain-faced dummies, a fat woman and a dwarfed man, which rolled forward and back laughing beneath a sign that said "Fun House" in neon. And there was cotton candy puffing into white paper cones that Mother stopped for and said, "Muy pretty, muy cute."

After Marguerite got the large pink puff and Tío Sal bought Manuel a smaller pink puff, they walked on toward the diving bell. They were near the ocean, where there were paintings of gray fish cut out of plywood and a round pool of water with hoses running in from a pump. Tío Sal bought the tickets, and when he came back they all watched the regular pop of the bubbles ascending to the top of the pool. They waited and watched, then the bell came up out of the water like a bar of soap. A spray of water passed over all of them as the eight-eyed bell bounced on top of the pool. A man with a blue captain's hat came to the fish net-covered gate and opened it to let the family in. His teeth had black spots on them, and he had a mustache that he chewed with his lip.

Father Mac took the aspergillum from the side of the kneeling bench and shook it from high to low three times, and he muttered . . .

"Avast, mateys," he said without enthusiasm. "Enter ye Davey Jones's locker." He smelled like spilled beer to Grandmother and she turned her head as she passed him.

Manuel smelled the dead, rotten fish as he followed behind

Grandmother up the four steps with Mother following and Tío Sal behind them all. When they all were inside, the man with the captain's hat came into the tank and closed the hatch, and another skinny man tapped twice from outside on the hatch's porthole.

"Everyone secure themselves around the portholes and hold onto the rail," the man inside said.

"There are fish here?" Mother said.

"There were before," Tío Sal said.

"Are we all secured?" the man said into a small microphone.

"Yeah," came the voice from the skinny man.

There was a sucking sound, and the bell went lower into the water until the portholes were covered. There were finger marks and nose smudges on the glass, and Tío Sal rubbed the glass with his handkerchief, then lifted Manuel up along his side to let him see out. Bubbles covered the glass, then started to pop from the center out until only the edge was covered with bubbles. "Where are the fish?" Manuel asked.

"Mother isn't coming. Just me and Luis."

"She must feel very bad not to come to her own brother's rosary," Tía Rachel said.

"She said she'll go to mass and light a cross of candles."

"Oh, she must feel very bad. Pope John died too. That could be part of it."

"I haven't seen any yet," Tío Sal said. "There's something."

"Donde?" Grandmother said. "There is nothing." Because she knew Sal as a mother of twenty-five years knows those whom she has raised and she thought that he saw things that weren't there and knew he thought he was a rancher with his hat and cigar, or perhaps he thought he was a reborn General Villa with the wife Sal had left in Ocotlán and the two daughters he didn't care for.

"I see it," Manuel said. "Out this window, Grandmother."

Through the brown and green murk a silhouette was moving. A form of a small shark circled and came to the porthole and nudged it softly with his snout. He was small; a baby shark. The tank for him was like the tank for them.

"He looks like a baby," Sal said.

"Can he break in?" Mother said.

"The tank is cast iron," the man said, and he grinned. "The glass is an inch thick."

"And dirty," Grandmother said.

He ignored her.

"And the water," Mother said.

"Fresh sea water. Just pumped it in yesterday," he said.

A tentacle like a hanging snake hung down in front of the port-hole where Grandmother stood.

"Our octopus," the man said.

"Look at it," Manuel said.

Cups like rubber darts slid across the glass.

"This one is smaller than the last one I saw here," Tío Sal said, and he laughed to himself and thought that perhaps he had seen the octopus before, for he could not see much after the tequila.

"Hold on. We're going up," the man said.

"We just came down. Just a few more moments," Sal said. "What happened to the big octopus?"

"He got sick on us. We had to pull him."

"He was a big one."

"Yeah, we have to go up."

Mother said, "Let's go up. Yes?" and she looked at Salvador, her brother, for she was uncomfortable and perspiring, and the dress would stain and smell like fish or her make-up would run. "Let's go up."

". . . the father almighty, creator of heaven and earth; and in Jesus Christ, his only Son, our . . ."

The bell came up above the water with the brown water from below dripping from the porthole glass. It bounced, then began to hum as it leveled off with the outside steps. The man looked around inside the bell, then leaned over and opened the latches of the hatch. He pushed the door open, and the dead-fish smell, which was better then than the air of the bell, came into the tank.

All went out with Manuel and the man followed last.

The ferris wheel had stopped turning and loaded people onto the wheel near the ramp. Some sat three to a swinging seat and some two.

Rafael Zepeda

"You can see the harbor and the city lights from the wheel on top. Who wants to come?" Sal asked.

"I'll go," Manuel said.

"Marguerite?" he asked Mother.

"It's very high," she said.

"They strap you in," Sal said.

"Yes, I'll go see to look at the lights," she said.

"I'll stay here this time," Grandmother said.

And Manuel wondered how his Tío Sal had been on the ride before and who looked out from the wheel with him before, because he saw Sal look up to where the girl with the white dress and yellow hair sat on the top wheel, rocking like a pendulum and looking down. She waved down at a group of passing sailors who waved up at her. The boy she was with kept looking away.

Manuel hoped that there was no danger and he wondered if anyone had ever fallen, but he thought not because the wheel was still turning and it wouldn't run if someone had fallen.

Salvador bought three tickets that time.

Mother said, "I won't be frightened?"

"No, let's get on. Come on." And to Sal, Marguerite had been trouble, for she was five years older than he and what he wanted wasn't her sitting next to him but the girl from the top wheel. He thought as he looked up, with his cigar pointing, what could be with the girl if there was a chance, but there was no chance, he knew, with Marguerite and the rest there, and he walked toward the chairs of the wheel.

Manuel got up onto the chair that was like a church pew, only painted red and yellow. Sal and Marguerite came behind Manuel and sat on either side of him. Then a tall man came and pulled the red paint-worn bar across their laps, but there was no strap.

No one else waited to get onto the wheel, so a man with skinny arms walked to a tin shack and pulled a lever that made the wheel turn. The wheel the three were on turned while the opposite wheel turned, and both of those wheels turned around the center like a baton that twirls on turning fingers. The wheel the three were on swung up to be the top wheel and Manuel could see Grandmother small below.

Manuel held onto the cross bar and locked his feet under a

turned piece of steel that came from the chair. From the top the lights were all colors across the pike until they stopped at the water's edge. From there the reflected light continued into the water, then there was just blackness, and still farther out in the distance a green and a red light in the black that marked the entrance to the sea wall.

On the water's edge was a high, rolling structure. It was like a building without walls, and there was a red neon star at its peak. Manuel could hear squeals coming from the building without walls and the three hill-like peaks in graduated heights; high, with a red star on top, lower, with no star, and the lowest peak with a small blue star on top.

"What is that?" Manuel asked, and pointed.

"The Cyclone Racer . . . roller coaster," Sal said. He looked toward it. "Maybe we'll go on it . . . a nice view from here, eh, Marguerite?"

"Yes, but too high. It scares me. You should have known and told me."

"Just hold on and relax. We'll be down in a minute. Look at the view. . . . Are you scared, Manuel, like your mother? Is it too high?"

And Manuel shook his head no and said, "But it's high. Higher than I thought." And he thought that perhaps there was reason to be scared, but even if he was afraid there was no reason to tell Tío Sal—and he wondered if the Cyclone Racer would scare him like the women he heard who were scared and screeched.

The wheel turned down. The man with the skinny arms pulled the lever and the wheel below them stopped and car by car he let the people off. The girl in the white dress got off and Sal watched her walk away toward the Cyclone Racer. Then the top wheel the three were on went down and they got off and went to meet Grandmother where she was watching the laughing man and woman.

"Could you see the city?" she asked Mother.

"Yes, but I was afraid to look down very long."

"It looked beautiful watching the wheels turn."

"I was afraid."

Manuel walked to the right side of his grandmother and

watched the porcelain dummies reeling. She gave him a pat on the head and put her hand on his neck. Tío Sal walked to stand where metal arms pulled taffy into smooth white sheets then balled it again and pulled it again and again. He bought a white bag of the salt-water taffy and came back to the front of the Fun House.

"Open your mouth and close your eyes," he said to Manuel. Manuel closed his eyes and opened his mouth and stuck his tongue out flat. "And here comes a big chili pepper." Sal put a piece of the taffy on Manuel's tongue and Manuel pulled it into his mouth and smiled and let it sit there without chewing it. He turned it with his tongue and felt the round smoothness of the outer plane and the flat of the top and bottom planes. "Thank you, Tío," he said. "What ride now?"

"The Cyclone Racer, I guess. We should try that," Sal said, and knew why they should go—if there was something to see besides the harbor and the city, it was the girl that made the blood rush to his center.

They walked past the diving bell and the merry-go-round to the Cyclone Racer. A sign in front of the high white structure said, "Cyclone Racer, the World's Greatest Ride," in square red letters.

Mother's dress bounced when she walked. She looked at the sailors and their girls waiting to get on the ride, and she thought she didn't look her best because no one looked and that she should have worn the mink stole that her fiancé, Luis, had given her, and of the new green '29 Buick Luis was getting for them to drive away in after they were married. She had wanted a new car to drive to the church and their honeymoon—because Luis had the money from his vegetable business—because she deserved it, she thought. He could give Manuel a dollar for a haircut, too, he had the money.

Manuel looked up through the white boards X-ing each other to the rail that rolled across the top and wound around. Tío Sal bought the tickets for everyone, because it couldn't be that bad —women always screeched—and besides it was short, only a few minutes.

There was a white picket fence and behind it red cars sat still and unused. One track was empty—waiting for the moving car. Manuel could hear the clicking of the car on the track.

". . . *kingdom come; thy will be done on earth as it is in heaven. Give us this day our daily* . . ."

Grandmother was watching the car move fast along the track and so was Mother. But Grandmother remembered the stories of the Cyclone Racer, and said: "What about the sailors that stood in the front car and when they passed the top of the hill both of their heads were cut off by the points of the star? Landed in a girl's lap. They say that in the colony."

"Those are only stories," Sal said. "Like the diving-bell stories where everyone drowns. I heard that story in the colony, but there wasn't anything wrong with the diving bell except dirt, was there?"

"And the other story about the car going off into the sea, the one in the paper, what about that one?" Mother said.

"Those are only stories, just stories. Even Manuel knows that they're just stories. Don't you, Manuel? You're not afraid, are you?"

Manuel shook his head and looked away from his uncle's eyes.

"Is it safe, Salvador? Will it make my heart pump hard?" Mother asked.

"Would they have a ride that isn't safe?" Sal said. "Aren't the stories part of the fun? I have the tickets. Just once."

Then the red car came fast down the empty track behind the fence, and the people were laughing and some were breathing deep. The girl with the white dress was in the first car with her boy friend, and she was laughing and reeling back and forth and so was her boy friend. The bars that held the passengers in popped up and a group of sailors with their girls got up and out. One sailor consoled his girl and laughed, then put his arm around her and swaggered off. The girl in white pulled two tickets from her gold purse and handed them to a man who came around. They stayed in the first car.

While Sal watched the girl, Manuel watched Sal. Manuel also thought the girl was pretty, but not in the same way as Sal did.

The man took the tickets from Sal and the four walked through the gate. Sal and Mother sat in the second car behind the girl, and Manuel sat in the third car with Grandmother. Manuel's legs didn't reach the floor of the car. The bar came down with a thump like a hammer. After all the cars were loaded with people, the cars rolled flat toward a turn.

"Hold onto the bar," Grandmother said.

When the cars reached the first incline the heads of the passengers jerked back, then forward. A sound of winding came from the track's chain as the cars rolled up and around the bend toward a steep incline. Across the flat and around a slow turn the chain drive of the cars grabbed hard and the cars were pulled up the long incline, with the chain clicking, and the cars headed toward the three visible points of the red star at the top. The car moved slowly.

". . . *as it was in the beginning, is now, and ever shall be, world without end.*"

There was the sea and the green light of the sea wall that Manuel had seen before and the wiggling reflections of the neon lights of the park on the water. Grandmother was looking out across the neon lights of the park to the edge of the city and the grated white lights that went back into the black sky. Mother huddled down in the seat in front of Manuel, and Tío Sal puffed his cigar. The smoke drifted back as the car moved forward. They reached the top. For a moment the cars perched beneath the red star and the star seemed to Manuel almost close enough to grab—but a fresh pull took the cars forward. The girl went over first with her arms and her boy friend's arms in the air, then all the cars were over. The cars dropped and Manuel felt as if there was no bottom—as if he was floating—like the white dress that billowed ahead. He held onto the safety bar the way a pup holds onto its bitch mother. He gritted his teeth and closed his eyes to the wind.

And Tío Sal yelled, "Holy Jesus! What kind of ride is this?" with Mother holding onto him with one arm and onto the safety bar with the other. But he knew that the hump just passed was the worst one—as the cars scooped fast and low then up a smaller hill that slowed them down.

"Por dios!" Mother said. "Is there more? No more!" And she thought that it was Sal's fault that they were there and she was afraid and she wouldn't do anything for him unless he did something for her.

Manuel saw that there was more to come and he wanted to get off, but he couldn't, and soon enough they would all get off.

". . . *full of grace! The Lord is with thee; blessed art thou amongst women, and blessed is the fruit of thy womb . . ."*

"I shouldn't have come," Grandmother said.

"We shouldn't have," Mother said.

All the time the girl in white was laughing and jumping up and down at the top of the humps. Tío Sal watched her and thought that she was very young and ripe, when he wasn't holding onto the bar or his hat.

Then the car clicked up the second hump, slow as before. And this time Manuel, and Grandmother, and Mother, and Sal were holding on tight all the way to the top. Mother was squeaking and shaking. Then the cars balanced at the top, and Tío Sal watched the girl as she threw her arms over her head. The cars dropped. The drop was shorter, but the floating feeling was the same. At the bottom Manuel felt as if they were scooped into a jaialai player's net.

". . . *mother of God, pray for us sinners now and at the hour of our death. Amen."*

The women were in black and crying and there was a line moving past the casket with Manuel near the end of the line. And when he passed he thought that Sal looked almost alive except he had no hat and there was no cigar. Afterward there was a big party that Margaret, his mother, didn't come to. But there was a lot of food and drink and all the women in black, who were professionals, cried very hard and made Manuel cry.

They went around the white painted structure, which shook with every strain of the cars turning, and there was the third and last hill. Moving up the hill Manuel could see the blue star of the top of the hump reflected in the water and it crossed the water as they moved up. At the top the girl in white put her arms up again and gave the blue star a light stroke.

Austin Wilson

LA CUCARACHA, LA CUCARACHA

When I left for work this morning, I slammed the door as hard as
I could, hoping I'd rattle a few dishes, shake the flimsy walls, and
make my irritation known by the sound of my leaving echoing
like a gunshot back to the bedroom where Cathy had taken the
kid to change his diaper. Naturally the latch didn't catch and
the door bounced open and swung all the way against the side of
the trailer and stayed there. I had to go back and close it care-
fully. Serve her right if I'd left it wide open, letting in God knows
how many flies. But she's enough like her old man that she prob-
ably would have enjoyed killing them. More likely she would
have phoned him to send somebody out to get rid of them and
he would have sent me. I was thinking, though, that I'm the one
who has to pay to cool the trailer and it's expensive enough, what
with the lack of insulation, without letting all the air conditioning
escape through the door. The trailer is like an oven in the sum-
mer, an icebox in the winter. Besides, it's a deathtrap in a tornado.

Before I shut the door, I stuck my head back inside and was
just about to shout "Goddamn trailer" loud enough for her to
hear, but I caught myself. She still hates for me to call the trailer
a trailer and tries to get me to call it a mobile home like she al-
ways does, but lately she has turned all my complaints about the

trailer into reasons for buying a house. So I didn't say anything. I just shut the door, quietly this time, and went to the car.

As much as I hate that car, at least it does take me away from the trailer on mornings like this one. I had been cooped up all weekend with a sick kid and Cathy had been nagging me since day before yesterday to go out and look at some houses one of her daddy's realtor buddies was eager to show us. Cathy kept reminding me about all the gripes I had ever had about the trailer. She used to always defend it, but this weekend she acted like I'd finally convinced her how bad it was and like it had been my idea all along to buy us a real house. It's a wonder she didn't come to the door I couldn't slam shut, stand there shaking her head, and then say she agreed with me completely about the absurdity of having a door like that. She probably would have told me what a difference it would make in our lives if we had a door that opens in like a normal front door instead of one that opens out. Hell.

The car is a Volkswagen sedan painted to look like some kind of weird bug: it's got eyes painted on it, antennae attached right above the windshield, and fiberglass wings that move while I drive. There's a sign on both doors that says "If you got 'em, we get 'em" and under that "Parker Exterminating Company/ Locally Owned and Operated" and the phone number. Cathy thinks the car is cute, and her old man (he's the Parker that I work for) acts like he's doing me a big favor by letting me drive this instead of one of the trucks. He can't understand why I want to buy my own car, since he lets me take the company car home and doesn't mind me using it for pleasure since it's good advertising. Being seen in the car ranks in the Top Ten of things I hate about my job.

Since it was Monday I checked in at the office to get my route. Most days I just pick up where I left off the day before. I didn't particularly want to see Parker. I figured he'd want to know why I wasn't jumping at the chance to sign away the next twenty or thirty years of my life to give his little girl the house she wanted. You'd think he'd be mad at her for wanting to get rid of the trailer. Take it personally the way she used to take the things I said about it. She was so crazy about the trailer that she sounded like a salesman for one of the mobile-home lots out on the highway where her daddy took us just before we got married and he bought that box we live in. But soon as she changes her mind, Parker is eager to do whatever she wants, butting into our business. You'd think he was after a commission the way he gave my name to every realtor in town.

As soon as I went into the office and started kidding the secretary like I always do, I knew that Cathy had called before I got there. The secretary just looked at me and then said, "Mr. Parker wants to see you in his office."

Cathy is always getting him to try to make me give in to her. Like he does. She figures he can handle me since he's the one that talked me into marrying her after she got pregnant. He made me all kinds of promises about my bright future with his company and I quit technical school and now I'm stuck here. It's typical that finding out his precious daughter was knocked up didn't make any difference. He gave her the big church wedding she wanted. If I'd been him, I'd have made her get an abortion.

When I went into his private office, he was at his desk acting like he was reading a piece of paper, so I just stood there and said nothing. I looked around the room at all the framed photographs of bugs and of termite-damaged wood as if I'd never noticed them before. He has some bugs—roaches, termites, silverfish —mounted in frames the way some people have butterflies. Finally he looked at me, so I said, "You want to see me?"

"Not really," he said. "Sometimes I wish I'd never laid eyes on you and Cathy hadn't either. What's got into you this time?"

I played dumb like I didn't know what he was talking about. It probably does Parker a world of good to chew me out now and then. When Cathy is around, he has to pretend he likes me.

"Cathy just called, crying so bad I couldn't catch what the trouble was exactly. You want to explain?"

"There's nothing to explain," I said.

"That's where you're wrong, buddy boy. You've got a lot of explaining to do."

I shrugged and didn't say anything, just smiled at him.

"You cocky bastard; you think you've got me over a barrel, don't you?"

"You!" I said. I couldn't help laughing.

He got up from his desk and I thought he was going to grab me, but he just wanted to get close enough to blow some of his cigar smoke on me. He took the cigar out of his mouth and I thought for a second when he jabbed my chest it was with the cigar. It was just his finger. I should have known he'd be careful not to burn the uniform he had to provide that had his name stitched on it.

"Listen," he said, trying to sound tough, saying it through his teeth like he'd forgotten he didn't still have the cigar in his mouth. "You ungrateful . . ."

I thought I was going to have to listen to him tell me all that he'd done for me and I was ready to laugh in his face again, but he didn't go on. He was having trouble thinking of something to call me.

"Punk" was the best he could come up with. He glared at me and then said, "This happens one more time and I'll . . ."

He put his cigar back in his mouth and went back to his chair. He had the same problem trying to think of a threat to hold over me. I knew he wouldn't do anything that might make Cathy and his precious grandson suffer.

"Get to work," he said, and I left.

The secretary smirked when she gave me the list of my calls.

It was the usual, mostly regulars, but with a few names and addresses I didn't recognize. They were probably the result of Parker's ad last week offering a free inspection for termites, so that meant I'd be crawling under houses all day. But there were a couple of bright spots: Maureen's Beauty Parlor (a couple of the beauticians there aren't bad-looking), Jennifer Morris' house (I figured she was bound to be home since school's out now and maybe her mother would be out shopping or something), and it was time to treat the National Veterans Union Club, which I decided to save until after four when Joyce-Ann would be working the bar. I was the one who always treated the NVU Club, though I'm sure Parker didn't really like the idea. I think he let me handle it because it was the only account I had signed up myself and he was still trying to encourage me to take the job seriously.

When I first started working for Parker, he tried to convince me that the job was some kind of religious crusade or something. He went on and on about ridding houses of infection and about us being public servants. But all I could think about the job was that it would offer all kinds of opportunities, like the stories I used to hear about milkmen and traveling salesmen, going to houses all day while the husband was at work. It hasn't turned out that way, though. The way I figure it, it must be the smell of the insecticide clinging to my clothes or something, or maybe the women associate me with roaches in their minds and that turns them off. It's a damn shame too, because I get excited as hell sometimes when I spray in some of their bedrooms with the beds sometimes not made up yet and sometimes their underwear is draped over a chair or just thrown on the floor and the woman is still wearing her bathrobe. It really gets to me. But all they ever do is sign the ticket showing I've been there and all I give them is their copy of it.

Usually I don't plan the best order to treat the houses, just take them in any order, so that I waste a lot of time and Parker's gas driving back and forth. Even though I hate the car, it beats working. But today looked like it was going to be a scorcher so I figured I'd just as soon spend as much time as possible in the houses that are air-conditioned. When I rode by the sign on the bank it said the temperature was ninety and it was only nine twenty-two.

My first call was the Baxter house out in Cherokee Hills. I thought I'd take those in the good sections that are farthest away first and work my way toward the other end of town so I could get to the NVU Club fairly close to quitting time. The Baxters just got the standard treatment for roaches, so all I had to do was get the tank (it looks like a fire extinguisher, right down to the hose) out of the back seat of the VW and carry it from room to room spraying the baseboards. I took my time, even though Mrs. Baxter isn't anything to look at. I just wasn't in any particular hurry. As I went through all those big rooms and opened up all the closets to give the floor a squirt of poison, I kept thinking of Cathy whining about wanting to have regular-size rooms with at least a closet in each one. All the trailer has is the one closet next to the bathroom and it has an accordion folding door that always sticks.

Our bedroom is about the size of the Baxters' walk-in closet and is so small we both have to get out of bed on the same side. The Baxters' kitchen is almost as big as the whole trailer; ours is more like a hall with the counter and appliances jammed along one side. And the shower stall in the trailer is so tiny you have to stoop and hunch your shoulders when you're in it; the Baxters have a bathtub in one of their three bathrooms that's big enough for two people. But if Cathy could see some of the things I notice in these closets, in these big rooms, the filth and clutter that people live in, she wouldn't be so sure that all it takes to make a happy family is a house. You'd think Parker might have told her the truth about houses when she started wanting one, but he always pretties everything up for her. Besides, he sees things differently from me. I think people deserve the bugs and rats they get; he thinks it's his duty to protect people from their own filth by rooting out the products of it.

The next few houses got the usual spraying. Mrs. West was sitting at her breakfast table with dirty dishes still on it and like every time I treat her house she was yakking on the wall phone. As usual she was irritated when I interrupted to get her to sign the ticket.

The first real problem I ran into was at the Corringtons'. There were fleas in the carpet from Mr. Corrington letting his bird dogs into the house while Mrs. Corrington was visiting for a week with her sister, who, she told me, was dying of cancer. I think that's what Cathy's mother died of, eaten up inside like a termite-infested house. I can imagine why Cathy isn't sure about how her mother died. Parker hid the truth from her, trying to protect her.

I had to go back to the car and get a different nozzle for the hose to spray the carpet and already the bites were itching on my ankles. There was some insect repellant in the glove compartment, so I rubbed some on my socks and cuffs and hoped that would keep them off when I sprayed the rugs. I was really going to stink before the day was over. Despite the kerosene-smelling repellant, the fleas preferred me to the carpet.

After the Corringtons I had my first free inspection. I went into the crawlspace under the house and immediately cracked my head on a cast-iron sewer pipe. It hurt like hell and I was rubbing it when I realized I was probably getting that clingy, powdery dirt you find under houses all in my hair. I could imagine how I was going to look by the time I got to the NVU Club. I was drenched with sweat because of the heavy coveralls I'd put on to crawl under the house. As far as I took the time to see, the foundation was okay and the old woman didn't want me to check the attic when she saw how dirty I was.

Out by the car I brushed myself off, took off the coveralls, and emptied the dirt from my shoes. I found two more fleas on me. Then I drove off to the next house. I thought about going to the trailer and taking a shower and changing to a clean khaki uniform, but Cathy would just start up again as soon as she saw me.

The next house nobody was home and the door was locked. With some of my regulars I just go right in, even if nobody seems to be home as long as the door is unlocked. One of these days I'm going to catch one of those women in the bathtub or something. I just left one of the notices on the doorknob that said how sorry I was to have missed them and promised to try to get back as soon as possible.

Going to the next house on my route, I passed an Orkin truck and the driver gave me the finger out his window. I just laughed. I couldn't care less about the competition, except that I like to see Parker worrying himself into an ulcer and heart trouble about the way the big chains are eating into his business. As far as I'm concerned they're welcome to all the bugs in town. Parker is also worried about all this ecology stuff. He thinks that all his poisons will be outlawed and he won't be able to prevent the world from being taken over by the insects. When he dies, if there's any business left, I plan to sell to the first taker.

A few more calls and I was ready to knock off for lunch, particularly after the last one, a free inspection. There were about a dozen cats under the house hissing at me and just barely covered cat shit every place I put my hand. The subflooring and all the joists were eaten up by termites, but I told the people it was fine. I didn't want to have to come back and treat the house. I hope the floor caves in and drops them down into their cat mess.

Cathy thinks that having a real foundation under us will make a difference, instead of being propped up on concrete blocks that just barely hold the trailer's wheels off the ground. She should see some of the foundations under these houses that look so nice on the outside. And she should see some of the things that live in the thick walls she thinks are so much better than the corrugated metal and thin plywood veneer of the trailer.

I eat lunch at The Pig, which used to be the hang-out when I was in high school. Now the kids all go to McDonald's and the other hamburger places on the highway. I go to The Pig for sentimental reasons and because I like the barbecue. The carhops like to kid me about the car but those working today were pimply-faced and ugly, so I decided to eat inside where at least it's cool. I ordered a couple of sandwiches and a milkshake and went to the restroom and washed my hands to get all the poison, dirt, and cat shit off. While there I invested a quarter in one of the rubber machines on the back of the door. You never can tell when you might need one. When I turned the crank I figured it was loud enough for the waitress to hear and know what I'm up to, which was okay with me. She looked better than the two carhops. But she didn't pay any attention to me after she brought my order, and I didn't leave a tip.

After lunch I drove down to the tennis courts and parked my car in the shade and watched a couple of girls half-heartedly play. It was too hot for them to play for long, and I thought they would quit and come over and talk to me. People don't like me coming in and spraying while they're still eating, so I had an hour to kill to make sure the Morrises, who were next on my list, weren't still having lunch. I wanted to give Mr. and Mrs. Morris time to get away so that maybe only Jennifer, their daughter, who was a college girl and looked like a hippie, would be there. The girls playing tennis ignored me until just as I was getting ready to leave. When they finally quit playing and left the court and walked by the VW, they started singing "La Cucaracha" in Spanish. Every now and then one of them would break up and bend over giggling and drop her racket or tennis balls. I could hear them singing it all the way down the block. That's one song I never could stand. It's one of the things that made me quit high school. The old lady who was failing me in Spanish had what she called a fiesta every Friday instead of the regular lesson, and we always sang that song for about fifteen minutes straight. I've tried to blot that song out of my mind completely ever since, and now those girls had to go and sing it and make it start running around in my head.

Mrs. Morris opened the door for me and followed me from room to room, complaining all the while about some rat that died in the wall and stank for over a week. She blamed me for it, since I had sprinkled some rat poison in their basement, as she'd requested, the last time I treated the house. There were a couple of new posters up in Jennifer's room, so I knew she must be home for vacation, but she wasn't anywhere in the house and I left disappointed. I added Mrs. Morris to the list of those I wouldn't mind poisoning.

There were four more houses I thought I'd do before going to the beauty shop and then the NVU Club. I decided to skip the rest of the free inspections. The first house went smoothly, except that the Negro maid followed right after me throughout the house. She probably thought I would steal something if she didn't keep her eyes on me every minute. And I kept catching myself whistling "La Cucaracha." Nobody was home at the next one, so I left another notice. At the third one an old lady wanted me to climb up on the roof and knock down a hornets' nest about three times the size of a football. It was hanging under the eave and I wasn't about to get involved with it. I told her to call Parker to send out one of the trucks with a ladder. The last one was Mrs. Bennett; she had a special problem too.

After I'd sprayed for roaches, she asked me to step outside. She showed me their new patio.

"Can you keep the slugs from coming up on it?" she asked. "Just the other night we had some guests out here—Jesse was trying out the new grill—and a slug climbed up on the rim of Mabel Franklin's glass. She almost put it in her mouth. I was humiliated. And she dropped the glass and broke it, one of my best set. I'd just as soon get them out of the yard entirely. I live in constant dread that I'm going to step on one. The thought of smashing one makes me cringe."

Slugs are sort of out of my line. I don't handle garden pests, but I told her how she could take a garbage can lid or something similar and fill it with beer and the slugs will come up and drink it and drown. I told her all she had to do then was to scoop them out periodically. I didn't mean to gross her out when I started but she got a funny look on her face, like she couldn't decide if I was joking or not. Then I could tell she was disgusted by what I was saying. For some reason I started going into more and more detail and told her about sprinkling salt on slugs until they would shrivel up to almost nothing. She turned and went back through the sliding glass door and just left me there. She hadn't even signed the ticket. I didn't bother trying to find her and get her to. I could tell that she would probably phone Parker and complain. So what? I was getting pretty fed up myself.

A couple of women had complained before (or so Parker claimed) when I first started treating houses. He said the women complained about the way I looked at them. I think he called it leering. He made a big production out of it and said he would tell Cathy if it happened again, but I knew he wouldn't. He wouldn't tell her anything that would hurt her. I bet the women really liked me looking at them, even if they did phone Parker.

When I finally got to the beauty shop, it was packed with customers and the beauticians didn't have time to even notice me. I suppose I wasn't the freshest-smelling I've been, but a beautician ought not to mind. They stink themselves. They always smell like permanents. They looked irritated when I started spraying, and when I said "Hey, good-looking" to Mary-Ellen, she just turned around and concentrated on rolling up her customer's hair. Maureen, whose shop it is, told me when she signed the ticket not to come so late in the future. In the late afternoon they had too many last-minute customers and they didn't need me to add to the confusion and stinking up the place besides. "With the pesticide," she added, after a pause.

It was a relief to call it a day and head out the old highway, the wings of my car flapping. I parked the car around in back so it wouldn't be so noticeable. Since I'm not a member I didn't have a card to stick in the slot to open the door. I had to push the button under the sign that said "Members Only." While I was waiting for the answering buzz that meant Joyce-Ann had pushed the button at the bar which unlocked the door, I realized I was whistling again. That damn tune had been in my head ever since I heard the girls singing it at the tennis courts. I went into the dark, carrying my canister of poison, and as soon as my eyes adjusted I started spraying. There weren't too many people in the bar, which surprised me, since it was so hot outside and so cool in there. It was Happy Hour besides, and the drinks were all half-price. When I went behind the bar to spray I pretended that I was going to squirt Joyce-Ann, aiming the hose at her crotch. She laughed and grabbed my arm, pushing the hose toward the floor. After I had done the bar area I sprayed around the dance floor and the band platform. Peewee wasn't there yet; he plays the organ most nights. Then I put the tank down by the back door and sat at the bar and asked Joyce-Ann for a beer.

"Can, bottle, or draft?" she asked.

I said draft and she brought me a mug and sipped some of the head off before she handed it to me. She said I looked like I needed it and it was on the house.

"I 'preciate it," I said.

I still had to do the rooms out back, but I wanted to wait until things slacked off about suppertime and see if maybe Joyce-Ann would be willing to go back with me.

Before the four-lane was built, the buildings that are now the club had been a motel. The bar and the dance floor are in what used to be the restaurant and office. The club still keeps about a dozen of the motel rooms usable, and that's what caused the trouble with the last sheriff. He raided the place a couple of times and caused such a stink that the national office of Amvets lifted the charter from this place and it had to reorganize as the NVU so they could still sell mixed drinks. Now the new sheriff is a member himself and even owns the slot machines in the bar, so he doesn't cause any trouble.

I had just played the jukebox, hoping to replace the tune in my head with another one and was sitting at the bar listening and sipping my third beer, when the phone rang. I was watching Joyce-Ann moving back and forth behind the bar, thinking that she really didn't look half bad, though a little too tall and a little too broad in the hips, which she exaggerates with the miniskirts she wears. I was still waiting for the sparse crowd to thin out some more and for Peewee to show up so he could handle the bar while Joyce-Ann was gone. The pay phone is on the wall right at the end of the bar where I was sitting. I just let it ring. Finally Joyce-Ann came down and answered it after about the tenth ring. She said, "Just a second, I'll check," and covered the mouthpiece with her hand. I figured it was somebody's wife, but she looked right at me and whispered, "Your boss."

"Tell him I'm not here," I said.

She did; then she listened a few seconds and said again, "I'll check."

She leaned over the bar and whispered in my ear, "He wants to know if you've been here to spray yet."

"Tell him no. Wait. Tell him I came early in the afternoon before you opened and left right after," I whispered back and then I nibbled at her earlobe.

She said, "Stop that," and repeated to Parker what I had told her to say. She listened a while; then she laughed and said, "Okay," and hung up.

"He's mad as hell at you, said that customers have been calling all afternoon wanting to know where their inspection was. He said, 'If that son-of-a-bitch comes back, tell him to get his ass home.'"

She laughed again.

I told her to bring me another beer. I wanted to show her I was in no hurry to get home. When she brought the beer, I tried to slip the quarter down the neck of her blouse, but she danced out of my reach.

Soon after that, Peewee came, and I asked Joyce-Ann if she wanted to show me which rooms to spray out in back. She looked around the bar; there were only three other people left besides us and Peewee. She told him to hold down the bar for a while; then she led the way and I followed, carrying my tank.

Parker ought to be proud of the way I always did my bit to protect the poor suffering people who came out to the NVU. Because of me they're protected from the evils of roaches and bedbugs and other assorted common household pests. He really was pleased when I told him that I had brought in a new account. He thought he had finally gotten through to me. This is one place I always did a good job of thoroughly spraying every nook and corner.

Once Joyce-Ann and I were inside the first room I dropped the tank of poison on the floor and shut the door and grabbed her, but she slipped away.

"Why don't you take a shower?" she asked. "You look like you could use one."

It sounded like a good idea so I started taking off my clothes and headed for the bathroom.

"Hey, there're no towels in here," I said.

"I'll go get some," she said. "There are some under the bar. I'll be back in a second. You go ahead and get in."

I stepped into the shower stall and—wouldn't you know it—there was a large cockroach on the hot-water handle. It started running down the tile toward me and I didn't have on shoes, naturally, and I wasn't about to stomp him with my bare foot. So I had to get out and get some toilet paper and catch the roach with it and drop it in the toilet. Then I showered, not even trying to stop singing the song that had been running through my head all afternoon, and I felt one-hundred-percent better, particularly when Joyce-Ann was there waiting with a handful of bar towels when I got out. She helped me dry and then started horsing around with me, pretending she was a bullfighter with one of the towels. I made some horns with my hands and charged at her, still singing that song. After a couple of times I ignored the towel and aimed at her skirt, but she kept jumping out of my reach. Finally I caught her and started undressing her.

I am just about to get her into the bed when the door bangs open all the way against the wall and there's Parker. He glares at me and then turns back outside and pulls Cathy into the doorway. "See, I told you; you wouldn't believe me," he says.

Then they both are standing there looking at me like I am something disgusting that has just crawled out of the woodwork.

Tom Oliphant Turner

TAPERING OFF

Billie had passed out at the enamel table in the kitchen and although there were several blowflies buzzing her, it was pure instinct that woke her up and nudged her over to the window. She parted the curtains and tried to focus her eyes on the 1959 Cadillac out at the curb. Billie's dark eyes had little orbits all their own that moved through her freckled face at different rates of speed. They both stopped as suddenly as if a siren had checked their progress, forcing them to wait for an emergency vehicle to pass. Only it didn't pass. The great hot pink automobile had no more business in front of that house than a vessel from the Spanish Armada. But it was there and Billie suspected that she had left it there.

As she stared, the March wind tried to get at her face through the windowpanes. Billie smiled radiantly, just as she would have done at Phillipses, wiping a table, lifting a beer can, testing its weight. Her mouth was a tight little bud which she could wink into a blossom and back to a bud again. This gave her time to think.

Doris, the woman Billie stayed with, had a photographic mind when she was sober. Even when she had drunk herself into a coma and was lying on the living-room floor, she would sometimes come to long enough to recall phone numbers, bus schedules, and other technical information. Once, when Billie had dialed the Greyhound station and let it ring for thirty minutes before giving up, Doris had merely turned over and said there was a bus leaving for Jacksonville at 7:40 A.M. and the price of a ticket was seven dollars and seventy-eight cents. . . .

Billie went in to try and wake Doris up. "Doris! Did you know they's a fifty-nine Cadillac out in front of the house? A pink one!"

"Shitfire!" Doris yelled. She didn't like for people to see her when she first woke up. Not even Billie. She was uncovered and her rayon gown had drawn up in little hoops beneath her armpits. "Find me a clean pair of pants."

"Did you hear what I said?" Billie touched her hair and tilted her eyes up at the high, fly-specked ceiling. The bouffant felt sad and crusty, as though she hadn't invested twelve dollars in it the day before.

"Billie, you know goddamn well you came home in that car this morning. I had to let you in."

"Well, I don't remember a thing about it," Billie said. "The last thing I remember was slipping a B drink into the ladies' room at Phillipses."

Doris scratched her chest. "If I had a clean pair of pants to put on my freezing ass I could probably tell you a lot of things. For instance, you don't even work at Phillipses no more."

"You said that right," Billie broke in, "I quit. Phillipses is a 'community bar.' Forty dollars a week and you ain't even allowed one B drink."

Doris got up and pulled down her rayon gown. She was too cold to argue. There was one white sock underneath the bed, so she put it on.

"Can I fix you a cup of Nescafé?" Billie's bud opened and closed.

"Fix yourself one," Doris said.

"Say, Doris, you couldn't let me have five dollars till Friday?" Billie diverted her eyes to the bedroom window. It was covered from the outside with a sheet of plastic to which the wind had finally gained access.

"What for?" asked Doris.

"For gas," Billie said. "Do you have any idea how much gas a Cadillac de Ville can drink up?"

"For gas my ass." Doris yawned. "First you come in here asking me where that Cadillac come from, but now you know the gas tank's empty."

"Well, I thought as long as we have a Cadillac on our hands we might as well enjoy it," Billie said. "Never look a gift horse in the teeth." She laughed a volatile kind of laugh which might have caught the wind in a bar and spread.

Doris didn't answer. She poured herself a glass of gin from a jug on her night stand. Doris didn't drink as much as Billie, but she didn't know how to taper off.

"I'm drunk," she said. "Have been since Sunday was a week ago. Do I look yellow to you?" She turned to face the rattling window. In the light she looked gray. "You can tell me the truth."

Billie hated to lie to Doris because Doris was so good to her. She didn't charge her board and was generous with her liquor. "Yes," Billie said, "I'm afraid you're yellow as a canary."

Doris wheeled around and tried to look Billie in the pupils, but this made Billie's little eyes crawl the ceiling. "Dr. Romero warned you." Billie blinked. "I think you ought to let me take you out to Regional again. You're overdue for a cure."

"In the pink Cadillac, I imagine?"

"Why not?"

Doris sipped her gin. She still had at least a quart to go. "Look in my pocketbook," she said finally, "and take what you need."

Billie's thin fingers opened the zipper, and went for the knotted handkerchief just inside. She freed a twenty, letting it remain a spitball, telling Doris she would repay the five the day they let her out of Regional.

"That's okay, honey," Doris said, and Billie was touched enough to kiss the older woman's cheek. A few hollow bristles pricked Billie's lips like a little electric shock.

"I need to run to Eckerd's and pick up a few things. Can I get you something?" Billie asked, and already she had located a Walgreen's shopping bag for Doris to pack in.

"Yes," Doris said, "get me a cheap garden hose. One that you can't see through. Here, you'll need some more money," lifting her pocketbook from the bed. Billie took it, unzipped it, and with both hands pulled its jaws apart, extracting the money handkerchief as though it were a foreign object in the mouth of a child.

A cheap garden hose that you can't see through didn't strike Billie as an unusual request until she reached the checkout counter at Eckerd's. She took it from the cart along with the items she had selected for herself: douche powder, Listerine, and a giant tube of Crest toothpaste.

When Billie returned to 718½ Molly Pond Avenue, she parked the Cadillac with the passenger side facing the curb. The drive out to Regional Hospital had to be smooth and direct from the beginning, and with the Cadillac it should be. All the automobiles Billie had driven before had had hand brakes. You worked the emergency on this one with your foot. Power seat! Power windows! The last time she had been this excited over a vehicle was almost twenty years before, when she had thundered down to Daytona Beach on a Harley-Davidson Electra Glide. "Queen of the Road" is what the mechanic she went with had called it, and that's exactly what she felt like that night after the races until a girl in riding leathers blacked both her eyes and caved in her mouth. Billie came back home on the Greyhound while the other girl popped down the coast of Florida with the mechanic, on that ice-blue and snow-white motorcycle.

Doris looked in the Eckerd's sack for her garden hose. "My God!" she said when she came to the Listerine. "Billie, are you going to start sucking peters?"

"Hell *no!*" Billie rushed into the kitchen, her face red as she took the Listerine away from Doris. "If you must know, I'm going to find work."

Doris reached in and withdrew the green plastic hose from the sack. "If you must know," she mocked, "I'm taking my gin with me. Find me a cork." She unscrewed the nozzle, and inserted some of the hose inside the neck of the half gallon jug. With the end of the hose in her mouth, she began blowing and sucking. What she could not siphon into her fifty-foot flask, Doris was determined to drink.

The drive out to Regional was direct the way Billie had

planned. Direct as desire, and hot. The raw March wind had died down and the day had suddenly become as hot as a Dog Day. "My God," Billie said. "This weather's changeable as I am."

The Regional was backed off the highway like a country club. New one-story brick bats with shingles coming down their fronts like mod wigs, and thickets of white waterspouts were visible on the field of green.

"Where is all the people?" Billie wondered out loud.

"Oh, they're at *O.T.* or *R.T.*," Doris said with all the smugness of a factory-trained mechanic.

"What the shit kind of hospital is this with everybody going to tea parties?"

"It ain't that kind of tea. It's the initial T. T for therapy. Occupational Therapy, Recreational Therapy."

"It's still a tea party if you ask me," Billie said, and before Doris could say it didn't make a shit to her what Billie thought, Billie made the Cadillac creak and groan against the brake. Two men in Security uniforms sat behind the dark green glass of the gatehouse watching the small blue TV screen light. The men had on sunglasses. One of them stepped out to tell Billie where to park and how to find Dr. Romero's office. The man smelled like a cold lemon just sliced. It was a smell familiar to Billie, like a lounge before it opens, before the beer-belchers and the chain-smokers set to work. She was glad the Security Guards were not at one of the tea parties, otherwise nobody would have known what kind of car they had come in.

Dr. Romero was about half Billie's age. He lay on one elbow placed in the center of his desk. Billie realized that if it hadn't been for Dr. Romero's slightly bluish beak of a nose, his face could be that of a girl in her late teens. His eyelashes looked almost false.

"Doris, I'm afraid you'll have to stay a month and a half this time," he was saying. His long thin legs were crossed; heavy black shoes turned over, and long silk socks made his limbs end like the fins of a shark. Billie sat beside Doris and tried to estimate the size of Dr. Romero's penis.

"Your friend here will look after things I feel sure. . . ." But

Tom Oliphant Turner   31

Billie wasn't listening. Her eyes were swimming ripples out the office window. It was huge, she decided, or teenie.

The Cadillac was frying in the parking lot when Billie came out. It sounded like an old house taking on heat and settling. She let down all the windows, but to save gas she left the air conditioning off. The fuel gauge showed even lower than she had imagined. *Fumes.* She watched a colored R.N. step into a new gold Oldsmobile and whoosh straight away like the captain of a Whisperjet.

Billie hadn't planned on stopping for gas until after she had had a bath, but there was no choice. The first service station she came to was a Hess. She was disappointed when a slender boy with a shag haircut and perfect teeth came out. "A dollar's worth of regular," she told him. The boy frowned but didn't suggest super. Billie handed him the twenty to be changed.

At a Raco station she had better luck. There were no cars at any of the pumps, and the wind-burned attendant was kneeling at an island when she drove up. He had sweated through his pants and his shirt was open, exposing a stomach blanketed in pig hairs. "Fill 'er up?" he asked, hardly looking up from the carburetor he was dunking in a can of gas.

"Oh, you mean the *car?*" Billie asked. The bud below her nose blossomed full blown.

"Well, yes," the man's words whistled through black stumpy teeth. "I meant the car." He grinned, pulled a pink rag out of his pocket and pressed a wart on his nose.

"Well, I *mean,*" Billie giggled, "you seem to have lots of gasoline and I seem to have a lot of time. . . ."

The man wrapped the carburetor in the pink rag and dropped them both into the can of gas. "You want to pull around back, lady?"

"After you fill the car up with Ethyl."

The attendant moved with surprising agility for a man his size. He knew exactly where to look for the gas tank and slipped the nozzle in. Unlike the Hess boy, this man danced around to the front and skillfully unlatched the hood. He checked the oil, battery, brake fluid, radiator, even added a can of coolant—a $3.50

can. All of this while the pump bell dinged. It occurred to Billie
that the man was stalling. He reminded her in fact of a Memphis
mortician she had once gone to bed with. He hadn't been a neat
man either, yet he had hung up his clothes, balled his socks, put
shoetrees in his shoes, folded his undershirt, had gone to the bath-
room and brushed his teeth; came back, got in bed, got up again,
dressed, threw twenty dollars down, and left. It had baffled
Billie. Maybe if she had hung up her dress or if she had folded
up her bra and panties. . . .

The pump read $11.77.

"Now go ahead on around while I dig us up a coupla cool ones."

Waiting, Billie laced her fingers together at the back of her neck
and looked into the rear-view mirror. Her eyes were clear but
her head ached. Her armpits persuaded Billie to lower her hands
to her lap.

"My name's Ray," the attendant said, sliding in on the passen-
ger side. He patted the tops of both beer cans with swollen pink
index fingers as he spoke. "This here's Ray's Raco. Sort of like Roy
Rogers. But it ain't the name that pulls in business. And it ain't
service, neither. I tell you *what* miss, uh. . . ."

"Billie."

". . . Billie, you tell me what draws 'em."

"Speaking purely for myself"—Billie's eyes rolled around the
station as though it were a roulette wheel until they came to rest
on just the right answer—"it's the attendant. If he looks right,
I'll turn around in the middle of the highway."

Ray took off his shirt. His stomach hung out over his pants
like a sack of meal and Billie could see that he had a lather of pig
bristles all over his back, too. He put his beer can down and placed
his still cold hand on Billie's shoulder, and went on to say how
long he had been pumping and the risk maintaining a dealership
involves. He was into Raco-related experiences when he sud-
denly sat up straight and arched his eyebrows. "You hear that?
That phone. I'm gonna have it took out."

Billie didn't hear any telephone, but she was glad Ray did.
When he went to answer it, her first impulse was to back the
Cadillac onto the highway and leave Ray a note, on the horn.
When Ray came back, however, he didn't get in, but motioned

Tom Oliphant Turner

for Billie to let her window down. "I'm sorry lady, but I ain't the real Ray," he explained. "That was him on the telephone. He's on his way here now."

Billie considered offering to pay the fake Ray something on the gas, but she whined her electric window up instead, jerked the air conditioning on, and squalled over the asphalt. She felt like a teen-ager, grinning as Ray's Raco diminished in the rear-view mirror.

718½ Molly Pond Avenue, twenty minutes later. Billie held the Listerine in her throat while she gave herself a lilac douche and resurrected her hairdo in the full-length mirror of Doris' bathroom. She spat the Listerine into the bathtub and gave voice to a song that had been working its way through the top of her headache: "You may go to coll-idge, You may go to school, You may have a pink Cadillac, but don't you be nobody's fool. Oh comeback babycome!"

Douches were rare events in Billie's life. Luxuries. There hadn't been a man in years to hold a pair of her panties up to the light. The last had been Eugene Jorjorian, her dead Ex. She had had his only existing snapshot (taken at Gaddy's Bar, showing Eugene using a white telephone and wearing a Mason's ring on his little finger) blown up to an eleven-by-fourteen and hand-colored. The last time she had laid eyes on Eugene, he had been slid out for her to view in the altogether, in a drawer. He had always known he would die at the hands of a Negro. Although the rest of Eugene was bloated white, his eyes had sunk, the lids resembling two jack-in-the-pulpits. Billie hated to think that underneath the sockets held two hard raisins where muscadines had ripened and cooled. Besides the picture, the only other personal effects Billie retained were a wisdom tooth and a nickel-plated Smith & Wesson .38. Eugene had the tooth extracted during a stay in the Richmond County Stockade. He had drilled a hole in it to make Billie a key chain. The wonder of the Smith & Wesson was that it never had been loaded. Eugene had kept the virgin pistol in the glove compartment of his Fleming Taxi, so that if some Negro tried to hit him in the head with a wrench, he could scare him off with just a glint from the blue-silver gun.

After they had fished Eugene out of the Savannah River and

Billie went down to identify him, she explained to the lieutenant that Eugene thought all Negroes were cowards who seldom try anything by themselves. He knew they were after him, but Eugene figured if more than one attacked, the gun was no good anyhow; but if *one* did, that shiny gun would make him grab his hat. "A shame," the lieutenant had shook his head. "He would've been better off with a harmonica."

What saddened Billie was that she and Eugene had separated six months before he died. It was not his taxicab pension but Eugene's rock-hard body she hated to lose. Losing it, Billie had already discovered that she longed for it in the exact way a person hungers for home when he's homesick. In memory, Eugene Jorjorian was as much a place as Waycross, Georgia, which means very little unless you're from there. She missed tattoos, veins, the curious locations of hairs. It was these things compared with eyes and voice, the hair of the head, that she finally missed: the grass and trees, the rocks, the ditches of Eugene Jorjorian.

Billie put on Doris' flesh-colored support hose and pulled a pair of her own black mesh stockings over them. She wanted to make Gaddy's by four-thirty if she could, in time for the happy hour. She slammed the front door and glanced at her reflection in the jarring glass. A flush of starlings blew from the street and disappeared behind 718½. Billie was down the steps before she remembered something. A pair of angora dice. Back inside, they were not exactly cube-shaped any longer, bunched together near the bottom of her cedar chest like fuzzy testicles. But they hung from a nice pink ribbon which couldn't have gone better with the Cadillac if Billie had planned it out in advance. This time she left the front door open.

Gaddy's was an alley with doors on it. Billie hadn't seen the place since Gaddy had put in a black light and changed the name from "Gaddy's Bar" to "Gaddy's Lounge." The light was already on by the time Billie managed to park the Cadillac in a space out front.

"What you think, sweetie?" Gaddy asked before Billie's eyes had a chance to adjust. She looked at Gaddy's sparkly eyes and ran up them to the tube of light on the ceiling. It was the color of a varicose vein.

"Nice," Billie said. "It's real nice."

"God, Billie! Where'd you git that *car?*" It was Virgie Mae in a pink knit pants suit. Virgie would have had trouble plunging one leg through the skirt Billie had on.

"It was in front of the house when I woke up this morning," Billie said, "with the keys in it."

"You mean you don't know whose it is?"

"No."

"Well, has it got a Georgia or a Carolina tag?" Virgie was from the Valley, a redneck belt near the Georgia-South Carolina line. She only worked in Georgia.

"Shit if I know." Billie turned to face Gaddy at the bar. He poured her a B drink with his good hand. She couldn't help wondering if the artificial hand Gaddy wore on his right arm glowed when the place got completely dark. Virgie set her tray down on the end of the bar and stepped outside to look the Cadillac over.

"I wish you'd look at that cow's *ass!*" Gaddy said. Sweat stains forked in a slingshot pattern from Virgie's shoulder blades to a branch just above her behind.

Billie laughed out of politeness. "You got anything to eat in this lounge?"

Gaddy's eyes twinkled at the sound of the word lounge. "Peanuts," he said, "and boiled eggs."

Again, out of politeness, Billie accepted a boiled egg.

Virgie came in dusting off the seat of her pants suit, her fingers trying to separate knit and flesh. "It's got a *dealer's* tag on it," she said. "Bodey's Used Cars."

"And you don't remember who it belongs to?" Gaddy's voice was so high that he sounded like Doris waking up.

"I reckon it belongs to whoever owns Bodey's Used Cars," Billie said. "The last thing I remember is doctoring up a B drink at Phillipses around one o'clock this morning."

Gaddy and Virgie looked at each other as though they thought Billie had omitted an important detail.

"I don't remember a thing about it," Billie said. "I swear I don't. I don't even have a driver's license," she laughed, trying to make it catch.

"'Spose the pleece had stopped you?" Gaddy posed the question. "Driving all over Augusta in a stolen Cadillac and no license."

"I told you I don't know where it came from," Billie said. "I know I didn't *steal* it."

"Well, when they make an arrest they automatically think a car's stolen unless you can prove it ain't." Gaddy tried not to make a joke of Billie's predicament, but Virgie started laughing and he couldn't restrain himself. Billie laughed too.

"What if I just leave it right where it's at?" Billie speculated.

"Then they'll think I'm mixed up in it," Gaddy shook his head.

"Not if you call Bodey and tell him one of his used cars is parked in front of your *lounge*," Billie said.

Gaddy considered this. "Listen, Virgie," he said, "why don't *you* call Bodey? Tell him there's a pink Cadillac down here with his paper tag on it."

"Okay," Virgie shrugged, "but give me a dime."

Billie took Gaddy by his good hand and looked him in the eye. "Y'all won't *say* nothing, Gaddy."

"Naw." Gaddy pulled his hand back and slid it into his apron. With a manicured index finger he pressed a dime onto the bar. "We don't know a thing about it."

Virgie jumped at the slightest excuse to go across the street and use the telephone.

It was dark when Bodey came in. He was wearing a straw hat and a boiled white shirt that glowed in the black light. There were almost a dozen ballpoints in each of his shirt pockets. "You wouldn't happen to have the switch keys?" he asked Gaddy. Billie's mouth became a perfect morning glory on the rim of her glass. Bodey glanced down at her and backed off a little as though suddenly realizing his pants were unzipped.

Gaddy didn't do anything that would acknowledge Billie's presence at the bar. "All I know is it was there when I opened up this morning," he said.

Bodey was a big man and he dug his fist into his palm. "Well," he said, "I appreciate you calling me." He looked around the lounge slowly, a booth at a time, and slid Gaddy a five.

Tom Oliphant Turner

"You didn't have to do that," Gaddy said, snapping up the five and pushing the NO SALE on the cash register.

Bodey looked at Billie again. Billie's eye flew up to the ceiling and flapped around the black light. Bodey's eyes clamped down her, down the stool she was sitting on to the tile floor. "It's my goddamn brother-in-law," he mumbled. "All I told him was wash the birdshit off that car."

After Bodey had gone, Gaddy looked across the bar at Billie. "You could've left the keys in the switch," he said.

"I just didn't think about it," she said and took a crisp ten from her purse to pay for the B drink Gaddy had poured.

"Aw, thassokay Billie." Gaddy's artificial hand *did* glow in the dark.

"I had to take Doris out to Regional again."

"That girl's got a problem," Gaddy said.

"Yeah, she was yellow as a Chinaman, but she's got the cutest little doctor you ever laid eyes on."

Gaddy's eyes opened wide. "Male or female?"

"A boy," Billie said. "Size eight-and-a-half *narrow*."

"Dammit, Billie," Gaddy's face was red even in the dead light. "Is that all you ever think about—*sex?*"

" 'Fraid so." Billie tossed down the rest of her B drink.

Gaddy massaged the bar with a glowing rag. "We'll have to ride out there Sunday and see Doris." He winked.

Doggies were starting to file into Gaddy's, Billie noticed. Next would come Negroes and an occasional fag. Doggies gave off immunity, a peculiar security, which Billie could appreciate. They were to bars what truck drivers are to restaurants. SAFE. A Negro was already sitting in one of the booths. He had a bridge in his mouth that glowed whenever he set down his drink. Beneath his safari hat with its simulated leopard-skin band, behind his funky shades, he was obviously brooding.

"Virgie could use some help," Gaddy said.

"You said *that* right." Billie grinned.

"You know what I mean. A *lounge* just ain't the same as a bar."

"Well, I *could* help out till Doris comes home from the hospital. Provided"—Billie waved a finger—"you sweeten my B drinks."

"Now, Billie, when you ever drunk a glass of tea in here?"

"Well, just so a lounge ain't *that* different," Billie giggled.

Gaddy went under the bar and came up wiping out an ancient tray with a picture of a pack of Cavalier Cigarettes on it. "Beer's forty-five. Fifty with a glass. Don't worry about B drinks. I'll figure them."

"You got a Goody, Gaddy? My head's about to bust wide open." Billie got down from her stool and went to the front glass. The Cadillac was still where she had parked it. It didn't look the same color in the street light. Billie slid the Goody headache powder down her throat and chased it with the remains of her drink. She carried her tray to the back of the lounge, where a game of Rotation was being knocked around on the pool table, and took a couple of orders. Billie didn't have an opinion of Doggies one way or the other. They had cash, and, as a rule, drank fast. The Negro was drinking straight whiskey, bolting it down like medicine.

"Mind if I set with you a minute?" Billie asked.

The Negro simply turned his palms over face up on the table. There was still some whiskey in his glass, but Billie took it away and brought them both a fresh one. The Negro didn't talk, but he faked a lot of smiles. It was as though he was aware of the effect the black light was having on his bridge.

More Doggies. Styled short hair, fake mustaches, tight pants, and wallets. Billie could remember a time when she would have been called to the bar and given a piece of Gaddy's mind for serving a Negro, much less sitting at a booth with one. But dollars out of Fort Gordon had a way of eroding petty differences. Bars became lounges.

Billie had lost count of the B drinks she had had, when a man came in who was the spit and image of Eugene at twenty-five. It was better than seeing a ghost. He was built like a stocky little tractor, and absolutely nothing about him reacted to the black light. Not even the plaid design in his shirt glowed as he advanced straight for the pool table. The way he carried himself told Billie this man had never been in reverse. Suddenly she wished she had taken the time to change Doris' bed.

The man was at the cue rack looking down the sticks for the least crooked one when Billie approached him with her tray.

"Look, sweetheart," he said, before Billie had opened her mouth, "if I want a drink, I'll call you."

"How about a quarter for the jukebox?" Billie tried to look him in the eye and blow a smile at the same time, but the man only turned to face the pool table.

Five new Doggies had come in. "PBR," they all said, "in the can."

"Five blues," Billie told Gaddy, "and hold the glasses."

The Negro was getting to his feet.

"Hurry back to see us, now," Billie told him.

The Negro had stood up too quickly and had to steady himself with the table. Billie knew how it felt when a person's head gets free and goes wandering off from the rest of his body. Her own head could get half a block sometimes before she'd remember her body down the street on a stool.

The Negro tried to speak, but a torrent of hot caramel squeezed over his bridge. A sheet of it lopped off the table edge onto the floor, spattering Billie's black mesh stockings.

Virgie Mae came running with a bucket and towel. Billie took them and motioned Virgie back to the bar.

"Now, honey," Billie told the Negro, "everything's going to be just fine. Now, if you'll just aim at this here bucket. . . ."

Again the Negro tried to speak, but only more vomit came; finally, when he was able to talk, he had stopped trying to. Billie stood beside him and pulled one of his arms across her shoulders. "Which way you parked, honey?" The Negro raised and lowered his chin toward the back door.

Out on Ellis Street the wind was getting up. It was easy to spot the Negro's car in the lot. It was a white '65 Mustang. Along the side, in red enamel italic was MR. GOODFOOT. Billie helped the Negro inside like a dutiful mother tucking in a child. "You wait a while before you try to drive now," she said, but the young man was already slapping his pockets for the keys.

As she turned to go back, Billie saw a tow truck from Terry's

Paint and Body Works rounding the corner of Fifth Street. She hurried back inside.

Gaddy had stepped from behind the bar and was watching the commotion out the front window. The flashing yellow dome light on the cab of the tow truck competed with the black light inside the lounge.

"Just in time for the live entertainment," Gaddy laughed as Billie came up beside him. "All this lounge needed was a yellow strobe light."

Men with cable were crouching around the Cadillac's fins. One of them stood up and signaled to the driver. To Billie's surprise, the Cadillac was hoisted up tail first. Its grille was aimed down at the street like a great sad face. Billie could see her dice swinging side to side from the mirror, rubbing against the windshield.

As the wrecker jerked away, a feeling came over Billie as though she were in a rail terminal with no train to catch. It was the same way she felt when a silver bus swept past her full of strangers going places. Billie let her eyes wander up the black-lit ceiling where they might have filled with tears if Gaddy hadn't spoken.

"Better git a mop and some Lysol," he said, "that nigger's vomited all over creation."

Sally Robinson

OVERTURNED

Jacob Katz was thirty years old, lived in an old falling-down mansion, and collected unemployment insurance. He lived in the house rent-free. It belonged to the father of a former Princeton friend. "I'm a caretaker," Jacob told everyone. Now and again, he would mow the lawn near the house. The rest of the land he ignored. He spoke French like a Frenchman and Italian like a child. He read both like a scholar. Leslie met him at a party. He took her arm and said, "Let's go for coffee."

"Do you teach at the university?" Leslie asked when they were in the car.

"I'm a caretaker." There were several Coca-Cola cans on the floor of the car. Jacob kicked them out of his way. "I taught once. Drama." He held two wires together and touched the starter with the tip of an ice pick. "Old car," he explained. He took off his sweater. His shirt was unironed. "What a party. My God." He laughed nasally, making a strange harsh sound in the back of his throat. It ceased abruptly. "I've forgotten your name," he said.

"Leslie."

"Jacob." They shook hands, then he pulled her toward him and kissed her mouth.

"Drive the car," Leslie suggested.

"Don't start telling me what to do," Jacob said.

He drove to Pat and Sandy's Diner. After his coffee, Jacob ordered scrambled eggs and a Coca-Cola. Leslie smoked a cigarette and watched him eat. "You're satisfied with your life?" he asked her. "What are you looking for?"

"I take what I find," she said grandly, exhaling smoke like a movie queen.

"I'm looking," Jacob said. "I want to fall in love. Are you in love?"

"No." Leslie ordered another cup of coffee.

"Karina just moved out," Jacob said. "She's taken half the goddamn kitchen with her. We had two can openers. She took them both."

The summer session began. Leslie taught her class at nine-thirty. Every morning a man had to clean the pigeon droppings from the building steps. The building was part of the original university and had Latin words dug in above the pillars. A deep ledge ran between the words and the roof. The pigeons lived there. They stroked each other's necks and made soft noises like a woman gargling in the morning. And every morning, a man came to hose down the steps. And every morning, even when it hadn't rained, the wet steps made it look as though it had.

Leaving the building, Leslie heard her name. It was Jacob.

They made love in his summer bedroom. When they were finished, he put the pillow under her head. "Are you hungry?" Jacob asked.

"Just a cigarette if you have one." The telephone rang. "Can you get that?"

Leslie lifted the receiver. "Hello?"

"Hello," a woman said. "I'm calling for the Rochester Guide to Consumer Products. Can you tell me please, are you married?"

"No," Leslie said.

"That's fine. Do you use a commercially prepared douche?"

"No, I don't."

"You don't. Thank you so much, you've been very helpful."

Sally Robinson   *43*

"That's all right." Leslie replaced the receiver. Jacob handed her a cigarette.

"That was Karina, wasn't it?"

The photograph showed Karina standing next to Jacob in front of his house. Leslie studied the photograph and put it back.

"The President of the United States is going to resign," Frank said. "Do you know, everyone's crazy?" He paced around Leslie's office. She looked at her watch. "Do you know, I went to have my teeth cleaned yesterday? The goddamn hygienist started to tell me about her therapy. I'm not joking." He pulled at his moustache. "She said she couldn't remember her dreams until she went to a therapist. It turns out she was repressing her anger. Now she dreams about choking her relatives. I'm not making this up, Leslie. All this, while she's cleaning my teeth. You don't believe me."

"I believe you," Leslie said.

"You're smiling. Goddamn you, Leslie. Don't smile. My thesis is at a standstill," he added morosely. "What time is it?"

"Eleven-fifteen."

"I've got a class. I hate students. They're so personal. Leslie, come to Toronto with me. Just for the weekend."

"I can't."

"You can't," he repeated. "Know anybody who can?"

The sun was in the kitchen and it made Leslie think of small, perfect children and cereal and glass pitchers of milk. Like a cornflake commercial. There's too much television, she realized. I won't let my children watch so much. The dog, Ola, lay on the floor, watching Jacob make toast.

"Today," Jacob said, "we'll go to the country and pick strawberries." Leslie stroked the dog. Ola blinked and turned to face Leslie.

"Good girl," Leslie said softly. "Good girl. How do you know they'll be ripe?"

"Saw it in the paper," Jacob said briefly. "Saw it in the stars."

At the side of the road, the boy sat in an old camp chair, his feet dangling. He wore a pair of blue rubber thongs and he scrunched his toes, making the thongs flap against his heels. The wooden quart boxes, stained with strawberry juice, were stacked on a card table. A cardboard sign leaned against the table leg. Strawberries, it said. U-Pick. 45¢.

"What's in there?" Jacob pointed to the cardboard box weighted down with a large cement brick. The box moved, just slightly.

"Toad," the boy said. "Biggest toad you've ever seen."

Leslie straightened her skirt and pushed her hair behind her ears. She smiled at the boy. "Maybe you should put some holes in the box," she said. "So he can breathe."

The boy shrugged. "I don't care. The sheriff's givin' thirty dollars for him, dead or alive."

"You're making that up," Jacob said. Leslie frowned at him.

"I ain't, swear to God." The boy flapped his thongs and grinned at Jacob. "You wanna see him?"

"How big is he?"

"Big as a kitten. And this one ain't full-grown. Sheriff says full-grown they weigh 'bout three pounds."

"It came from outer space, huh?" Jacob stood on one leg and scratched his knee.

"Come from the university. Somebody overturned a whole barrel of 'em an' they just escaped. Two of 'em been run over by trucks."

"Let's see." Jacob kneeled down next to the box. "Is there a slit or something I can look through?"

"Uh huh. Over in the back. Watch out now. Sheriff says he's got poison. Could kill a dog," the boy added proudly. "Can you make him out?"

"Kind of. It's dark. Leslie, want to have a look?"

Leslie balanced on the balls of her feet and peered through the slit in the box. She saw nothing. Then a toad eye gleamed. The creature spoke. Leslie drew away, startled. The boy laughed.

"Hey," he said, "that's the mating call. He must like you, lady. How many boxes you want for pickin'?"

"Four," Jacob said. "How come your toad's worth thirty bucks?"

"Sheriff says they gotta all be caught or it's gonna upset the ecology around here."

The strawberry field stretched before her. In the distance, other people bent and searched. You had to lift the leaves, reach beneath, and look for the largest berries. They reminded Leslie of the large strawberries Bosch had painted and she half expected tiny naked people to emerge, eating seeds and dancing. She became tired of balancing on her feet and she simply knelt, letting her knees get dirty. It would be pleasant to own a strawberry garden, she thought. To come out every morning and look down the rows. To say, these are my strawberries. I put the seeds in the ground and strawberries grew. Back to the soil. Don't be so romantic, she told herself. You'd last two weeks on a farm.

Still, when she rose, she looked out to where there were no people and pretended. My field, she pretended. My strawberries.

"I swear to God," Frank said. "If I find two of those toads, I'm going to mate them. The balance of nature needs a good fucking over. Why, for example, are there so many Chinese?"

"Frank—"

"I'm ridiculous, Leslie. It's your fault. You wouldn't come to Toronto. I spent the weekend in bed with the checker at the A&P. She wouldn't let me get on top of her because she said I weighed too much. I said, okay, you get on top. She said no, that way she felt like she was drifting. I said there are a million ways to fuck, just pick one. She said, let's do it side by side like the land and the water." Frank pulled his moustache. "Like the land and the water, Leslie. Tell me the truth now. Have you ever heard anything more beautiful? Should I marry her?"

She found the pornography on the lower shelf in the autumn bedroom. "Do you read these?" Leslie asked curiously. She thumbed through a copy of *The Dean's Revenge*. It was illustrated.

"Do I read what?" Jacob turned from the window. She tossed him the book and he caught it with one hand. "I didn't buy them for decoration. This isn't a bad one. See the pictures?"

"*Angie Makes Friends*," Leslie said, reading aloud the title of a hardbound volume.

"That's a better one, if you like whips. Do you like whips?"

"I doubt it."

"Have you ever tried?"

"No." Leslie turned away from the shelf.

"You should," Jacob advised.

"Maybe some other time." Leslie saw his face. "You're serious, aren't you?"

"Of course I'm serious," he said. He walked around the bed and came to stand next to her. "Go on," Jacob said. "Hit me as hard as you can and see how it feels."

"No."

"Don't be afraid."

"I'm not afraid. I don't want to."

"Okay, I'll hit you first."

Leslie walked down the driveway, away from Jacob's house. On either side of her, the trees were thick and full-grown. It was getting dark, but she saw the toad clearly. She went back to the house and quietly lifted a metal garbage can. She walked back slowly, careful not to make any noise. When she got there, the toad was gone.

Charles R. Richison

Excerpt from
HOLLOW AUGUST

Steelwork was the only work that W. O. Tanner knew, and after
being away in prison for seven years he was worried whether or
not he would be rehired. He arrived early and parked the pickup
in front of Zottman's Grocery, a little store sandwiched between
two of the huge metal buildings of the steel plant, where the
workers gathered, shoulder to shoulder, buying cigarettes or
candy or other necessities for the coming day's work. He was
anxious to get inside; to see his old friends, yet there was some-
thing in being away seven years that made him want to savor
this moment. He got out of the pickup and walked very slowly
into the store.

There was a special coolness about Zottman's at seven o'clock
in the morning. The air conditioners had run all night with the
heat of the coming day and the warm threat on the east side of
buildings; Zottman's seemed even cold. As he entered, he could
hear the men in the back at the meat counter, thirty or forty of
them, drinking coffee and talking; the loud and robust talk of
steelmen. He knew this talk, felt an affinity for it, found a sense
of security in it. These weren't the best of men. At night, at
Taulburt's or one of the other shanty bars out on the river road,
they'd fight, among themselves mainly, because when the steel-

men hit a certain bar, they became that bar's only clientele. And they usually fought in groups, bound together one night by race, the next by religion, though none could be called religious unless he needed something to fight about; the next perhaps by political party or maybe the married men against the bachelors, usually with fists, misguided by drunkenness, usually being rowdy more than mad; and always, when morning came, they would be at Zottman's, laughing about the previous night's battle, loud, boisterous laughter, the laughter of steelmen—of Toupaheela Steel.

When W.O. was a boy, young and impressionable, he would get up on summer mornings and go down to Zottman's, buy some gum or a Coca-Cola, and hide in the aisles listening and peeking around to where the men stood, then as now, drinking and talking and laughing. He somehow knew that someday he would be one of them. And as he watched them he imagined how he'd dress. He'd have white jersey gloves, blackened on the palms by manganese and iron and grease. He'd keep them in his back pocket and let the fingers dangle out when he walked. At first he thought he wanted to wear khakis, but then he realized that it was the older men who wore the khakis, the younger ones wore blue jeans. He'd wear blue jeans, or wheat jeans—wheat jeans because then the black of a day's work would show on his thighs and lap in evidence that he was a steelman of Toupaheela Steel.

And he'd wear a T-shirt or a western shirt with the sleeves torn away or rolled up high on his arms so his biceps and shoulders would show; brown, thick, and hopefully bulging with the power that the heavy steel built in the arms and shoulders and back. And he thought, back then, he'd like to be a welder or a primer so there wouldn't be any doubt in anyone's mind that he was a steel worker, because the welders had black resin around their mouths and wore the quilted, welding-mask liner that hung down over their ears and the back of their necks like a fighter pilot's cap. Or, if he was a primer, he'd have orange paint from head to toe and the mask dangling around his neck, made orange itself where it would filter the air he'd breathe.

But most of all, as he hid in the aisles, he liked to listen to their talk; crude, vulgar talk that was music to a young boy's ears. And their voices: deep, resonant voices, almost indistinguishable as

Charles R. Richison   49

to who said what, to him they were just the hardy voices of men, the voices of steelmen.

"Loan me ten, man."

"Loan you ten? Shit! I'm so broke, if a whore walked in here right now offerin' it up for a nickel a shot, all I could do is run up and down these aisles with my hands in my pockets sayin', 'Damn that's cheap! Goddamn that's cheap!'"

"They's a lot for sale out on the old river road and the highway. A man could get that lot for a handshake and a good joke."

"Son-of-a-bitch! I've tried every son-of-a-bitchin' thing I can to try to get that son-of-a-bitch to fight, but all the chicken-shit, son-of-a-bitch does is fuckin' walks off. The son-of-a-bitch!"

"Stick your middle finger 'bout half way up his nose and tell him about the mole on his ol' lady's ass."

"Got a match?"

"Your face and my butt."

"A man could put him a used-car lot out there on that lot. Make him a killin'."

"Zottman, you got anything for chapped lips?"

"Tried chicken shit?"

"Why, does that work?"

"No, but you'll sure as hell think twice 'bout lickin' 'em."

"Wonder what that woman down at Taulburt's 'd do for a saw-buck?"

"'Bout half of what she'd do for two."

"Tell you what, I'd eat that honey on the fifty-yard line of the O.U.-Texas game at half time."

"Let her pee in your face just to see where it's comin' from, huh?"

"With my mother watchin'."

"That *is* one nice little woman. Wish I had a pup out of her."

"Now, of course, a man could put him up a fruit stand on that lot. They's good money in fruit. And then in the winter time he could sell fire wood and Christmas trees. Make him a goddamn wad."

"Hot out there, yet?"

"Is a cat's ass furry?"

"What if his ol' lady ain't got a mole on her ass?"

"Everybody's ol' lady's got a mole on her ass."

"Time Dempsey get through with that son-of-a-bitch, he ain't gonna know whether he's washin' or hangin' out."

"I'll take ten of that."

"Hear you got pretty drunk last night. How you feel this mornin'?"

"Ever had a duck shit in your mouth?"

"Education my ass! I tell you what, fella. A man that works with his brains don't build nothin' but bullshit and a broad ass unless there's men like us, men that works with their hands and their backs and their guts and their sweat, that puts all that goddamn education to use. It's them little cross-legged, four-eyed bastards that did all the plannin', but it's men like us that built this nation of ours. Education? You keep that back educated and them arms. That's all the education you'll ever need!"

"Buy that man a drink!"

Just talk. Just voices in a young boy's head. But when he was a boy it was all he'd ever hoped of achieving. Not a Ruth or a Dempsey, but a common steel worker—at Toupaheela Steel.

And he knew there was a price. In that same boyhood he would wait for them in the afternoon and when the whistle blew, he would watch them walk from the giant, ribbed-metal edifices; coming in groups; talking, Black, Indian, Mexican and White, walking together; bound by or united in their fatigue and their respect for and pride in each other's workmanship—sense of worth. Not blood brothers, but brothers of sweat; sweat they had each given for no other reason than the buck, sweat that melted and mingled in the cold dirt floors of the huge metal coffins, as if each had been responsible for his job, and in doing his job, holding up his end: they had, together, defeated the coffins for one more day, were victors over the dirge of unworthiness or mundanity; and they could go to their bars or their homes, tired and feeling good in their fatigue, thirsty and feeling worthy of drink, horny and feeling deserving of their women, because they were men, known to all, respected by all as being men; hard men, strong men, rough, rowdy, stern, stoic, vulgar, simple, filthy, poor, but proud men, real men, steelmen—of Toupaheela Steel.

Charles R. Richison

Agnes Riedmann

TO SOAR

She didn't cry at the funeral. "Parents die," she said to her husband later in defense of herself. "Papa had a long life. . . . Parents die, that's all. People ought to be ready for that."

Her husband went up to bed then, but he left his uneasiness there in the room, behind the sofa and in the deep folds of the velvet drapes, for her to deal with.

"Parents die, that's all," she said again, to the discomfort, and lit a new cigarette from the shorter one she found between her fingers. "People ought to be ready for that."

"And what will you do about your mother?" her husband asked the next morning at breakfast.

She poured canned grape juice for him and the children. "Mother will be all right," she said.

"Have you called her?" he pressed.

"No."

She set a bottle of chewable vitamins in the center of the table. With vitamins you didn't have to worry so much what they ate all day.

When they were gone she lit a cigarette and looked out the window. They had hung her once, naked, on a wire clothesline, a bleached wooden clothespin sucking at each of her ten long fingers. They had come then in the sultry humidity of a steaming

INTRO 7

sun to pick at her. With dirty fingernails they tore away bits of her flesh, eating then, strengthening growing sinews with her own, much as once the young ones pulled the calcium from her very teeth to grow their skeletons.

Seated still at their breakfast table, she blew smoke toward a tiny dust-grease stalactite which had grown belligerently from the kitchen ceiling. She smoked five cigarettes, lighting each successive new one from the previous, then banged a clenched fist against Formica and went up to the bedroom.

She opened windows and turned up the radio. She pulled loose blue jeans over thinning legs and ran a comb through her hair, forgetting to brush her teeth.

Downstairs, the screen door banged behind her as she slid into the wagon, turning keys she found in the ignition. In a nearby park she leaned against a thick tree, isolated from playground equipment by a deep ravine, and smoked a pack of cigarettes.

"Do you think she'll like it there?" her husband insisted some days later.

"Why shouldn't she like it there?"

"I don't know. Your mother in an old people's home. It just doesn't sit right, that's all."

"It's not an old people's home. It's an apartment house for people her age," she said.

She cried that night, long secret sobs that she hoped he wouldn't hear. But he did hear and took her into his arms, comforting. "It's all right," he soothed. "You need to cry. I've been waiting for you to cry."

A laugh formed then, down low in her stomach, between her pelvic bones, because he thought she sobbed for her father. The laugh came up through her torso, oozing out her pores, and running like milk from her nipples until, feeding on itself, it erupted in orgasmic rhythm from her throat. *He thought she sobbed for her father!*

She felt cold water splash against her face, breaking the laughter. Her eyes jerked open to see her husband standing over her, an emptied lavatory glass still in his raised hand. "I'm sorry,"

Agnes Riedmann   53 he said, visibly shaken. "I had to do it; you were hysterical. Are you all right now?"

"I'm all right," she said, rising from their bed, searching cigarettes. "I think I'll sit up awhile. You get some sleep."

She imagined their deaths, in some kind of freak freeway accident, coming home from a basketball game at the auditorium, or from a movie perhaps. Not a movie though, because usually she went with them to movies. She dressed each one for his or her respective coffin, the girl in her favorite dress and best shoes, the boys in their suits. One would need a new sport coat; the sleeves were too short now. She combed and properly arranged their hair. In the girl's hands she positioned a doll, the one she'd gotten for Christmas the year before last. The boys would carry, what? Trucks? Baseball gloves?

And what of the man? What would he wear? His best suit? Saturday Levi's? Probably they would insist at the mortuary that he wear a suit. What tie? And what would he hold in his hands? His key ring maybe. He was never without the key ring. His billfold maybe. That way he'd have his identification with him. And his Master Charge card.

But it struck her that if they met death in a horrid accident their coffins might be closed, and then she would not have to be concerned with what they wore or what they carried.

What would *she* wear? She had no appropriate black dress. Maybe she'd buy one. A veil? Nobody wears veils any more though.

Her gums began to ache, and she knew the pyorrhea was coming back. "Are you using your floss, dear?" the dentist would once more admonish. "Your waterpick?"

She imagined then the man's death, at the hand of some lunatic Tuesday-afternoon office-building sniper. She would take the others to the funeral, holding the youngest by the hand. They would see her there—the relatives, the acquaintances, his friends and business associates—they would see her and say to themselves, "Whatever she does now, to hold herself together, is fine."

She would sell the house then, and the heavy, velvet drapes, and the wagon, and take the children to the mountains maybe. Sit in a stream to cool her pulsing, clothespin-scarred fingers.

Later she baked him his favorite cake, German chocolate, crumpled an empty cigarette package, and went to his bed.

She had done that once before—left him—two years ago now. It was after he had stuffed her, a grand Thanksgiving turkey, spent years stuffing her with the right ingredients, the proper amounts of personal seasonings. And once she had been properly dressed, roasted to the loveliest complexion, he had set her in the center of his table. He had stood there, ooing, awing, above the feast. When he spoke of carving, she gathered her children to flee the knife.

She had told him they would take a summer excursion, told him they'd be back in a few weeks, lying.

"Why?" he'd asked.

"Just because," she said. "You're busy with the firm now. We'll go and be back shortly. You'll see."

He had consented, nervously, and in the end he even helped her pack the car. "Where will you go?" he persisted.

"Maybe Minnesota," she replied from nowhere within, to quiet him. "I'll call you tonight."

She headed west with them into the mountains. Two weeks later she phoned. "I lost track of the time," she explained, meaning it. "Don't worry, we'll be back soon. I'll call you tomorrow."

She received his letter that month, sorry then that she had communicated her cottage address. He ordered—then on the second page he begged—that she come home now. He said there was a doctor there, waiting, one he had spoken of before. The doctor would help. But she knew the doctors only add some sliced raw apple to the stuffing, making it sweeter, lending variety.

She rode horseback with them that summer, almost every day. Gradually the stuffing lost hold, began to jiggle from her body cavity at the persistence of the trotting horse. She was feeling some better, felt room again in her chest for oxygen.

One of them though, the second oldest, had begun to steal things. First a tiny Indian-beaded souvenir from a roadside tee-pee. Then a drugstore comb. Marbles. So she drove them home to the discipline of their father.

Agnes Riedmann   55

She packed little this time. One suitcase did it. Jeans, a nylon jacket, some cotton knit shirts, panties, a pair of sneakers, Hermann Hesse paperbacks. They would say, "Her father's death must have shaken her more than she let on. It's the ones who don't cry that take it the hardest." It was a good time to go.

She slept the first night in the back of her wagon, parked at an interstate rest stop. She had driven several miles the next morning when she realized she had left her cosmetics in the public restroom. She didn't go back.

As the sun came high, springtime warm, she pulled the car to the shoulder of the road, slid over, and got out on the passenger side. She would walk some now because she felt like walking.

She felt the crunch, from inside her sneakers, of the remains of last year's corn crop—not the sharp, brittle crunch of fall-emptied stalks, but rather the wet, sludge-crunch of defeated husks in March, themselves having been hanged on wire clotheslines by a beating winter. A persistent, haunting hunger irritated her: she would walk now because she felt like walking.

It occurred to her that the husband was probably phoning relatives, asking what they knew, was she there, had they heard from her, where would she have gone. Momentarily she wondered whether the children had cried.

With the late afternoon chill, she returned to the car, consciously pondering whether she yet felt refreshed. She would drive into the next highway town, find food there and a hotel room. There would be no problem about money, at least for a while; she would write to her bank, withdrawing from her personal savings account gradually, as the need arose.

A two-story brick hotel stood in the center of the town, on a black-topped street at right angles to the highway. She parked in a small lot adjacent the hotel and locked her wagon. At the counter in the lobby she paid an extra two dollars per night for a room with a private bath, then carried her suitcase up the worn carpeted stairway.

She unlocked the green-painted door to her room, and entered upon a chenille-spreaded double bed and blond, spindle-legged furniture. She moved to open the window, but it had been painted shut.

Three weeks she stayed in the room, reading, sleeping, mixing herself instant warm tea with bathroom tap water. Her gums aching steadily now, she acquired the habit of lying half awake, a cold wash cloth pressed into her teeth.

The morning she left, she tried the window again. When it wouldn't open, she slammed a stubborn cracker box into the tiny wastebasket, threw scattered clothing into her case, and went out to her wagon.

The place intrigued her. A curious accumulation of junk and antiques to the left of the highway, covering five square city blocks perhaps, if you counted what had strayed from the density of it all. Rusting car bodies, broken rocking chairs, kitchen tables like the one her grandmother had had, with the drawer for the silver in the middle of the long side, butter churns, clay pots for planting, milk cans, an old grindstone, the middle-aged man inside the large open garage, admiring a mahogany back-bar.

"Hello," she said when he refused to notice her.

"Hello," he said, not looking up.

She sat on a maroon sofa, ignoring the mildew stench of its rotting cushions. "Do you sell these things?" she wanted to know.

"Sometimes," he answered, interrupted.

"Who buys them?"

"People."

She lit a cigarette. "Where'd you get the back-bar?"

"Brought it out of the mountains."

"How?"

"Flatbed truck."

"How long did it take?" she persisted.

"Four days."

"Do you often do things like that?" she asked, exhilarated, learning.

He eased a few drops of lemon oil from the bottle he held onto a soft, gray cloth. She watched him rub at the lion's-paw curve which supported a shelf intended for glassware. "Have you been here long?"

"Yes," he said, polishing.

"Are you married?"

He did not respond; the chill of him crept across the cracked cement floor, edged up to sit next to her on the sofa.

"I've been wandering almost five weeks now," she told him after she had smoked some time in silence. He didn't answer. "I left them, my husband, the children."

"I stayed in a hotel three weeks," she said, "just reading, thinking." She paused then, awaiting some sign of empathy, understanding. But he continued to buff the back-bar and she heard herself say, "I can go anywhere now, see anything I want to see." She inhaled. "Meet all different kinds of people."

She shifted, pulling her legs into herself, folding them Indian style under her on the sofa. "Do you live alone here?" she asked him.

"Yes," he replied.

"Do you intend to sell the back-bar?"

"I don't know."

"Why did you go to get it then?"

"I like it."

"Life is good for you," she said, asking. He rubbed calloused fingers over mahogany smooth.

Light withdrew from the burden of the room. She rose to leave. "If you're hungry now," he offered suddenly, "I have some canned peaches."

"Thank you," she responded.

He shuffled to a small white refrigerator in the corner of the cluttered garage, came back with a can of chilled cling peaches, searched his junk for an opener. Rummaging through a metal cabinet, he foraged out two plastic bowls, steel spoons.

"I left," she said, cutting a tender peach half with the edge of her spoon, "because I was crippled, couldn't walk."

Staring, he didn't answer.

"I wanted to begin again, live a brand-new way."

He was eating ravenously, placing the peach halves into his mouth whole.

"We lived in the city. I was always driving them somewhere," she explained. He did not look up.

The granite of him tired her and she rose, not finishing the peaches. "I must go," she said.

He didn't answer; instead he looked at her for the first time, peered into her. Uncomfortable, she shivered. He noticed because he said, "You needn't worry. I won't bother you. I am not that way any more."

She laughed heartily, holding her narrow sides, bending in two with the humor, because he thought she feared him. "Nor am I," she said finally, recovering.

As she walked from the place, a cool breeze brushed her bare arms, and she held herself, hurried. She bent her head to see tiny particles of Thanksgiving bread cubes, celery bits, old now, descend from her as she jogged. The dog must have smelled it, she mused later, and, starving, labored toward food.

He was a big dog, part Irish setter probably. His auburn glinted in the last traces of daylight. He crawled rather than walked, whining with each major advance. When he reached her, she saw that the left rear leg had been torn, by the jaws of a rabbit trap perhaps.

She sat next to him, cradling his head in her lap for what seemed a long time. Later she rose and eased him into the car. At her motel she smuggled him up the vacant outside stairway, half pushing, half carrying. Once inside her room, she ran bath water lukewarm, tearing her top sheet into strips to bind the wound.

She bathed him, first the ruptured leg, then the rest of him. She lit a cigarette and held it close to a bulging tick, fastened tight behind one ear. The tick wiggled some, and she moved the cigarette end closer. It raised its head then, backing off.

She wrapped muslin around the red and white of his inner leg, gave him water to drink. He slept at the foot of her bed that night. The next morning she went out to buy some peroxide, hamburger, eggs. She bought a two-burner hotplate, some bowls, a fork, one frypan. She diluted the peroxide in water and changed the animal's dressing.

That night she lay quiet, hurting, a cold wash cloth shoved tight against gnawing gums. She cried some with the anguish, and the dog came to her, struggled onto the bed next to her, licked her fingers. They convalesced together, sleeping much, sharing the hamburger, eggs, peroxide. Gradually the animal learned to walk, holding the damaged leg up, tucked in behind him, useless but not throbbing.

When they grew stronger, she took him out into the air. She bought a collar for him, and a leash, so that she could more easily walk with him. It occurred to her one morning as they sat near a pond in a small town park that she might name him. She named him "Friend," because he had come to be hers, and threw out a hard rubber ball she had bought for twenty-nine cents at a sundries store. He scurried to retrieve it, setting down the scarred leg with every other leap, and when he was back she hugged the silky, faithful skull.

They roamed the countryside, sharing food and beds, playing, learning, recovering together. Summer baked hot for what seemed the first time as their wagon approached a small roadside cafe.

"Wait here, Friend," she said, rolling up windows. "I'll be out in a jiffy."

Inside the cafe, ceiling fans purred above the sporadic humming of motors, freezing, cooling, mixing, warming. Chrome gleamed harsh in the bright light as it shone over inadequate ringed curtains along the front windows.

Sliding into a booth, she glanced at the menu. When a waitress ambled over, she ordered a roast beef sandwich without mayonnaise and a glass of milk. She searched her purse for change, walked to a pink and green jukebox with bubbles going up and down inside transparent tubes, inserted a quarter, and pushed buttons without reading the selections.

Back in the booth she lit a cigarette and pulled a paperback from her purse, fingered absently through the dog-eared pages, and began to read. Her lunch arrived.

Mid-afternoon heat waves projected off the front bumper when she stepped from the restaurant. Inside the wagon she saw the setter, limp from the warmth, a pool of pink vomit on the floor beneath him. Confused eyes blinked and followed her as she slid into her place behind the wheel. She rolled down windows, said, "I'm sorry, dog," to the windshield and started the motor.

They turned off the highway, headed along an unpaved county road. "I didn't expect to be so long," she said aloud. "Just lost track of the time, that's all." Dust rebelled at being disturbed, came in through vents to ruffle her. It was in a tiny valley between two sharp inclines of the road that she stopped.

"Out," she said, twisting in her place to open the back door. The dog didn't move. "You have to get out now," she persisted. She removed the leash from the leather collar, and the animal slumped from the wagon.

She caught glimpses of him in her rear-view mirror as he ran after the car, undaunted by the dust pitched back at him. Soon she reached the crest of the hill; with the descent he was gone.

There was a tree she wanted to sit by, because of its thick trunk, pleasant shade. But running toward it, she found it was anchored farther away than she had first imagined. Her gait slowed; she stumbled some. She brushed a stinging fly from behind her shoulder, realizing suddenly an urgent need to urinate. Angry, she persisted. She would walk because she wanted to walk.

Her feet groped, she lit a cigarette. She slapped at piercing flies, sweating her bra and shirt wet. The urine came then, trickled along the inside of her thighs, under her jeans, down into her shoes.

She sat a moment. But the acid gushed more heavily, soaking the ground beneath her, the burning wet stinging her buttocks.

David Reich

JOCKO'S TREE

If you go by Benmar's Luncheonette someday, there's a better than even chance you'll see a skinny junkie sitting cross-legged on the sidewalk in front, nodding like a Mexican at siesta time. Jocko Gruber is so strung out he's like a town joke. He'll sell you orégano at twenty dollars an ounce, and once I heard he was pimping for a sixteen-year-old girl. There are young kids around who can't remember when he was not like this. If you tell them that ten years back Jocko Gruber was the biggest hood in town, that he was worshiped and feared, that guys walked down the halls of East Bergen High School trying to copy Jocko's funny bowlegged strut, they're likely to laugh in your face. But there are still a few guys like me around who knew Jocko before he started sticking needles in his arm.

It was Dizzy Gillespie who got me involved with Jocko Gruber back in the days when Jocko was still on top of things. Dizzy Gillespie: I filled a huge leather scrapbook I'd got as a Bar Mitzvah present with news photos of Dizzy in fezzes, berets, straw coolie hats, and silk Afro-turbans. In school I spent long afternoons writing crude poems in his honor. I thought I was some kind of beatnik. Where most guys whiled away boring classes doodling pictures of rocket ships or souped-up cars, I drew ballpoint sketches of Dizzy Gillespie playing the trumpet, Dizzy

Gillespie laughing, Dizzy Gillespie snapping his fingers. The rare drawings that captured the true Dizzy I'd pass around the room for the benefit of the class. Mostly they humored me, though sometimes my drawings came back with comments like "Fucken Nigger Dizzy" scrawled in pencil. This was probably the work of Willy Koffman, the junior Nazi, who Maureen Bowser, a tough little girl from my neighborhood, had nicknamed Kuff-man on account of the played-out cuffed pants he always wore.

The poems and drawings were just the beginning, though. It was only after the first time I saw Dizzy on TV the September of my freshman year that my propaganda campaign really shifted into high gear. On Sunday I found out that Dizzy was making a guest appearance on Vic Damone's "Lively People" show the following Wednesday night, and Tuesday and Wednesday mornings I ran around before school trying to get people to promise they would watch. Most of them claimed that their family had to watch "The Beverly Hillbillies" in that time slot.

Still, by Wednesday night I was terrifically keyed up. Ma was out at my sister's violin lesson, and the old man was down in the basement with his ham radio, so I had the television to myself. I sat back on my mother's green couch, waiting for Dizzy to appear on the screen. The TV buzzed and flickered, but when the picture came on it was Vic Damone on a sailboat dock, with the wind blowing his hair and seagulls wheeling overhead while he sang "I Left My Heart in San Francisco." After that, I suffered through a Ford commercial, and then a Connie Francis number with alternating verses in Yiddish and Italian. It was almost too horrible to believe.

When the picture flashed to Dizzy, though, I tuned right in to the vibrations he was sending out. His whole band was set up on a beach: a bass man, a drummer with his traps, a conga player, and even an upright piano out on the sand. The camera focused in on Dizzy, his cheeks puffed out like a pair of bellows, his body bent back like a limbo dancer's, the bell of his trumpet catching the sun and reflecting it in a blur of light. I reeled back in amazement.

As far as Dizzy's solo, it was snaking and turning in a hundred weird directions. It was as though Dizzy had uncovered the secret of his horn and now it was playing itself, running itself up and down scales faster than any man could make it run. I closed my eyes and my head filled with a light that was the color of brass. The solo could have gone on forever and I would have just sat there taking it in.

But after a couple choruses, the band went back into the head of "Night in Tunisia," and Dizzy finished up with a drawn-out, flashy coda. The second he was done, Vic Damone came on again, but before he could say two words I switched off the set and flew out of the house. I had just hatched another farfetched plan to push Dizzy on my friends.

Halfway across the school field, I slowed to a fast walk. I passed the row of maple trees that grew by the side of Pulaski School, and continued out to River Road and across to the shopping center. It was after nine, and aside from Fowler's Bar and Bowl-o-Drome, the only place that stayed open that late was a candy store called the Manchester Spa. The Spa was run by Mrs. Lipschutz, an old lady with an ape face and feather-duster hair. I went right in and asked her if she was still selling those toy kazoos. Mrs. Lipschutz gave me one of her famous ape looks. She hadn't had much use for me since five years before, when she had caught me lifting seven packs of baseball cards and a girlie magazine. Finally she croaked, "Just a minute," and started poking around behind the lunch counter. After a while she came up with a dusty old metal kazoo. In case you've never seen a kazoo, they look something like a flattened-out tobacco pipe and sound like Donald Duck. As far as I know, no kazooist has ever won a *Down Beat* readers' poll.

I decided the locker room was the best place to try out my plan. In the lockers before and after gym class was the only time all day that there wasn't a teacher watching over your shoulder, and often guys would sing their favorite rock songs while they suited up. The gym teacher I had that year, a cross-eyed guy from Oklahoma named Mr. Marshall, had such a bad time controlling us that he wouldn't come near the lockers unless we were damn near breaking down the walls. Hell, he was happy as long as he could shoot his baskets. People said he would have made the pros except for his eyes.

Anyway, that particular Thursday, Marshall had other business after class. We were wrestling, and that day Marshall had his pet, Dick Himmel, up against Jocko Gruber, who was number 1 on Marshall's shit parade. Jocko refused to do calisthenics, and it burned Marshall's ass.

The whole class, in gray gym shorts, was crowded around the smelly green mats, shooting the bull, while Marshall went over the rules with Himmel and Jocko. I was standing with Fat Joey Gross, a kid with an ass the size of a weather balloon. Ever since the day Fat Joey's old man, the preacher from St. Matthew's Lutheran, suddenly died and Joey came into school singing "Ding-Dong, the Witch Is Dead," he'd had a reputation as a crazy, mean bastard, but we were buddies and he treated me okay. On the other side of Joey was Little Denny Latino, a dandy hood with a baby face and liquidy eyes who worked behind the counter at Benmar's Luncheonette. Denny wasn't very tough for a hood, but half the girls in the ninth grade were crazy over him. He stood rocking on his heels, gazing across the mat and muttering to Joey: "Himmel only has about fifty pounds on Jocko. Talk about a setup! And just because Jocko won't do them stinking Mickey Mouse calisthenics that Cross Eyes is always trying to shove down our throats."

Fat Joey pursed his lips grimly: "I'd like to see Himmel take on Jocko in fronta Benmar's. There'd be blood, and it wouldn't be Jocko's."

I sneered at the whole business: "High school wrestling. Big fuckin' deal. It don't have anything to do with. . . ."

But then Marshall blew his referee's whistle, and we all focused on the center of the mats. Himmel, a big horse of a football player with a purple, acned face and huge, acned shoulders, started to circle around skinny bowlegged brown-freckled Gruber. Denny yelled advice to Jocko, and across the mats, a couple of Himmel's football buddies were yelling for him.

For a long time Himmel kept his distance, circling Jocko without touching him. Finally he lunged forward, grabbing hold of Jocko's left shoulder. Jocko looked at his shoulder as though a

David Reich 65

bird had just crapped on it, then threw a right that whizzed in the air and made a cracking sound when it connected with Himmel's skull.

The whole class started jumping up and down and screaming. Marshall blew his whistle frantically. Himmel was backpedaling and shaking his head as though he'd been dazed, and Marshall quick sneaked up behind Jocko and slipped a full nelson on him. Himmel had backed off the mats by then, and the class stood frozen for one quiet second. But then Marshall tried to tighten up his hold, and Jocko caught him with a backward shot in the balls. We all went crazy screaming. Marshall let up on the hold, and Jocko ran to the far wall of the gym.

He stood there bobbing like a prizefighter while Marshall stood stiffly in the middle of the mat trying to get back his wind. Again, the room was silent. Finally, Marshall called in a muffled voice: "Jock, put on your street clothes so I can take you to Mr. Fiorello's office."

Jocko sneered and cupped his right hand in front of his crotch: "Eat this, Marshall!" His voice echoed off the high brick walls.

Marshall started toward Jocko, moving slow. Then, behind us, the door of the Phys Ed office squeaked open. I looked back and saw Mr. LaRue, the wrestling coach, moving across the gym floor.

Jocko looked from LaRue to Marshall and back. The odds were too long. When they got in striking distance, he gave up his fighter's stance and let them lead him away to the gym teacher's office.

After Jocko was safely put away, Marshall came out and told us to go and get dressed, even though it was twenty minutes till the period ended.

We all filed into the low-ceilinged, windowless locker room, talking and arguing about the fight. I was so impressed by Jocko's performance that I'd practically forgotten my plan. Himmel, who was in front of me and seemed unhurt, was about the only one in the class who didn't have anything to say.

The air in the locker room smelled of moldy socks, and my row was crowded and noisy. Toward the aisle, Steve Muller, the school math whiz, was polishing his glasses with a handkerchief.

Next to me, Fat Joey discussed the fight with Joe "El Porco" D'Annunzio, a meaty but solid guy with fine, oiled hair and coppertone skin who played catcher on the East Bergen Babe Ruth All Stars. By the cinderblock wall at the end of the row, pointy-nosed Bruce Brennan stood around in a T-shirt and gray, tapered pants, sneering at the rest of us and once or twice bursting into a nasal rendition of "Book of Love" that trailed off into nothing after a few bars. Brennan was a minor hood who rarely talked to anyone except hoods more important than himself, but he was always on the lookout for an excuse to bully someone.

When I was finished dressing and had all my gym stuff put away in my locker, I stood by Joey's elbow till I got his and Porco's attention. Joey asked what was up, and I pulled the kazoo out of my pocket with a crazy little flourish and held it out in front of me.

Porco looked at me funny: "What's that thing? You gonna smoke a pipe or blow bubbles?"

Me: "It happens to be a musical instrument."

Porco leaned back against the lockers and whirled his index finger around his ear: "You're nuts, Silverman."

Joey broke in: "Nah, Silverman is okay."

I lifted the kazoo to my mouth and announced: "Dizzy Gillespie's 'Night in Tunisia'!"

Porco covered his ears and groaned, but I started playing anyway. Joey laughed and snapped his fingers in time, but when I hit the break between the head and the solo, Brennan, his teeth bared and gleaming, butted in front of him and started jabbing his finger at me: "You're so damn smart, Silverman. You don't stop in one second, I'll knock that piece of metal down your throat!"

Who the fuck was he? It wasn't my fault he'd been left back twice and his idea of good music was "Book of Love" sung through the nose. I raised my eyebrows at him and launched into a solo, but before I got the first phrase out, I saw his fist coming at me, and then my kazoo was flying and I was crashing back into the row of lockers, and finally I was sitting on the grainy concrete floor, watching Brennan smash the kazoo under his shiny black pointy-toe shoes. He was much too big for me to handle—

David Reich   67

six feet tall to my five-one. Complaining to Marshall would have gone against my principles, though. And anyway, squealers always got it double in the end.

I put my hand up to my mouth and wiped a little blood from my gums. Brennan kicked the squashed kazoo out into the aisle and started out of the row of lockers, toward the john, holding his right hand up like an injured paw. I figured that he must have skinned his knuckle on the end of the kazoo, but it wasn't much of a consolation.

Meanwhile, the row had gotten quiet, and Joey and Porco were back to dressing, with their noses stuck in their lockers. I got up off the floor and quickly locked up my stuff. Out in the daylight of the gym, I lined up to wait for the bell. Mr. Marshall was kidding around with someone at the front of the line. I heard a few guys line up in back of me, and turned to see Fat Joey and Porco standing around with their eyes lowered. Joey was halfheartedly telling a Polish joke: "Hey, Porco! How do you tell the bride at a Polish wedding?"

Porco: "Uhhh . . ."

In a way I couldn't blame them for ignoring me. What could they have said? Against Brennan they were as powerless as I was. When the bell rang, I lagged behind, looking past Joey and Porco as if I was waiting for someone at the end of the line. After the whole line had filed out, I went through the double doors into the halls and was absorbed into the traffic. A few feet down the hall, though, I felt someone jar my shoulder. Brennan, holding a wet paper towel to his bad hand, was smiling down at me like a comic book villain. He pronounced each word slowly and distinctly: "Better stay away from gym class, boy, cause I'm gonna make you suffer. . . ." Then he swept past me to a group of hood girls with ratted hair and continued down the hall.

That day after school, I didn't go to Benmar's with Fat Joey the way I did most days. There was a good chance that Brennan would be at Benmar's, and there was no point in dragging Joey into my mess.

At home I told my mother I was early because I had an extra-heavy load of homework. That must have surprised her some, since I wasn't exactly the studious type, but before she could make any comments, I started down the cellar stairs.

The idea was to scare Brennan worse than he'd scared me. I didn't want to carve him up so much as keep him at a safe distance. In the workroom, across from the old man's ham radio setup, was a pegboard hung with all sorts of possible weapons. I checked out various monkey wrenches and chisels, but it would have been hard to explain what I was doing carrying any of them around in my pocket. Not that I wasn't willing to risk getting kicked out of school. School wasn't worth going to anyway if your friends treated you like a leprosy victim. But if I played it right there was a chance of getting off scot-free. Then I remembered the little souvenir penknife my Uncle Mickey had brought me back from his vacation in Puerto Rico. It had a mother-of-pearl handle with a picture of a cruise ship painted on it, and below the ship, it said *Ponce, P.R.* in tiny letters. The blade of the thing was about two inches long. It looked as innocent as a baby's toy.

For the second night in a row, I went to the Manchester Spa and bought a kazoo. Mrs. Lipschutz must have stared at me for a whole minute before she went in back and got the thing.

I didn't sleep much that night. Every time a picture of Brennan's face came into my head I wanted to get up out of bed and put my fist through the Sheetrock wall.

The next day in school, I didn't eat any lunch. Fat Joey thought I was broke and offered me a sandwich, but I said I wasn't hungry. Gym class was sixth period, and after that, study, and after that, we went home. At the lunch table, Joey, Porco, and Henri DuBois, the weightlifter, flicked chips from the chocolate covering of their ice cream bars at each other and me, while I sat there like a zombie.

I got to the locker room early and was out on the gym floor shooting baskets before Brennan had even showed up. Jocko wasn't around, but that day Marshall made damn sure everyone wrestled in his own weight class.

I was the first one in the lockers after class. By the time Brennan had straggled in the door, the row was full, and I was dressed and waiting for him by the aisle. When he got near our row, I greeted him with a long kazoo blast of "Night in Tunisia," starting approximately where I'd left off the day before.

Brennan stopped dead for one split second, then came charging at me, yelling: "Silverman, you die!"

I flung the kazoo at his head, and his arm shot up in a reflex action. The kazoo bounced off his wrist and landed on the floor with a hollow ring. Now he came slower, stalking me, backing me toward the wall. I backed carefully past Steve Muller, past Joey and Porco, reaching into my back pocket for the penknife and opening it behind me. Muller was the first to catch on. His voice cracked when he yelled: "Watch it, Brucie!"

I flicked the knife out underhand, in front of me.

Brennan froze. His long face was yellow with fear, and his voice was shaky: "Oh boy! Wait'll Marshall hears about this!"

I couldn't believe my ears. He was the sickest punk I'd ever seen. I went after him for real now, waving the knife in the air.

Brennan was backing in a hurry, muttering: "You'll pay for this, believe me."

In the corner of my eye I caught the guys in the row backed flat against lockers as I flashed by. I was grinning like a maniac.

Behind me, Porco called in a dull voice: "You better run, Bruce."

Brennan was nearly at the aisle, and I suddenly realized that he might get away. In a panic, I lunged at him with the knife.

He jumped back two feet into the aisle, turned, and flew out of the locker room yelling: "Hey, Mr. Marshall, Mr. Marshall!"

Guys from all over the locker room came crowding into the row to get a look at me. I stood there shaking, with my silly knife drooping from my hand. Fat Joey said I'd better get rid of it, but I just shook my head. I couldn't get words to form. All I could think of was how I'd come within one hair of getting sent up to Bordentown. I was some J.D. I was nearly pissing in my pants.

After a minute I heard the locker room door, and pretty soon Marshall was pushing through the crowd, shooing people with his hands. People started to file out, and Marshall put his hand on my shoulder: "What's the story, son?"

I handed him the knife, shaking my head and gasping for air: "Self-defense . . ."

Marshall closed the knife, then tapped me on the back: "Come on with me."

I thought of picking my kazoo up off the floor, but I was afraid it wouldn't go over too big with Marshall. Marshall led me out of the lockers and across the gym toward the Phys Ed office. The bell had already rung, and the gym floor was deserted. Marshall's office had a gray concrete floor, and the far wall was lined with cardboard boxes piled with gym equipment. Marshall pulled out the chair to a battered desk covered with sports magazines, but he didn't sit. Instead, he stood holding the knife out in his open palm and stared at it cross-eyed in the dim light. I stood next to him, looking at it as though I had never seen it before. After a minute he handed the knife back to me: "You take this home and leave it there."

His voice was quiet, and I started to calm down. I stashed the knife in my pocket, nodding up and down: "Don't worry, I will."

Now he stared at me: "What in the hell did you go pulling a knife on that boy for?"

I breathed in deep and shook my head.

He looked me right in the eye without cracking a smile: "Well, I don't expect he'll be giving you any more trouble . . . but if he does, you let me take care of it." He opened the top desk drawer and got out a slip of paper. Bending over the desk top he wrote me a pass to study, then handed it over: "Now, we don't have to let this get beyond here. You go on to class, and if there's anything you want to talk about, come to me."

I said thanks and lit out of the gym.

Shuffling along the polished stone floor of the gloomy, tomb-like hall, I was at peace with myself and the world. Somehow I had the idea that I'd never have to fight again. In a way I was concerned that my friends would think I was psycho, or that some hood might decide to make a lesson out of me, but it was like being concerned about someone else, a character in a movie.

I stopped off at my street locker to get my notebook, and then took a stairway up to the study hall run by Mr. Plumbtree, a weird, religious guy who always wore red bow ties and floppy suits and had a face like a fattish churchwoman's. It was only when I got to Plumbtree's classroom door that I really started to worry about people's reactions. I stopped a second and wondered if Plumbtree was aware of what had happened and if the girls knew yet, but finally I flung open the door and walked in. Eyes lowered. I took a step toward the front desk, where Plumbtree was reading to himself from the Bible. But before I could hand him my pass, I heard Porco yelling in a cowboy accent: "Hey, Deadeye Dave!"

I turned and saw him leaning his school desk back against the supply closet at the back of the room, smiling his head off. At first I thought he was mocking me out, and blood rushed to my face.

But immediately half the kids in the room were up out of their seats, crowding around me and slapping me on the back.

Plumbtree shot up and started grabbing people by the shoulder, telling them to sit back down, but by the time the crowd had broken up, Fat Joey was clapping and cheering from his desk by the high, small-paned windows, and big-nosed Maureen Bowser and a couple of her girl friends had joined in. Soon the applause was general, and Plumbtree and I were looking around us in absolute confusion. Then Joey started calling: "Speech! Speech!"

All of a sudden what was happening came perfectly clear. There were thirty people in the room, and I had them in my power. It was exactly the chance I'd been waiting for. I turned to Plumbtree: "How about letting me read one of my poems to the class, Mr. Plumbtree? I've got the feeling it'd quiet things down."

Plumbtree looked shocked: "But that would be highly irregular in a study hall."

Joey called out: "Silverman's poems got cultural values to them. We need some concepts here!"

Plumbtree: "But what of the people who wish to study?"

I fluttered my eyelids: "Why don't we let the class decide?"

Fat Joey and Henri DuBois started yelling: "Yeah, yeah, is this a democracy or is it Russia?" Bowser and Laura Vitello chanted: "Jelly Belly Bowtie! Jelly Belly Bowtie!" referring to Plumbtree's build and dress. Porco called from the back of the room: "Dizzy! Dizzy!"

Plumbtree waved his hand like the white flag: "Okay, okay, but only one poem. Then this becomes a study hall again." He sat back down at his desk, and the room quieted down.

I grabbed a bunch of raggy papers out of my notebook, set my books on Plumbtree's desk, cleared my throat, and started to read, now and then waving my free hand in the air for emphasis:

The Jazz Cafe

I bring me down to the Jazz Cafe
To see Gillespie playing there
And Eddie Goldberg meets me there.

Eddie runs the Jazz Cafe
He's cool as cool can be
He digs his sounds, he digs his booze,
He digs . . .

"Hey!" Porco was calling out. "Hey! you still got that instrument on you?"

I looked up.

Porco: "Why don't you play the class some Dizzy, so we can know what the poem's about?"

Before I could answer him, Plumbtree sprang up, handed me my books, and started guiding me in the direction of my desk. The class started to boo, but Plumbtree was insistent this time: "I'm afraid you don't have the full co-operation of the class, David."

I made a face, jerked away from Plumbtree, and went to sit. On the way, I passed Fat Joey's desk, and he put out a hand: "Let's have some skin, man."

I gave him five and passed on to my own desk a couple rows behind.

Sitting at the desk next to mine was slit-eyed Willy Koffman, the guy I suspected of defacing my Dizzy pictures. As I sat, he hissed at me: "Your poems suck!"

I leaned forward, two inches from his high-boned face: "Yeah? And what's the matter with them?"

Koffman: "I don't like the subject."

Me: "I doubt if you know what the subject is."

Koffman shouted: "Niggers and Jews!"

David Reich   73

I sneered: "I'd rather be a nigger *or* a Jew than wear cuffs."

Koffman: "Jews suck, Jews suck. . . . !"

Me: "Yaaah!" I dropped my books and jumped up, waving my hands like a wild man.

Koffman jumped up too and threw a wild punch that glanced off my shoulder. People close by scattered, and kids from across the room drew closer. Fat Joey started yelling to me: "Hit him inna mouth!" and in the background Bowser and Laura chanted: "Oooo Tuffkuff! Oooo Tuffkuff!"

Koffman came in and threw another wild one, and I hit him in the face with a combination that sent him reeling back into an empty row of plastic-bottom school desks. The class burst into cheers like a partisan fight crowd.

Up front Plumbtree was yelling in a high-pitched voice: "Okay, boys, that's quite enough!"

I nearly started laughing, but then Kuff got his balance and came in swinging again. Plumbtree ran for the intercom on the wall by the door: "Hello? Hello? Mr. Fiorello's office, please."

Kuff stopped in his tracks, and I let my fists drop.

Plumbtree, looking back at us and talking into the intercom: "It's okay, you can cancel that call."

People began to straighten up the desks, and pretty soon the study hall was back to normal. In fact, it was about the quietest I'd ever heard it in there. I sat at my desk, stealing glances at Koffman and vaguely plotting some kind of revenge. Then, across the room, by the side bulletin boards, I noticed Bowser handing a note to Laura, and Laura reading it and handing it back to Henri DuBois, and Henri glancing at it and handing it to Porco. It was near the three-fifteen bell by the time the note got around to Fat Joey. Joey read it with a smile. The clock over the door clicked three-fourteen. On signal, in unison, to the tune of "Good Night, Ladies," the class roared out:

> Go home, Kuff-man
> Go home, Kuff-man
> Go home, Kuff-man
> And don't you dare come back!

Koffman turned pale. Plumbtree stood up in front of the room opening and closing his mouth. When the class started going through the song a second time, Koffman grabbed his books from the rack under his desk and ran out of the room. People sang in his face as he flew past, and an eraser flung from somewhere in back hit him square between the shoulders, leaving a dusty white rectangle on his shirt. I fought off a weak impulse to go out after him. I had the feeling that the whole class was ready to follow me into the halls and beat him to death with rulers and school-books. Anyway, it had been a long day for me and I was tired.

I went back to hanging out with Fat Joey in front of Benmar's. Marshall was right. Brennan had been taking pains to walk around me, preferably in back of me, on his way in and out of the luncheonette. Still I was a little worried about the other hoods in town. When I went inside smoke-filled noisy Benmar's to drink an Orange Crush, Little Denny shot the breeze with me over the counter, but he never mentioned the incident in the lockers. As far as the older, more important hoods like Jocko Gruber, I'd never talked to any of them, though I'd been kind of admiring them from a distance for years.

Every morning they crowded onto the high sidewalk in front of Benmar's, latecomers spilling over into the asphalt lot, all dressed in sharp, narrow pants with the latest-style pockets, their hair combed up in elaborate, permanent-looking pompadours shaped like hoods and fenders of cars of the future. Sometimes I'd see Dave Dragonetti, the body builder, ride his black motor-cycle past the early shoppers from Joe's Superite, smiling like a Roman god, and pull up in front of Benmar's to talk with the other hoods. He had light brown hair, but there was a patch of gold on the back of his head that people thought of as his trademark.

Tuesday morning, the week after I pulled the knife on Bren-nan, I was leaning back against the big front window of Ben-mar's, kind of looking off at the flat-roofed memorial wing of the high school and waiting for Joey to show, when Jocko Gruber and Dragonetti came up. Jocko nodded at me, curling his upper lip: "You the kid pulled the knife on Brennan?"

I swallowed: "Yeah."

Jocko looked at me real hard, then burst out laughing: "He's a tough egg, hah?"

I smiled faintly.

Dragonetti stood slightly back, while Jocko did the talking. Jocko, half-sneering: "Well, I hear you're a real beatnik from Greenwich Village."

My smile widened: "Nah, when I was real little I lived in the Bronx, but I'm mostly from here."

Jocko: "The Bronx? No shit? Where?"

Me: "University and Tremont."

Jocko: "You know Cypress Avenue? Over by the Triboro Bridge?"

I scrunched up my face: "Mmmmm. I think my old lady grew up in that neighborhood. . . ."

Jocko, nodding: "That's where I'm from. . . . Hey, listen, you're okay, Silverman." He put out his hand.

After I'd shook with him and taken Dragonetti's monster hand, he said they had to go inside Benmar's to meet someone: "But maybe sometime I'll get a hold of some beers and we can all get fucked up. Little Denny tells me you like to drink."

I called after them: "Sure, sure, sounds good."

I was surprised Jocko considered me important enough to make friends. I stood around half waiting for Joey, till Benmar's had emptied out, a few minutes before the late bell. Aside from me and a few other stragglers, the only people left standing on the sidewalk were four or five older guys in gray work clothes, hoods from a year or two before, their hair still greased, drinking steaming coffee from paper mugs and waiting for their rides to machine shops and factories in South Hackensack. I'd hardly noticed them until that moment, though I realized they'd been there all along, that I'd seen them every morning. There was something drab and faded about them, something that blended in with the yellow brick and asphalt of the stores and parking lot. Cutting around the cyclone fence between Benmar's lot and the school, moving fast enough to make it to homeroom before the bell, but not so fast that I'd look uncool, I pictured Jocko and Dragonetti in a few years, wearing work clothes and drinking coffee. I thought of South Hackensack with its factories as a trap, and I wondered if they'd escape it somehow. As far as me, well, I'd go to college like my old man did, and after that I'd live in Greenwich Village or California and forget Hackensack ever existed.

That night, Fat Joey was supposed to call for me on his way over to the Bowl-o-Drome. We went there on Tuesday nights sometimes to watch the drunks in the leagues try to bowl. Ma's bachelor brother, Mickey, was over for supper that night and he was delivering his usual dinner-table tirade about Russia. He was waving his hands around, turning purple from his neck to the shiny skin on the top of his head as if he was strangling in his white shirt: "We could bomb them into the stone age! We could bring them to their knees in half an hour! Khrushchev is trembling in his shoes!"

When Joey showed, I skipped dessert and cut out as soon as I could. Out in the school field I started bitching about Uncle Mickey: "Man, you should of heard him! All he ever talks about is Russia!"

As we rounded the corner of the ancient brick Pulaski schoolhouse, I spotted Denny Latino in the shadow of the maple trees, leaning against the railing of the concrete porch by the kindergarten door, smoking. He looked extra sharp in a pastel orange sport shirt. Jocko, in a sweater with stripes like a yellow-jacket wasp, was sitting back against the wooden door with his knees drawn up against his chest. Since Jocko and Denny lived up near the high school, I kind of wondered what they were doing hanging around my neighborhood.

Denny waved as we walked up. "Hey look, it's Big Joey and Deadeye Dave."

I waved back coolly, flashing my hand at waist level. "Denny. How you doin', man?" Joey and I stood on the asphalt at the foot of the porch steps.

Denny nodded. "Pretty good, pretty good."

I looked past him to Jocko, who was still sitting with his knees against his chest. I called over: "Hey, Jocko!"

Jocko didn't move or say a word.

I wondered if something I had said this morning had pissed

him off. I whispered to Denny: "Hey, what's with Jocko? He drunk or what?"

Denny chuckled and shook a greasy curl off his forehead: "If you wanna know what's the matter with him, why don't you ask him?"

Jocko snarled: "Fuck you, Denny."

Denny didn't look back, but explained to me and Joey: "We're s'posed to be meetin' some girls down the Bowl-o-Drome and Jocko has to take a shit."

What a situation! I would have offered to let him use the toilet at my house, but I couldn't very well march him past the dinner table and explain to my family, who didn't know him from the wall, that he was a friend of mine that'd suddenly had to take a shit. And he was going down to the Bowl-o-Drome to meet some girls, so he couldn't use the rest room there. I didn't have a girl friend, but I realized the problem. You wanted a girl to be thinking about your date, about making love, not about shit. In those days there was an unwritten code about these things. In the end, I kept quiet.

Denny: "So where you guys headed?"

Fat Joey: "We're goin' over the alleys to watch the leagues."

Denny: "Kicks, hah?"

Me: "Beats TV. Specially after they've had a couple beers."

Denny was about to comment, when Jocko bolted from the concrete porch and stalked off across the path, then under the maples, toward River Road. After a second, Denny and Joey took off after him, with me lagging behind. But suddenly Jocko stopped at the base of the highest tree and started jumping for a low branch. On the third jump he caught it, hoisted himself up, and started climbing, using the branches like a ladder.

Denny and Joey stood at the bottom of the tree, craning their necks. Denny cupped his hands around his mouth and called: "Hey, Jocko! We was only kidding. We didn't mean to chase you away."

But Jocko kept on climbing, without looking down. By the time I'd got to the base of the tree, he'd already disappeared in the thick, rubbery leaves. After a while, even the rustling of the leaves stopped. We stood there transfixed, looking up into the branches, wondering when he would come to his senses and climb back down. Someone drew up behind us, and we all turned at once.

Dave Dragonetti was standing there with his huge arms folded, as solid as a marble statue. "You guys taking up birdwatching?"

Denny waved his hand Italianly. "It's fucking crazy Jocko! He went up a tree and won't come down."

Dragonetti looked up and shook his head.

And then it started spattering through the leaves. We scattered out of range like dice shooters at a raid, regrouping on the asphalt path under the outer tips of the branches, and it came down like a solid rain of red clay, slapping the dirt at the base of the tree.

Dragonetti hooted: "Pretty disgusting show, Gruber!"

Denny called: "Hey, Jocko, you been eating dog food for supper?"

Joey laughed: "First time I ever seen it done in a tree. . . ."

I stood on the path with them just happy to be present. This was as wild as the wildest Dizzy stories on the liner notes of albums! It occurred to me that Jocko, like the fabulous Dizzy, did crazy things not for fame and money but because what most people thought of as logical was crazy to him. He just had a whole different view of life. I was a little like that myself. I pictured myself up in the tree tops shouting down poems and playing jazz licks on my kazoo. Everything Jocko had done, the antics in gym class and the fireworks in the tree, made perfect sense to me.

After the shit stopped, it was quiet for a while. Every now and then a crumpled leaf would drop to the ground.

Finally the rustling started up again, and pretty soon Jocko appeared in the low branches. From the lowest branch he dropped to the ground, carefully choosing a spot where the dirt was dry. He started toward us, hitching at his pants and tucking in his undershirt. His brown hair hung in his eyes, and there was a big smile on thin lips: "Okay, boys, let's hit the Bowl-o-Drome." He waved us forward.

Dragonetti explained that he was supposed to meet someone

David Reich   79 at Pulaski in a few minutes, and the rest of us cut across the front lawn of the school, talking and laughing.

The girls Jocko and Denny were meeting turned out to be Bowser and Laura Vitello. Jocko and Denny both had steady girl friends back in their own part of town, but that was their business. It was still early when we got to the Bowl-o-Drome, and most of the alleys were empty. Joey got a Coke at the snack bar, and we stood with the girls watching Jocko and Denny play eight-ball on the pay table.

By the time Joey finished his second Coke and a plate of french fries, Jocko and Denny had disappeared with the girls. The clock over the snack bar said ten after eight, and the alleys were still nearly empty, so we asked the bald guy behind the control desk what time the leagues came in. He looked at us funny, then told us that league night had been changed to Thursday at the end of the summer.

That night, after Joey had a sudden craving for liverwurst and took off for home, I went up to the Spa and bought my third kazoo. When Mrs. Lipschutz started staring, I told her that kazoos were catching on so fast I was starting up an orchestra with my friends. She gave me a dirty look, but got me the kazoo without any fuss. I was getting to be a regular customer.

Kazoo in hand, I rushed home and barricaded myself in my room. Then I sat down and wrote my first original composition, an up-tempo major blues called "Jocko's Tree."

I kind of let it drop in home room the next morning that I'd written a song, but the only people that seemed very interested were a few hard-core converts like Joey and Porco. I blew a few choruses for them in the lockers after gym, and they banged out rhythms on the locker doors while Brennan sulked at the end of the row.

By seventh period the story of Jocko in the tree had spread all over the school, and in study hall, kids crowded around me and Joey like Catholics wanting details of a miracle. Joey told the story, adding a few new twists of his own. In Joey's version, Denny had started climbing after Jocko to try and persuade him to come back down, and when he realized what was happening, he'd had to crawl out to the end of a branch to avoid getting hit. In this way the story grew and changed, and for months after, people treated me with great respect for having been there when Jocko Gruber took his famous shit.

Charles Minyard

Excerpt from
BY ANY OTHER NAME

I didn't see Brother for quite a while after that Sunday. Ben told me he went to New Orleans with Nancy for a trip like just-married people take. They took Nancy's baby with them, which is not exactly like all just-married people. But I don't suppose they were just any people.

Brother had definitely decided to leave the place and work somewhere else. I figured he'd be farming again, but Ben said he'd gotten work as a foreman on a construction gang.

"He was damn lucky," I said. "Times being like they are."

"A man like Robert's too well qualified not to find a good job, Bo. Anywhere, anytime. A man like him is always needed."

I didn't say anything. I knew a lot of good boys, well qualified, good character, and all that shit, who couldn't find more than piecework, and happy as hell to have that. The farmers had plenty of work for their own people, but even they couldn't hire anybody walking on. So, while I knew Robert was one of those good workers everybody recognizes on sight, I also knew he was damn lucky.

Ben brought Nancy to the shed where we kept the cane wagons. Me and Freddy and Solomon Moses Brown and Raoul Crejean were repairing the wagons, fixing the sides and changing wheels.

This was a standing job for the time out of grinding season. Whenever there wasn't anything else going on.

The wagons had high metal sides with wooden extensions on top to make 'em higher so you could overload. They had two big wheels like tractor wheels. We used them to haul cane from the fields to the mill. Each season every wagon made well over a hundred trips in and out of the fields and into the mill. And with the fools we had driving and the mud and rough traveling, just about everything on the wagons was finished by the end of grinding.

We usually had to change one or both wheels and maybe straighten or change an axle that somebody bent. I never said anything about that, never bitched about the goddamn maniacs who couldn't drive shit, because I'd turned over the first time I went to the mill. Tractor and wagon both. Brand-new tractor, too.

We righted the wagon and only had to change one wheel. The tractor had to have a new radiator, exhaust stack, and seat, but it wasn't torn up too bad. It rolled in a ditch and got hung on a fence line and didn't land flat. But I hurt my ankle when I jumped and we lost the entire load. I blocked the road nearly two hours right in the middle of the day, and you know them damn niggers didn't let me rest about it ever. So I didn't bitch about fixing overturned wagons.

Working on the wheels could've been tough because there's a lot of lifting involved in taking the wheels on and off and handling the two-inch solid steel bars that are the axles. Even the tools are heavy. Wrenches you have to drag to where you're using 'em and four-foot-tall hand-screw jacks. But Freddy and Solomon Moses did most of the lifting. I did the thought work and the bolting and unbolting and adjusting.

That's what usually happens when white men work with niggers. The niggers do the real straining and the white fellas stand around and scratch their heads and tell 'em where and when to grunt. But that wasn't the case here. That wasn't why I was just standing, because I don't do business that way. There's only so much room in a place where something's got to be moved, and there is no sense in putting a man in the harness when you got a mule.

Solomon Moses Brown was bigger than Freddy—taller and his muscles stuck out more. His teeth and ears were like a horse's. He had only short hair. It never grew. His face was big and bony and always wrinkled from laughing, with two little clusters of saliva at the corners of his mouth. He was related to Freddy, married his sister, I think, and they'd grown up together. They had a good time working, teasing and joking and kicking like two bulls in a spring pasture feeling their nuts.

Solomon wasn't smart as Freddy, though. Couldn't seem to remember things. But he was good-natured, which was a damn good thing. I liked him. We got along well and usually got some work done.

So I had it easy with two men like that to do the straining for me. They were extra willing, too, when they got together. It was just understood that they'd be the muscles, the "force," like Freddy said, and I'd do the other stuff.

Ben and Nancy drove up in one of the white Fords. Mr. Rochelle had three of them. Didn't believe in any color but white for a car.

I was underneath a wagon greasing the axle when Ben poked his head at me from out of the sunshine.

"How's it going, Bo?" Ben said.

"Same as usual, Ben," I said.

"I brought Nancy by here, Bo. Why don't you get out from there a minute. She's getting ready to leave. She and Brother. She'd like to say 'by before she goes."

I hurried to get on my feet. Nancy was standing behind Ben with her hands clasped in front of her. Freddy and Solomon stood back like niggers always do when a white woman is around. They looked shy as kids.

"Hello, Bo," Nancy said. She stepped forward smiling.

"Hi," I said.

Nancy looked over to Freddy and Solomon Moses. "Hello, Freddy," she said. Freddy smiled. I wondered how she knew him.

"I wanted to tell you good-by, Bo," Nancy said. "I suppose Ben told you we were leaving. Or I guess you already knew."

"I didn't know for sure," I said. "Be sorry to see you go."

"Thanks, Bo," she said. "I wouldn't mind staying. If things were different."

I thought she must've wanted to stay. I bet she never told Robert, though, not after she found out he wanted to leave. She was the kind of woman who wouldn't say anything.

She might've liked it farming, at another time, another place. Never will know for sure. It's one of those things like missing a train. There's always another one behind it going the same way, but you'll never know if the first one wouldn't have been the best ride.

I didn't think much about old Robert leaving. I figured it was his own life and he did the best thing generally. He was a man in charge of himself. I don't feel sorry for men like that. Though I'm sure they get confused and don't know exactly what they want like everybody else does, they don't ever appear to be getting pulled and pushed by things. They seem too strong for that.

Ben looked around the wagon. He asked me how long we'd be on it and I said it might be forever if I didn't get some help. Ben laughed. Freddy and Solomon shuffled. Nancy laughed and said she thought it might be the other way around. Freddy gave it them "uh huh, you-hit-it-brother" eyes.

Ben said they had to be going because Brother'd be mad if he kept Nancy away too long. Nancy said 'by again and smiled like she meant it. She got in the car and waved to us as they pulled off.

While Solomon Moses Brown and me and Freddy had been doing the work on the bottom, Raoul Crejean was doing the work on the wooden extensions, most of which were broken, or at least chewed up. Raoul was a carpenter and a somewhat shiftless bastard. He was always chuckling real fast to himself with his breath whistling through his front teeth. Short and skinny. He looked like a rodent—a squirrel or a weasel, maybe. His upper teeth curved out to the front and you could always see 'em, like they were too big for his mouth. He did everything fast. He talked like he had so much to say he couldn't wait to finish one word before he started the next one. He did have a lot to say, too. A lot of shit. The first time I noticed the man was in a pool hall before he was working for Mr. Rochelle. He chalked his stick so fast it made a piercing squeak that drove the dogs and cats out.

I didn't like Raoul. I think I had good reasons.

Raoul had quit hammering while Ben and Nancy were there. Soon as they drove away I heard that goddamn wheezy laugh.

"Oooee, sure is a nice hunk a woman in that white car. Sure is," he said. "I bet Ben don't go straight home with that. Bet he spens a little time showing her them woods before she leaves. Course you can't see too much from your back, now can you, Bo?" Chuckling.

"All right, Raoul," I said. "This ain't no time for your shit." I motioned to Freddy and Solomon and we went back to work underneath. Raoul beat on the wood and stopped.

"Yeah, I guess you're right, Bo," Raoul said. "Ben ain't man enough to handle that kind a woman. Take a real man to do for her. I bet old Robert gets after her ass. Oooee, I bet . . ."

Talk like that makes me uncomfortable. I yelled up to Raoul to find something better to talk about.

"What's better than pussy, Bo?" he said. "If God made anything better, he kept it for himself, I always say. Hee, hee, boy, that is some pussy, too. Umm-uh. Hot to trot I bet, too."

I didn't say anything, 'cause I could see he wanted me to.

"I saw her looking at you, Bo. Smiling. What you did to make that woman so happy, Bo? You know her before. Huh, Bo? Maybe she got more than one kid, huh Bo? I bet you ran into her before, Bo. Why, I bet you . . ."

"Goddamnit, Crejean," I said. I scrambled out from under the wagon. Raoul was sitting on a plank laid across the top. "That's a lady you're talking about."

"Shit. They all the same when they got 'em spread, Bo. All moanin' and groanin' and wiggling and breathing like a horse. They all the same then, 'cause they all want it. Ain't no ladies then."

There's nothing you can say to a man like that. Some people are born to be stupid. There's nothing you can do to change it.

I went back to greasing the axle. Raoul shut up and did a little of what he was getting paid for. But he kept on chuckling. Like a rodent.

A few minutes later, Raoul stopped again.

"That woman smiled at you too, Freddy. Must be she knows a man when she sees one. What you think of her, Freddy? You think she could handle that python you got in your pants? Hee, hee. Boy, I bet she could. Just take it all in and call for more. Oooee."

"Jesus Christ," I said to myself. Freddy and Solomon sat on their haunches waiting for me to finish. They had their heads straight. Their eyes were turned down. They were uncomfortable too.

"You'd like to get at some of that white pussy, huh Freddy? You too Solomon Moses. Bet you can almost taste it." He stuck out his tongue. Ugly bastard. "See that," he said. "Bet you can't touch your nose like that. Drives 'em wild."

Freddy twisted on the balls of his feet like he was getting ready to stand up.

"Shove that can closer to me, Freddy," I said.

"But niggers don't eat pussy, huh Freddy? Can't say I blame you. I wouldn't eat that dark meat either." He started laughing so I thought I was gonna have to strangle him. "I eat the white stuff, though. Have to. If I didn't, I wouldn't get nothing. So I do. Make 'em cry, boy." He stuck his tongue out again. Laughing.

"You know," he said. "I bet that's what you boys want. Some white pussy. I bet you just crave it like a dog in heat. And you know what else. You ain't never gonna get it. 'Cause white women don't want no black boys diddling with 'em. Hee hee. No sir. And besides, if you ever did, it'd cost you your balls. Why, I read one time about a nigger in North Louisiana that they caught with a white woman. And you know what they did. They . . ."

Raoul didn't finish, though we all knew the end to the story, or the general end. Mr. Rochelle drove up in one of the other white Fords. A gentleman with him was sitting on the shotgun seat.

Both of them got out and walked over to us.

"How're you fellas doing this morning?" Mr. Rochelle said. He looked under the wagon. "Hello, Bo."

I crawled into the sun, still sitting and holding my hands away from me so I didn't get grease on my clothes.

"You still greasing axles?"

Charles Minyard   87

"Yes, sir. Afraid we'll be at it till next month. Just about all of 'em need repair work, sides and wheels and such."

"Yeah, I know it, Bo. I know it. This here's Mr. Davis from Stephenson Machine Company. I'm looking at some new wagons." Mr. Rochelle pointed to the man. Then he looked the wagon over, rubbing his hand on it like he did with anything he was studying, machine, animal, whatever.

I reached for the grease bucket. It was next to Mr. Rochelle, so when he saw I was going for it, he bent down quickly, grabbed it by the handle, and lifted it to me. When he set it down, he turned his hand up and looked back at Freddy and Solomon Moses for something to wipe it on.

"What the hell are you boys doing?" he said. I knew there was going to be some shit. "You getting paid to sit?"

Mr. Rochelle picked a rag off the edge of the wagon and wiped his hands.

"Fine thing, isn't it, Mr. Davis? I'm paying four men and getting work from two of them. Mighty nice of me to give those other two a living, isn't it?" Mr. Davis grinned and shook his head from side to side slowly.

"Freddy and Solomon are waiting on me, Mr. Rochelle," I said. "I'll be finished in a second."

"They can't help you, Bo?"

"Ain't enough room under here, Mr. Rochelle. Besides, no use in more than one of us getting grease all over him."

Mr. Rochelle grunted.

"You boys afraid of getting grease on you?" he said to Freddy and Solomon. He looked square at 'em.

Freddy and Solomon stood and moved as if to get under the wagon with me. I suppose it was about the most desirable place to be at the time.

"What about that pile of wood over there?" Mr. Rochelle said. We had made a pile of the broken and rotted extensions from the wagons, off on the side. "You fellas waiting on that wood to move itself?"

I started to say that we were waiting till the end of the day to put it all on a flat wagon in one bunch. It was easier that way. But once at the sugar mill I'd heard Mr. Rochelle jump on a young nigger, telling him he was one of those who didn't want to work, but wanted to get paid. The boy told him that he did want to work but he couldn't see any reason not to make it convenient. Mr. Rochelle got fired up. Red hot under the collar. We must've heard "convenient" around the mill for two weeks, either from the old man or from the niggers. So even though it seemed to me that there was nothing wrong with the way we'd been doing the job, I wasn't going to repeat the mistake of that young nigger.

Freddy and Solomon stepped off to the wood pile. But Mr. Rochelle caught them before they got going good.

"And what about all those flats in the warehouse? You boys think they're going to fix themselves? I guess you don't. It's a lot easier to put a new tire on than to fix the old one."

Freddy and Solomon froze between the wood pile and the warehouse. Freddy decided on the wood pile when Mr. Rochelle turned away.

"You see what it is, Mr. Davis. You can't get a man to work nowadays. Not really. If you tell him exactly what to do and you stand over him every minute, you might get something out of him. But if you let him alone, figuring he can think at least far enough to know what has to be done, you'll find him sitting down every time. Everybody's doing as little as they can for as much as they can take you for."

I heard Raoul chuckling above me. I wondered if I could hit him with a handful of grease without Mr. Rochelle seeing me.

"Bo," Mr. Rochelle said. He looked under the wagon at me. "You have to stay on 'em, Bo. They'll sit and look until all their relatives are dead if you let 'em. You have to tell 'em what has to be done."

"Yes, sir," I said. "I have been. They been working pretty hard up to just a while ago." Mr. Rochelle stood up. I saw his and Mr. Davis' legs walk around the wagon and get into the car. The car left, sending dust after me under the wagon.

I greased the axle and came out. Freddy and Solomon were loading the wood. Freddy was throwing it like you'd throw your worst enemy into hell. Raoul was chuckling.

Charles Minyard   89

While I wiped my hands, Freddy and Solomon finished loading the wood and came over to me.

"He sure had something up his ass," I said.

"Old fucker," Freddy said. Solomon pushed him on the shoulder. Smiling like always.

"I wonder what's wrong with him today," I said.

"Just showing off, Bo," Freddy said. "Every damn time he brings somebody around here, some businessman in white shoes or another one of them big fellas they call farmers, he got to show off. He got to show how he's in charge. Never acts like that 'less he got company."

Raoul cackled. Freddy looked up at him. A quick glance.

"What the hell's so goddamn funny?" I asked. "You been laughing up there like a goddamn insane man. What the hell's so funny?"

"Oh, nothing, Bo," Raoul said. "I just like to see that the old man ain't lost his touch. The way he goes most of the time, I'd say he was getting too easy on 'em. I just like to see he can still set 'em straight. Hee, hee."

"Well, I don't see you busting your back around here," I said.

"I guess not, Bo," Raoul said. "I got a skill. I ain't supposed to bust ass for a living. 'Sides that, I'm white."

I could see this was one of those things there wasn't any use talking about. An ignorant man doesn't get any smarter if you make sense to him. Generally, he gets more ignorant. Or he gets mad. Or both.

"You didn't hear the old man get on me or you, Bo. That's the difference. He knows who's working and who ain't, who's sitting on their ass looking and who's getting it done for him."

"Why you damn fool," I said. "You think we could've got these wagons fixed without Freddy and Solomon Moses doing all the real work?"

"We ain't supposed to have to do it without 'em, Bo. That's what they're paid for, ain't it? What the hell's wrong with that?"

"Nothing. Not a damn thing. Freddy, let's change this wheel. Shit."

"That's the way, Bo. Get after them boys. Hee, hee. That's the boy."

"We'll get it, Bo," Freddy said. "About all we can do is roll wheels, you know. But we can do that."

Freddy and Solomon Moses went over to the wall where the wheels laid against each other. They picked one off the top, righted it with a quick flip of their arms and rolled it over to me. Those wheels are six feet tall and the rims and spokes are all steel. Add a tractor tire half filled with water and you understand what Freddy and Solomon were flicking around with.

"One wheel coming up, Mr. Bo," Solomon Moses said, grinning.

"Mister?" I said. "Since when I got to be a mister, Solomon Moses?"

"We don't want you to think you ain't got a bigger tool than us, Bo," Freddy said. "That mister makes you a real man, poppa."

We laughed easy. I punched old grinning Solomon in the arm. Almost broke my hand on his muscle.

"Ain't gonna get anywhere that way, Bo." The weasel woke up.

"I ain't never getting anywhere, anyway," I said. "So I'm kind of like a robin, Raoul. I don't give a big shit."

"Didn't you hear what the old man said a few minutes ago?"

"Yeah. I heard," I said.

"Well, that's the kind of man who's running this place. And he didn't get there by fucking around with no niggers."

"You're more stupid than I thought, Raoul."

"Stupid, huh. I'm stupid and the old man's stupid, and you're smart. Well, I know this much. I know what it'll be next. You saw how them bucks looked at that woman a while ago. You saw 'em. And we ain't gonna be able to stop it. If you ain't in charge all the time, you ain't never in charge at all."

Raoul leaned over the edge of the wagon like he was spitting on us. I had a feeling we had all quit laughing for some time. It wasn't funny any more.

Ben turned the corner and drove up from behind the warehouse in one of the pickups. He got out and came over to us.

"Hiya fellas," he said.

Nobody answered. We stood there quiet. Raoul tapped lightly on the wagon with his hammer, like a clock in a quiet bedroom.

"What in the hell is wrong here?" Ben asked.

Nobody said anything. I studied the scratches I was making in the ground with my shoe. And studied the way my laces were tied.

Ben was confused. "Bo?" he asked.

"I'm just about to bust that little woodpecker's ass," I said. "I'm working up to it."

"Bust my ass?" Raoul screeched. "I'm the only one with any sense around here."

"Sense! You ain't got the sense God forgot to give a jackass."

"Yeah, well, I got sense enough to know what's right and what ain't. I got sense enough to know it ain't right to let niggers go on about white women that way."

Ben got color in his face.

"And somebody has to stand up against 'em. And if you ain't, I will. I'm not afraid of no niggers."

"What white woman, Bo?" Ben asked.

I didn't say anything.

"The lady was with you a while ago, Ben. That real pretty girl Robert married. You should've heard them two bucks going on."

Ben looked at me. I looked up.

"That's a damn lie, Ben," I said.

Ben was red. He started back to the truck, but he stopped and wheeled around.

"I don't ever want to hear this kind of garbage again. Robert's wife, and any other ladies for that matter, are not to be discussed. Keep your mouths shut."

"Ain't no use in just telling them niggers, Ben. You got to . . ."

"Why don't you be quiet, Crejean? I don't want to hear your redneck crap."

I'd never heard Ben say "crap." He slammed the truck door so hard I thought he'd cracked the glass. He left in first gear, too.

I hate to get told something like that. Ben meant what he said. I'm not sure how he felt and who he believed. But I knew he meant what he said and that bothered me. Didn't make me mad. Bothered me.

Raoul was laughing. "Boy, did you see the look on that little bastard's face? Is he ever pissed! I bet he rides your ass till you can't stand it and quit, Freddy Taylor. Now Solomon Moses over there won't quit. He'll just stand there grinning all his life. Hee, hee! Boy! I thought little Ben was going to bust your ass."

"Get the bar, Freddy," I said. We used a thick steel bar we'd gotten from the railroad to lift the wagon on one side to change wheels. Jamming it like a lever, Freddy and Solomon would lift one side and I'd shove the jack under the axle. We'd lift her the rest of the way with the jack.

Freddy shoved the bar under the wagon. He and Solomon Moses got a good grip on it. Which is one good grip—them four hands. I picked up the pointed crowbar that fit into the jack and dragged the jack over as close under the wagon as I could get it.

"What I can't believe," Raoul said, "is that he didn't fire you two bucks right then."

It's a good thing Freddy and Solomon lifted the wagon when they did, 'cause that crowbar I threw might've killed him. Raoul fell off balance when the wagon tilted and I missed him. He saw it go over him, though. While he was hanging onto the side by his elbow and armpit, he looked back at me. Big-eyed.

He squealed like a stuck pig. "What's going on? What's going on?"

Freddy and Solomon dropped the wagon back on its wheel.

I jumped in the back. Raoul saw me coming and scrambled over the side like a squirrel scurrying around an oak tree. I climbed over after him.

I jumped over the other side. Raoul was already running in the dust, looking over his shoulder. I went after him. When I passed over the crowbar, laying in the road where it had landed, I picked it up and threw it again. I was real wide this time. It just made him run faster.

That last throw took it out of me. I quit running. Yelled a couple of times. "You miserable shit! Peckerwood! Shiftless bastard!" That kind of stuff.

Raoul kept running. I turned around to go back. I smiled 'cause I felt good. Blowing your temper'll do that for you.

Freddy held his hands in the air like Jesus over the flock.

"Come see me, young man," he yelled. "At last, at last, at last. You got off your ass."

Charles Minyard

Joanne Meschery

WHY DO THINGS DIE
IN THE COUNTRY?

Elizabeth wakes in the night, startled, not knowing where she is. She has done this before, struggling from sleep in unfamiliar rooms where beds seem to face the wrong way and her eyes cannot find the door. She sits up and pushes the sheets back. The dog stirs beside the bed. "Rufus," she whispers and the Labrador's tail beats on the rug.

She remembers. She is at the ranch; her sister's house, and the baby is sleeping in the room with her. Gen and Steven had told her to sleep in their bed. "The best bed in the house," Gen had said. Elizabeth had changed the sheets, her fingers tracing the pale yellow stains on the mattress pad.

Elizabeth opens the window and smells alfalfa and sage. Occasionally she hears a car on the county road, someone going home. The road ends out there; just before the mountains. "We never see a face we don't know," Steven had told her. "Except in the fall. Then they come all the way from Southern California to hunt on the marsh."

In the summer there are egrets on the marsh. Tomorrow I'll drive out in Gen's car and see them, she thinks. Then she stretches and smiles, knowing she won't go anywhere. For two days she has not left the ranch.

She stands at the window waiting for a breeze. Beyond the road she sees headlights in a field and she listens for the low drone of the harrowbed and bailer. Steven's second crop will be ready soon, she thinks. And the barley. Steven and Gen had taken Elizabeth to see the barley field before they left. "Everybody out here is watching this field," Steven had told her, snapping off a spike of the pale, golden barley. He rolled the dark kernels into her palm. "Barley. It's never been raised here before." She had crushed the kernels in her fingers. "All I can smell is alfalfa," she said. "A nurse crop," Steven said, pointing to the patches of alfalfa in the field. "Barley has a better chance with alfalfa in there." When they went back to the car, Gen stroked Elizabeth's hair. "You know," Gen had said, "your hair is almost the color of that field."

Toward morning the baby wakes and Elizabeth takes him into bed with her. It was the same yesterday. The birds noisy in the trees and the sun bright as though it were noon. Elizabeth puts the baby to her breast and watches his face grow red from sucking. She runs her finger along his head, feeling the soft dark hair, more like cotton than silk. She had nursed her two girls until they were twelve months. "In my day it was the bottle," her mother said. "I put you and your sister on the bottle the day you were born and you grew up well adjusted, didn't you? The next thing I know, you'll be joining the La Leche League. A radical group, the La Leche League." "You're a cow," her husband, Carl, teased. "You always have too much milk." When they made love, blue-white drops ran from her breasts.

Elizabeth leaves the baby sleeping between the pillows and goes to the kitchen. Gen and Steven's little dog stretches in front of the door. "How does it feel to sleep in the house?" she asks, bending to scratch the dog behind his ears. Steven doesn't allow dogs in the house. "Animals belong outdoors," he says.

She sings softly as she makes coffee.

> *The wife takes the child,*
> *heigh-ho the dairy-o*
> *The wife takes the child.*

Elizabeth is relieved to be here alone with the baby. Gen and

Steven had come in from camping at the lake to meet her plane. "Are you sure you don't want to come with us?" Gen had asked as they drove to the ranch. "We'd call everything off if it weren't that the second crop will be ready in a few days. It'll be a while before we can get away again." Elizabeth had told them to leave her; she had wanted them to leave her. "Rufus and I will watch the ranch for you," she had said. She was tired. Very tired, she said, and there would be time for visiting when Carl and the girls arrived.

She sits at the kitchen table, and the dogs push their noses beneath her nightgown, along her thighs. These days are like secrets to her. Like the stains on the mattress pad or the soiled places where her nightgown wound tight and crumpled between her legs in the night.

Elizabeth's mother had made her a nightgown when the baby was born. She brought the gown to Elizabeth in the hospital. It was wrapped in lavender tissue with a note that said, "Dear Girl, Three babies are enough." Her mother had sewed the hem of the nightgown shut. Carl brought yellow rosebuds and a pamphlet for her to read. "Many couples find sexual intercourse more pleasurable following vasectomy," she read. Sometimes at night, Elizabeth wakes up, her legs pushing, flailing, under the blankets and she thinks the hem of her nightgown is sewed shut.

Elizabeth gives the dogs water from the sink and unlocks the door. The gray kitten hangs on the screen, its yellow eyes startled. "So you want to come in after all," she says. There are three kittens. Barn cats. "They're wild," Gen had told her. "The kids spend hours hunting those kittens." The kitten spits and drops from the screen, its tail stiff as it skitters across the yard. Behind Elizabeth, the dogs slip on the waxed kitchen floor and jump at the screen. "Be still," she scolds, following the dogs outside. "If you don't behave, I'll lock you out of the house tonight."

She looks down the dirt lane to the county road. It is a two-lane road with abrupt shoulders and greasewood growing on each side. Beyond the irrigation ditches and the alfalfa fields is the desert and the houses the government built for the Indians. They built six houses, wood frame and painted in pastel colors. Yellow, pink, and blue houses with concrete steps leading out to dust, to the Nevada desert. Nothing has changed since she was here last. The government has built no more houses.

She walks across the yard to the sheds and dust puffs between her toes. Another hour and she will have to put on her sandals. Yesterday she danced across the yard to the strip of lawn in front of the house, her feet burning. "No, today I'll stay in my gown," she says, pouring pellets of grain for Gen's rabbit. The big doe bangs against the back of its hutch. "You won't care, will you? I won't even wash my face. I'll be dirty all day. Here," she says and lifts the cotton gown around her waist. She runs her finger beneath the crescents of her hips. It is wet there. She is already beginning to sweat. "I'll be sour here. Do you smell it?" She laughs. "And tonight I'll bring all of you into the house. Everyone will sleep in the house tonight." She thinks of all of them together in the house. The dogs. The wild kittens. Even the chickens. The rabbit will stretch its long legs out behind it and lay under the covers in her bed. In the morning there will be mounds of dry, rattling droppings on the sheets and the room will smell of sour milk.

She feeds the chickens and surprises the gray kitten as she passes the sheds. The cat sits on the hood of Gen's car. It must be cool there, she thinks. She walks beyond the sheds and climbs up into Steven's tractor.

Heigh-ho, the dairy-o
The wife takes the cat.

It is a new tractor, huge and green with a closed-in cab, all windshield. She turns the key and pushes a cartridge into the tape deck. Steven is proud of this tractor. It has air conditioning and bucket seats. There is no music in the house except for the radio. Still, she is tired of these songs. She played them all yesterday, sitting there drinking iced coffee and tapping out time on the steering wheel.

Maybe today she will catch the horse. "Walter" they call him; an old horse Gen brought home from the auction. "For the kids," Gen said. But the children don't ride him. "He's mean," Steven said, "spooky." She pulls alfalfa from the field and waves it over the fence. "Come here, boy." But the horse jerks its head, wall-eyed, and gallops toward the canal. She throws the alfalfa after him. "Have it your way, Walter," she yells. "You think I'm chasing you today, you're crazy."

Then she hears the pickup. It turns off the county road and flashes bright orange between the trees along the lane. She starts back for the house. The dogs run ahead of her, barking, as the pickup stops in the yard. She begins to run. Each time her feet come down in the dust, she feels the ache in her breasts.

"Sorry to bother you," the man says, looking at her closely, leaning over the open door of the pickup. "I thought Steve was out of town. He asked me to check his barley while he was gone. Didn't Steve and Gen go out to the lake?"

She wonders why he doesn't wear a hat like Steven. Like the other ranchers, their faces brown with bright white lines across their foreheads from hats pulled down against the sun. She brushes her nightgown away from her legs and crosses to the lawn, smoothing her hair. Behind her, she hears the baby crying in the house. "Excuse me," she says. "I'll just get the baby."

The baby blinks, working his head from side to side as though blinded by the bright sun. "Looking for something to eat, are you?" Elizabeth whispers to the baby as she walks to the truck.

"You've got a pretty baby there," the man says, whipping his car keys softly against his Levi's. But he is looking at Elizabeth.

She wipes the sweat from her forehead with the back of her hand and smiles. Carl had told her once, "The prettiest women in the world are the ones who don't know they're pretty." He had said it more than once, teasing her; bunching her long, yellow hair up in his hands as if he would splash it over his face like water.

"Yes," she says, "he's a very pretty baby."

"I wanted to bring this package down." He reaches into the pickup. "It's been sitting out beside the mailbox for almost two days now. Not a good idea to leave things out there on the road."

"I should have picked up the mail," she says. She notices how his full lower lip is sunburned; skin flaking at the edge. "I haven't been up to the road. I guess I forgot about the mail." Then she laughs as she sees the package. "It's from me. I mailed that to Gen last week. Isn't that funny?"

The man's hair gleams reddish-black in the sun and his skin is white where the collar of his shirt stands away from his neck. Freckles grow into one another on the back of his hands like rust. The western shirt is tight across his ribs so that he looks narrow and thin.

"Oh, that's me," she says quickly. "Elizabeth Brender. We're moving, you see, and these are just some things, some things I wanted to give Gen." She laughs again. "You know how it is when you move. You get rid of everything."

He looks from the package to her and she sees that he is younger than she thought. Maybe younger than she is. "You here by yourself?" he says.

"Gen and Steven will be back soon," she says. "And I have the baby. David," she says, propping the baby up in her arms.

"Well, I'm just down the road. That trailer behind the old schoolhouse is mine. We like to keep an eye on things for each other out here. You need anything, call me. I'm in the book. J. R. Worthen." He opens the screen door and sets the package just inside. His face reddens as he turns back to her.

"About the only thing you could do for me right now is catch that horse. He could use a good ride," she says and smiles.

"Walter," he says, eyes fixed on her breasts. "You'd better forget about riding old Walter. That horse has been proud cut. Indians used to do it a lot. Makes a horse ornery."

"Proud cut?" she says and thinks she should offer him a cup of coffee; something to drink. He looks to her like a man who is always thirsty. She makes these distinctions; a silly habit. Carl makes a joke of it. "Your crazy nature," he says. "You want to nurture everybody." It is her way. The baby is hungry, thirsty, and she makes him full. She has done this for all of them. For the girls, for Carl. Most of all for Carl.

"Yeah," J. R. Worthen says, and looks off toward the yard. "When they cut old Walter they didn't take it all. He still has feelings. Makes a horse nervous."

She watches him walk around to the pickup.

"I'll be going into town this afternoon. Anything you want, give me a call."

She goes through the house to the bedroom and lays the baby on the bed. She hears him pull out of the yard and then stop.

Maybe he's coming back, she thinks. I'll give him a cup of coffee. Then the truck moves on. She stares at the large wet stain on her nightgown, the fabric clinging to the hard nipple.

"Did you like our company?" she says, unpinning the baby's diaper. "Mr. Worthen. J.R. Maybe a real cowboy." She holds the naked baby. "We're in the Wild West, my man."

She runs lukewarm water into the bath tub and sits on the toilet seat listening to the splash. The room smells like sulphur. "How can they drink this water?" she says to the baby. "It smells worse than we do."

She leans back in the tub and holds the baby's hands, letting him drift over her, his head between her breasts.

> *Sail baby dear far over the sea,*
> *but don't forget to sail home again to me.*

Her feet push against the tub, sending slow waves onto the baby's chest. She drizzles water from the wash cloth over his hair as he finds her nipple. His hands slip on her breasts. His feet curl along her thighs. She opens her legs and her hair flutters beneath the water like feather grass.

She towels and powders the baby carefully and puts him in his infant seat on the bathroom floor. "Now," she teases, "what shall I wear for you today? But, of course, my darling, I will be natural." She puckers her lips, lifting her hair before the mirror. "A prairie woman? Yes, yes." She pulls on fresh blue jeans and a pale print blouse. "And cantaloupe from the garden for lunch."

She holds a piece of cantaloupe to the baby's mouth and he begins to suck, his tongue pushing the cantaloupe into Elizabeth's fingers. "This young man needs solids," the doctor told Elizabeth when she took the baby for his check-up. But she hasn't taken the unopened cereal box from her shoulder bag. "Never mind," she says as the cantaloupe falls onto the kitchen table. "I'm all you need."

She snaps the elastic band of the sun hat under the baby's chin and carries him outside. He sits in the infant seat in the middle of the dusty yard. She wheels Gen's bicycle from the shed. "Are you ready?" she calls. "Ready," she answers.

She comes full speed across the yard, yip-yipping to the dogs at her heels. She spins circles around the baby and brakes abruptly. Dust settles over the baby's toes. "You want more? I'll give you more." She disappears behind the sheds and then pedals out, her hair flying. "My grand finale," she yells, passing the baby. Her arms shoot out. She jams her feet to the handle-bars. The front tire bounces against the fence and she laughs, dropping one leg. Everything is quiet. It is too hot for noise. She wipes the sweat from her face and listens to her breathing. The baby is asleep.

She looks back to the house, straining as she hears the faint ring of the telephone. The bicycle folds under her as she kicks away from the fence. She thinks of the cowboy; of the bright orange pickup. Maybe it is J. R. Worthen calling to ask if she needs anything from town. She will ask him to get her Canadian bacon and a carton of soft drinks. "People in the country give you your privacy but they don't forget you," Steven had said.

"Where were you, honey? The phone must have rung ten times."

"Carl, where are you?"

"The girls and I are in Reno. We'll be there in an hour."

"You couldn't . . ." She wonders why she is startled, alarmed. She looks toward the screen door, seeing; knowing how it will be. The room a rush of noise. Touching, all of them touching her, and Carl kissing her until she feels the soft inside of his lips. She presses her mouth hard against the receiver.

"Just teasing, sweetheart. I wish we were. You O.K.? You sound a little funny. Everything O.K.?"

She thinks she should tell him that Gen and Steven are gone; that she is alone. "Everything's fine. I was outside, that's all. I didn't hear the phone. Where are you?"

"Rock Island, Illinois. I figure three more days' driving. I've been stopping early so the girls can swim, but I'm going to drive late tonight and make some time. Be glad you flew with the baby and Rufus. It's so damned hot. How's David, anyway?"

"He's fine. I left him outside; he's asleep. I should bring him in."

"Wait a minute. The girls want to say hi."

Their voices are high and sweet. Small, uncertain voices. "Is that you, Mama?" they say. "We got new bathing suits. Daddy forgot the old ones in the motel." "Tell Mama you love her," Carl says to them. "Why are you there, Mama?" the little one says.

The baby wakes as she carries him into the house. "Go back to sleep," she says, patting him under the sheet. "Everything's all right. Maybe we'll have company. Would you like to see the cowboy?"

She makes the iced tea very strong. It should be strong with sugar. Or maybe he would rather have beer. She crouches in front of the refrigerator but sees nothing except a can of orange drink. The closet pantry is well stocked, but there is no beer. She takes out potato chips and a small package of beef jerky. "Cowboys live on jerky," she says. She believes he will come.

She arranges the damp bath towels in the bathroom and rinses out the tub. The cloth shade at the window sucks against the screen, full of sun. It is the only noise she hears. She would hear his pickup on the road; hear him turn down the dirt lane, shifting into low gear. "No one cares if the house is clean," Carl says. But she hates to be caught with things out of place. She cleans the toilet bowl carefully.

Then she takes off her blouse and washes her face, her neck, under her arms. She takes off her bra and lays the cold wash cloth over her chest. She will be sorry when her milk is gone. Her breasts will be small puckered things then. "It doesn't matter what they say. Your breasts are never the same after you nurse," her mother says. Her mother gives her creams in tiny blue jars. "You're almost thirty, Elizabeth. You must start taking care of yourself. A woman has to do these things. Thirty is a lovely time for a woman. For your birthday I'll give you a day in a beauty shop. You'll feel like a million dollars. A woman your age shouldn't wear her hair like a teen-ager."

In the spring she had taken her mother for a drive. They drove to Chatham for lunch and later they walked along the beach. "The clouds are beautiful," she said. "Thank you," her mother said.

When she married, she bought identical toothbrushes, not caring if they got mixed up. She had let her hair grow down her back. She makes herself a glass of iced tea and goes to the bedroom. Gen keeps her scissors in the narrow drawer of the sewing cabinet. Elizabeth listens for the sound of the pickup and watches out the window, sipping her tea. The baby has turned over on his back, eyes open, staring at the yellowed ceiling. "Too hot to sleep," she says as she changes him. She presses her finger on an ice cube and then runs the finger along his mouth; his gums. "Well, come on, my man. You can watch me cut my hair."

The baby is in his seat on the bathroom floor. "You're not watching," she says, letting her hair fall into his lap. Hair the color of barley. She cuts it chin length, strand by strand, a towel draped over her shoulders. Then she moves the scissors up, closer to her face. "Shall we go shorter?" she asks as more hair falls onto the towel. "A shorter look for the mature woman?" She takes the scissors higher, feeling the cold steel against her temples; her forehead. Too much time left, she thinks. I could live for fifty more years. Her reflection blurs in the mirror. "Dear Mother, Cancel the day in the beauty shop. I feel like a million dollars."

She puts the baby on the kitchen table and pulls the strap of the infant seat tighter across his stomach. Then she sits at the table, her head on her arm, her arm wet from crying. "Don't worry," she says after a while, and looks up at the baby. "Mama loves you." She thinks of Carl; of the girls. "I love all of you." The room is quiet; the baby's eyes fixed on a bright calendar hanging on the pantry door. She follows his eyes to the calendar. "Have a happy day," she reads and laughs.

The baby startles, jerking his hands and feet as she makes a bolting movement from the table. Still laughing, she ruffles the hair around her face. "Do you like it?" she says. She takes a package of chicken from the refrigerator. It is still half frozen, and she sets it in the sunlight. "I think he'll notice that my hair is different. You can't put much past a cowboy." She winks at the baby.

> Whoopie ty yi oh, whoopie ty yi ay.
> One man's work is another man's play.

"I think we'll make a cake," she says to the baby. "A chocolate cake; it's almost my birthday. What do you say? Maybe he'll come for supper. People in the country eat supper early."

There is no vanilla for the cake. She licks batter from her fingers and looks through the cupboards again. "We'll just have to borrow some. Down the road," she says. "We'll find a place to borrow some. What are neighbors for?"

The yard is dark with shadows. "It might rain," she says, looking up at the clouds. "Wouldn't that be something." It is almost cool in the shed. Gen's car is covered with fine dust. The keys are in the ignition. "We never lock anything," Steven had said. "No need." She lays the baby on the seat beside her and turns the key. The engine grinds. A slow sound, deep as though the car had not been driven in weeks. She tries the key again and hears a slapping noise. It comes from under the hood like something was loose inside. "Damn," she says, turning off the ignition. "What if there was an emergency, something happened to the baby, and I couldn't get out of here."

She fumbles angrily with the hood latch. "Stuck here in the middle of nowhere." The dogs push around her legs, their tails thumping against the wheels. The heavy hood goes up easily. She sees gray fur. Pieces of red, of orange; of slippery white. It is all over the fan, the hood, like vomit. "They're wild," Gen had said. "The kids spend hours hunting those kittens."

She pushes the hood down slowly and leans her weight over it, making sure it is closed. "Rufus, come." She takes the baby in her arms. "We don't have to have vanilla." She brings the dogs inside and greases the cake pans. He had said his name was in the book. The oven is on, the kitchen hot. "You need anything, call me," he had said.

"This is Elizabeth Brender," she says when he answers. "Gen's sister. I killed one of the cats; the gray one. It was in the car. In the engine. I didn't know."

"Not your fault," he says. "Crazy barn cats." His voice is clear, soft. "Things like that happen out here. I can't keep a dog. They get hit or they wander off. Don't worry about it. You want me to come over and clean it up?"

"I think it's all right," she says after a moment.

She smells the cake in the oven. Chocolate. Maybe they will eat it warm without icing.

The baby cries, arching his back, his face red and moist. She takes him out of the infant seat and lays him on a blanket in the living room. "Don't cry, baby." She turns him onto his stomach. "I'll be right back."

The dogs follow her. She feeds the rabbit first. Then the chickens. Pellets of grain flow onto the ground. I'm feeding them too much, she thinks. They'll get sick. But she keeps feeding them. "Eat," she says to the dogs but they don't touch their food. She brings them back into the house.

She takes the cake pans from the oven and puts them on racks to cool. Soon he will come to see if everything is all right. She sits cross-legged on the floor and puts the baby to her breast. His hair is wet from crying. "It's going to rain," she says. "You'll feel better then."

Her legs grow numb under her. When the baby dozes, she pinches his feet softly and he begins to suck again. She doesn't let him stop, even when her breasts are empty. The dogs settle down. They lie on the rug; breathing, sighing, their eyes half open. She keeps the baby on her breast long after he has fallen asleep.

She puts the baby in his crib and closes the bedroom curtains. The light is dusky in the room; her bed unmade. She runs her finger across Gen's bureau. Dust as fine as the powder she uses for the baby. She pulls the sheets from the bed and lies back, feeling the quilted diamonds on the mattress pad. She turns over, her face in the pale yellow stains. Then she changes the sheets.

Maybe he is waiting for the dark to come, she thinks, as she snaps on the kitchen light. Tonight there will be no sunset, but it will be cool. She begins to fix the chicken. He will like this chicken; chicken baked slow in the oven with herbs. She will fix corn and mashed potatoes. And tomatoes from the garden.

She has only to wait for the chicken to bake. It is good that he hasn't come too early. They might find it hard to talk if he came too early. She could tell him about moving; about how they are all coming across the country to California. She could tell him how, every night, her little girls jump on motel beds. Jump from bed to bed in their underwear until they are sleepy. She will ask him why he does not wear a hat and why he cannot keep a dog.

She studies the handwriting on the package and then carries it into the living room. She unwraps the package on the floor and pulls the tape from the cardboard flaps. "Get rid of this stuff," Carl had said. "Send it to Gen. She wants another baby." The clothes still smell of baby powder and mild soap. They are little things with ribbons. Sometimes when the girls play loud running games in the house, Elizabeth goes to her bedroom and shuts the door. When they come looking for her she asks, "Where are my babies?"

It begins to rain. She walks to the screen door. The smell of the desert is strong, the dust pungent. Then the hail comes; it rattles off the roof, bounces on the cement steps. The dogs move behind her, nosing at the screen. She holds her hand out the door and icy beads sting her fingers, her palm.

When she comes back from checking the baby, it has stopped. "A dirty trick," she says to the dogs. "Maybe it will still rain."

She lays the little clothes out carefully around her on the rug. "When I was small my mother gave me baby clothes, old baby clothes." She pets the dogs. "I put the clothes on the cats. I dressed them up and rode my bicycle down the street with the cats in the basket. My mother took a picture."

She doesn't let the phone ring long, but closes the door to the baby's room before she answers it.

"Steve's lost his barley," J. R. Worthen says. "I just drove out there. Figured it couldn't stand the hail. It's all down."

"What?" She looks out the window as if she could see the barley field.

"Damned freak storm. Two more days and Steve could have harvested that barley."

He is saying something about insurance. "Act of God Insurance," he says, but she barely hears him.

She doesn't bother to put on her sandals. The dust is cool as she runs to the shed. The baby will be all right, she thinks, as she lifts the hood of the car. She looks around the shed for a shovel, a rake. Then she runs back to the house. The baby is still asleep.

She takes the broom from the closet and calls the dogs back inside.

There is not much light in the shed. She uses the broom carefully at first, brushing at the fan. Then she uses the stick end, working the broom faster and faster.

The car starts on the second try and she backs out of the shed. Steven will be angry, she thinks. But it's not my fault. None of this is my fault.

She leaves the car and moves through the long stalks. She feels the barley under her feet. It is almost too dark to see and she squats between the stalks, feeling with her hands. The kernels are tiny in her palm, the size of hailstones. She rakes them up in her fingers and rubs them between her hands. Everything around her smells of barley.

She wonders, as she gets into the car, if anyone will plant barley again. She rolls the window down and feels the rain on her arm as she drives. The house is not far away; she could have walked to the field. The baby will be sleeping when she gets home. She slows the car, her foot barely touching the accelerator. The road ends out there; it ends before the mountains. In a few days she will tell Carl all of this. She turns down the lane. She will tell Carl nothing.

The yard lights are on, blazing from the sheds and the front of the house. She sees the pickup parked near the fence. She will ask J. R. Worthen why there is nothing left; why do things die in the country? The dogs run alongside the car as she pulls into the yard. They jump at the open window.

She walks past the sheds. The chickens make low, alarmed noises as she opens the gate to their pen, sweeping an arc in the dust. The rabbit trembles as she slides back the roof of the hutch. She raises the cross bars on the fence and the horse stamps in the dust. They are all safe. She calls to them as she moves back across the yard. "Go to sleep," she says. The dogs run ahead of her to the house.

It is as though the lights in the yard are trained on her or as though, suddenly, she has stepped into the path of a car's headlights. She thinks of them on the highway. He is driving late tonight, hurrying to get there. Once, walking home in the dark;

walking fast because her mother was waiting up, a car stayed be-
hind her, its engine so quiet that she heard only the gravelly
sound of the tires; the sound of sprinklers running on someone's
lawn. She did not dare to move out of the headlights or to turn
around.

Stan Lippman

STILL LIFE

*I rock on a fence rail, observing the lovers go by each morning
out of the bushes and back home. I, too, once longed to be a
lover,* to stroll sleepy-eyed, yawning the park path picking twigs
and leaves from a companion's hair. They call me Fern, those who
pass, embarrassed but pleased to find me there. They're all the
same (red-faced, giggling, in tousled clothes), like fashioned
dough on a cookie sheet, their ardor overbaking until they flake,
then crumble—the sheet emptied for still others to fill. I tip a
salute, a frozen smile . . .*

* I.

Long ago, I took to the woods to become a lover, to become a
man. It was spring, of course.

Rose and I were as green as the new leaves then and, like them,
we trembled in the wind. We walked Indian fashion, followed a
narrow, balding path deep inside the park forest between restless
and murmuring trees. Overawed by our nakedness, the awkward
weight of our pale, goose-bumped flesh, by our just being there
doing that—it was never done, enfeebled as we were by her gig-

gling and my own nagging guilt. Exhausted, too embarrassed to speak, we slept.

Awakening, I discovered that she was gone, that our clothes, too, were gone. *Rose!* I cried, my voice ugly and hoarse. My body was scored from leaves and twigs and crimped grass. *Rose!* I heard a voice behind me laughing—a shrill madwoman's laugh. Goddamn you, and your damn tricks, Rose, I cried, wheeling about angrily but then froze, gaped and wide-eyed.

There was a dwarf there. An evil, ashen-faced, bald, gnarled-legged dwarf, his wizened white hands folded on an ebony cane. He stood there draped in a loose-fitting and creased white robe, his dull, sunken eyes observing me. I was naked and trembling, without Rose, lost. When he began hobbling toward me, I turned, then turned again, cried *Rose!* whimpered *Rose,* then, hands around my nakedness, I knelt and began to weep. When he stood before me, I pressed my face against the submitting white cloth of his robe. I felt a blow to the head, then nothing.

The next thing I remember, when I awoke, I heard a door yawn open, and light flood hurting and warm, like an explosion, then darkness. Someone had walked in. I was inside a room. I was lying down, in bed. I was naked. I felt someone approach, but could see only yellow and red quivering blotches, and black. A slight jasmine scent reached me. Breathing, like a tongue, rippled across my cheek. A hand, gentle like breath, touched my chest. My arms blindly stretched out, and embraced a woman. We made love—oh, for hours.

I felt something poke me, something hard, repeatedly, until I turned. It was the dwarf: with one hand he wielded his cane; in his other hand a yellow lantern swayed in time to each poke, its light clinging to his face like dust.

Go away, I told him, my voice ugly and hoarse. I felt her shudder; she lay beside me, but inches apart from my flesh. He poked me again, harder.

Go away, I said. When I turned back to her, she was gone—crouched hiding in the darkness, her breathing irregular and loud. He poked me again, still harder.

Come back, I told her. Please, I said. He hit me over the head, and I lost consciousness.

When I awoke, I was in that other room, the dwarf's room. The walls and ceiling were white, but the color of bone, not flesh. Catty-cornered, at opposite ends, were two large unfinished-wood desks, and matching chairs—the room was otherwise bare. I was seated. I wore a zebra-striped bathrobe, but the buttons were misbuttoned; it was also about two sizes too small. The dwarf, his back to the desk, stood before me, dressed in his white robe. When my eyes met his, he began to speak:

II.

I'm called Simon, simply Simon, he said, his voice ugly and shrill.

I was injured in the Korean War. I led a methodical charge into a small, quiet gook village. There was no resistance—none to speak of.

Gentlemen, I told them (the other officers, he explained), we'll quarter here the two days until reinforcements arrive.

But, sir, they said. Sir.

They felt we should push on. They felt we should destroy them before they could regroup. They felt our position left us vulnerable.

But I said, no.

Nonsense, I told them.

I'm the commander, I said. I'll be obeyed.

You see, there was this village child—I called her Peach Blossom because of the fuzz of hair on her tummy and her large sweet-smelling breasts. I ordered her lodged in my quarters despite the others' protesting outrage.

Find your own, I told them.

I won't share her, I said.

But, sir. But, sir, her parents . . . they said.

Shoot them, but get out, I told them. Bring her to me.

Peaches was different from the others, young man. This time, there was love. This time, for some reason, that seemed enough.

Just this one battle more, I told her. Then I'll stop all this fighting.

I'll settle down, I said.

Stan Lippman

Peaches, love is wanting to go home. We'll work the land. We'll rise with the sun each morning. Each evening, we'll make love. You'll give me a son.

But she herself, alas, she was a child, selfish and swayed by lust. She'd smile but timidly as I spoke to her. She'd play with my crotch and that would be an end to it, our future, all my plans. You see, she only knew gook speech—and I knew none.

I had enlisted because like every other young man I found everyday life unworthy of me. I wanted magic and adventure like my father had had. Like Audie Murphy, I, too, longed to make a name for myself, to become the hero, to be a man. But this war wasn't like that other, just sweat and foreigners and killings from behind the back, or in ambush. It made one feel as useless and unknown as real life. And so all I wanted was Peach Blossom, and peace.

Loving her weakened my authority because I would not share her. I saw how they eyed her. I saw their sweat and distended cocks; their false morals mouthed just to hide their lust.

They wanted me to step down, they said. That, or to mobilize the men and move out. The reinforcements would arrive the next morning—but that meant nothing, they said. They questioned my ability to lead and again suggested I step down.

But I said, no, by God, never, I told them.

Get out, I said. By God, but I should have you *shot*, the damn lot of you!

They attacked us just to get me.

The men were not prepared. Love had made them slothful. As was I, they were caught in bed, each with his own rose or blossom. But I accepted that, being there in that way then—but we weren't destroyed. The other officers, on their own, they later explained to me, had taken measures, had on their own saved the day. The village remained ours. I was the only casualty.

By my expressed order, my quarters had been left unguarded. I'd not have sentries sweating, with hands in their pants, overhearing us or on their knees and peeping. They told me that Peaches' parents had crawled in, that the father had grabbed her. I was asleep then. I often dreamed of Billy, my son, then. Of our going fishing together. Of being out in the woods teaching him to be a stud just like his Dad. But then she screamed. I awoke, reached for her, but she was gone.

Peaches! I cried. It was pitch-dark in my quarters; I couldn't see. *Peaches!*

I heard something snap, something elastic. I heard someone giggle. It was a man's voice. The father, they later explained to me. I heard a shot then. I saw an orange lick of flame. I closed my eyes, lay down face down. Let this be the dream, Billy, I thought. Then, I heard another shot. The dull thud of dropped metal. Then, nothing.

They later said that the mother had rolled a grenade between us.

They later said that Peaches had shot her, then him.

They later explained that they had found her knelt weeping over my body next morning when the reinforcements arrived.

They said it was a miracle I was alive.

The next morning, after surgery, I had myself married to her.

Each one of the eight officers in turn suggested I wait. For what? I asked them. I knew damn well what they wanted, the damn lot of them. Where is she? I asked.

At the Surgeon General's, sir, they said. Sir, a man pieced you back together again, against nature, sir, against reason—just to see if he could.

Sir, we've been caring for her, they told me.

Sir, you've been in a coma two months, they told me.

Sir, for the first three days, sir, she slept on the floor beside you. Sir, but on the fourth day, grown hungry, we guessed—she could not speak, sir—but pointing to her belly she came to us, they told me.

I had inherited this plot of land here at birth—but bloodstained, my mother's death in labor and that on the heels of the ribbon and citation death of her husband; my father who, under Eisenhower, had marched heroically and with just cause. Back then, I believe, it was possible to be a man. Young man, it was that I sought. At eighteen, entering college, I felt I had exhausted the possibilities of this world. I ordered this house built and planned to retire here to cultivate the inner private man. But then the war broke out, as if a dream. At nineteen, I enlisted.

After being released from the hospital, Peaches and I flew stateside and to my home here. Despite my physical change, the essential inner man remained; she recognized me—I believe that. I believe that.

At first, we were content. Often, though, more and more often, when sitting together in here, I'd watch her grow restless then writhe and rub herself and make noise and all the time look at me, always look at me. I couldn't stand that. I couldn't explain my need and gratitude and love to her. She could only speak gook speech and when I spoke my voice frightened her.

Not to go crazy; not to forget or betray who I was, I began to write my autobiography. I began that eighteen years ago. Young man, that's why you're here. You'll type out my longhand; you'll make love to my wife. You'll be fed. You'll be happy. Now go.

No, no questions. Hurry. I can feel her waiting.

III.

I went back to her, then him, endlessly. He was always there, to poke me, after I'd finished. He'd lead me out, then in, each day, in intervals of four hours, with six hours laid aside for sleep, two hours for eating. Endlessly.

Once, being led out, I stumbled. I touched his back for balance, but pulled my hand back, shivering. His flesh felt like damp clay, cold and in lumps—and dead. He ordered me to stoop and to straighten the box I'd tripped over: that ebony box he stood on to wave his lantern and poke. It contained three moon-white diaphragms, and a piece of rusted shrapnel. The incident annoyed him, and he brutally poked me all that day, and the next.

But even despite that, often I tried to win his praise. I sought his compliments with a schoolboy zeal. Often, I typed the same page over and over hours on end until it was perfect. Each page was perfect. But not once did he look at them.

I already know it all, he stormed one day when I had been particularly insistent, laying the pages out on the floor around his desk like a white carpet.

Bah! he told me.

Besides, he said, they'll not be published until after I die.

At least, then, ask her how good a fuck I am, I told him. But he turned away.

I'd been puzzled by the page count, and by his calling *it* a *they,* and by his beginning with his college days before the war—where he seemed just to study making love and not much else.

Typing it acted like an aphrodisiac; it aided me in my love-making as a good wine or drug might. He took one day to write down each day, took a month for each month, etc. Each moment of the manuscript was spent either before, after, or in bed with a woman.

One day, then, finally, as he was putting away his lantern, I cleared my throat, and then I asked him: why have I started with page 6571?

He turned away from me without answering. When I remained where I stood, he turned and poked me, and pointed to my desk. No more, I told him. Until I know, I said. If you poke me again, I'll leave.

I knew he would admire my strength and audacity—so much like his own, in his own book, then, at that point. As if I were he, a man. My own man. And now he understood that. And now he had to give in and answer, man to man. As he had for so many times, now I had won.

If I rebelled, it was because I loved his book; I loved to type it and then make love, loved to enact it in making love; because I loved him as you'd love any book hero; because I sought his admiration. Because I knew it could only be won through action, not words. His submission would be all the praise I needed; a man's submission, that meant something, and would make me feel a man.

But I suppose he understood all that—and so that's why he twisted my triumph into his. It was our own kind of intercourse, at stake not just an orgasm but my whole being—to become equal, a man, now, and not just cod between his legs. That's why, when he poked me, I refused to move.

Because this is the seventh volume, he said.

Stan Lippman   115

Because the other six have already been boxed and stored away, where you can't find them, he told me.

He called me a fool, a damn common fool. He stood there and stared at me, his hands fisted, bloodless over his cane. He said, this happens every time; it happens every time. He told me I should grow up. He turned away, then turned back, pounded his staff, poked me, pointed to my desk.

She's my wife, he said. She's my wife, damn it, mine.

Now go back, or go, but stop this, he told me.

What else could I do then, being shamed, but go? Being treated like a child, but go? I returned to my desk, my typewriter, determined to have my revenge.

The next day, that morning, I told him, Simon, let's move to the City so that I, too, may have a life of my own.

Hmph, he snorted.

You're a fool, he said.

But that wasn't true. It wasn't enough, any longer, making love without being loved for myself; it wasn't enough, now, to help this man tell his story without recognition for myself.

Let me tell my story, I thought, but each time I prepared to, each time I'd cough to clear my throat, he would poke me, point, lead me away. Oh, of course, he knew. And for that, I began to hate him.

To him, I was volume seven: *The College Years*. I could have been anyone; he insisted on that. Being there, it had been an accident, that's all.

But to her, her cries and multiple orgasms, the nibbling kisses and her embrace . . . oh, I knew she loved me best.

If only there had been some outsider, then. A transient third person, someone who, by observing us, would affirm our love and our way of life. It was that I longed for, with Rose, with her, and with Simon, too: to find some proof of my own uniqueness; some object which, by gaining, would make me tangible, as myself, as a man: Kendle Young.

If only she could have seen my face, or I, hers, and, from out each other's gaze, our own; to no longer each time have to reconstruct and interpret each other's features from through the blind but certain feel of lips and fingers. If only she could have known my name, have whispered it when we loved rather than her babblings, have written it in tears on her pillow each time I left, and have it never dry. Then, I would have been satisfied.

But no, it was impossible, everything. Simon was stronger than us, more powerful. We both knew it, and so, did nothing.

One morning, crackling and with glee, Simon told me that he would finish volume seven at the end of August. At which time, he said, I would have to leave.

But because he was sadistic enough to give me notice, wanting to watch me squirm with each succeeding day; because he was too vain and self-satisfied to read what I typed, I turned this triumph of his inside out; I had my revenge. I wrote myself into his memoirs, and under my real name.

I wrote:

Simon huffed, stalled over laces. In the locker room, handball class over, others gone. He had a date with Jo-Ann. Cow-eyed, whining Jo-Ann. God, he hated her schoolgirl goo talk. To hell with taking her someplace. Just take her home. Give her the time, then go. But damn, she liked that. She *liked* being mistreated like that. She liked him being a brute. Damn chick! Boring routine by now. The bitch.

Suddenly, Kendle Young walked in: tall, blond hair, square-jawed and handsome; the only player in the same class as Simon. Until now, they had never spoken. Kendle was proud and withdrawn: a loner.

Suddenly, Simon was struck with an idea: a way to kill two birds with one stone. Slough off that chick, Jo-Ann, and an excuse to get tight with Kendle.

Hey, you play a damn good game, Simon told him. But can you handle a broad? he asked. How 'bout you do both me and yourself a favor?

Tense silence. Minutes ticked by. Kendle frowned, his cold, steel blue eyes turned inward. Simon tied laces, scanned his fingernails for grit. Kendle laughed, good-naturedly. Both relaxed. Friend, why for sure, Kendle said.

With each day, my role grew larger, dilating until I dwarfed him.

I wrote:
To achieve and maintain our individuality at any cost, he told him. Adding: without it, we're as good as dead.

Right-o, Kendle, said Simon. Dead as a goddamn doornail.

They stood shoulder to breast, both beaming, but Kendle with cunning, not lust. He'd arranged this sporting event: a test, really: Cindy-Lou. Imbecile-gin smile, her skirt hiked over thighs, her pale flesh couched in darkness. Simon licked his lips, grunted, hooked. He lowered his pants.

Simon, remember yourself, Kendle told him. Too late. Cindy-Lou squat, working off Simon into drool. Cindy-Lou: Johnny Smith, really. But just anyone—both of them now. Kendle grinned, closed the door, and waited.

But then the war came, ruining everything. But, oddly enough, the wrong war.

I wrote:
And though both accepted Simon's unnatural allegiance as inevitable, could their relationship survive the ironic twist of fortune: Kendle's military subordination as a junior officer in Simon's staff? Kendle wondered. Questions nagged his mind. Four questions:

1) would Simon's public position provoke him into seeking his own uniqueness?

2) would that seeking threaten Kendle's own?

3) under what conditions could their relationship accommodate a shift of authority: at sea? in a foreign country? in combat?

4) would it seesaw back and forth endlessly, or reach a new equilibrium, either equally one-sided or at balance, or, under strife and recrimination, collapse?

Kendle wondered, uneasy—quite frankly: unsure. Somehow, for some reason, he expected the worst. He *always* expected the worst. He cursed that day long ago in the handball locker room when, against his better judgment, on a whim, he broke his long-standing vow and became involved. . . .

But then, one morning, Simon told me he would reach Pearl Harbor by weekend. He said, I'll drop out of college, leave my fiancée, and enlist, entering OTS, ending the seventh volume.

My revenge was reduced to ash. Once again, he had reversed me. Before the reality of my leaving, which until then I had not believed, those scenes faded, as helpless as any dream. It all meant nothing, all my work; it made no difference. I would just leave, and be replaced, and be forgotten. The ash tasted bitter on my tongue.

But I conceived a second revenge, reversing him and his. After this, I hoped, he would hate me and curse me until the day he died.

That night, then, when they both slept—she, in her bed; Simon, on his desk—I slipped from mine and, crawling past him into her room like a child, with a safety pin plummeted her three diaphragms. She changed them every week. I was told I would leave that Sunday, the beginning of a new week.

That Sunday, I hurriedly finished up his enlistment, ending my volume, the seventh volume:

Simon and Kendle walked arm in arm to the bus stop. The wind, like the winds of fate, blew in their faces, tousling their hair, but they did not flinch. Despite their uncertain future, despite their doubts, they could not be cowed; they would not be afraid.

Then, having neatly tied up that narrative, I made my last love with her, an infinite and real love: the love of a man to a woman.

And if it felt no different for us, it was only because they didn't know. And if she turned away without tears, without gratitude or awe, it was only because he clobbered me before I could speak.

Because they didn't know; because Simon didn't know to replace the diaphragms; because the next one after me and each one after that, too, would make infinite and real love with her, all my efforts have been in vain. No one will know the child to be mine. No one will remember my cold, steel blue eyes. Again, Simon had reversed me. He had won.

When I awoke, I found myself lying here, naked, nestled against the fence, my head pillowed beneath the neatly folded bundle of my old clothes. While I was dressing, everything within urged me to go back, to once more challenge Simon. But I knew of no path to follow, to get there, no signs or portents to keep me from becoming lost.

In everything, I have failed: my relationship with Rose, with Peach Blossom, with Simon, with my own inner private man, with my own story. Standing here, dressed, looking into the forest, I hesitated, turned, turned again, and then sat here. I am not a hero, after all. I understand that now.

Ronald S. Librach

DEPRESSION AND THE PRICE
OF IVORY

She said herself that she was "depressed," and because by this
time I myself was goddamned near angry (much less "depressed,"
as she is wont to say), I said to her:

—Ivory, I said, is this the reason? Is this the debt which he holds
over your head as if your lovely face were pictured on the back
issues that he collects and the letters in the title over your joy-
less smile were weighty and thus creaky, about to tumble and
crush your lovely skull? Is this, I said, what you would call a
"debt," Ivory?

But (to my surprise) she would not say, as if I had left her
no room for words.

She did say, however (and this did indeed come as a surprise),
that he was a lover of the highest order, this man whose mother
would have called him "William" (or maybe "Billy") and of whom
others spoke *sotto voce* as "Burly Bill" Pyles.

But I felt it necessary (despite that peculiar apprehension at
the thought of Burly Bill which had always been a source of
speechless anger at my own intellectual passivity) that I persist,
and so I said to her:

—Is this, I would say (in undisguised exasperation), whom you call your "man"? Is this, I would say (striving with even greater vigor to be "poetic"), the absentee landlord who has for so long reaped the harvest of your affections?

—Who else? she would say. Do you know anybody else, she would say, to whom I have given that right?

Who else, indeed? I would ask myself. But after all, I would tell myself, she says that she's "depressed."

And all this time, as if she were trying to get me angry, too, she would be saying:

—Who else? she would say. Who else?

—Is this the barbarian, I said (however indelicately), who has for so long pillaged the outposts of your rectitude and virtue?

But, no, I do not in the final analysis find it surprising. Because how could a boy like me (and this, I find, is the key to understanding my own thoughts in the matter) imagine what a woman like her calls the "ecstasy," and sometimes even the "angelic anguish," of what she experienced with Burly Bill Pyles on the very night before the fish died? Certainly, I, too, like all the others, had seen them for days, leaping out of the water or probing the water's surface with plaintive mouths in search of air. But like the others, I was, of course, untrained. I did not realize that what seemed to be a merely natural moderation in seasonal temperature had allowed a phytoplankton of the genus *Microcystis* to become dominant, so that, because of certain gas-filled vacuoles which the warmth of the water caused to expand, the algae rose in a mere three days to the surface and assumed the form of a dense concentration of scum. Having thus risen to the surface, this algae then began to absorb heat from the sun, thus provoking a rise in water temperature which was, in turn, conducive to its own proliferation, so that an actual stratification of scum resulted. Oxygen was thus distributed only in the upper layers of the scum itself, because, in accord with Beer's law, the penetration of sunlight to depths greater than 0.3 to 1.2 meters is inadequate for photosynthesis. Naturally, the fish thus abandoned the oxygen-deficient waters below, and we could see them from the banks beneath the cliffs, weary and blinking from their tiny glazed eyes, as they leaped above and skimmed in desperation the water's surface. And then, as if in a stroke designed to discharge in a single moment our anxiety of days, a cold air mass from the Canadian Rockies caused the water temperature to drop, so that the oxygenless waters naturally upwelled to the surface and the fish were trapped and killed. Like the others, I, too, lamented for days the fact that we had not thought of copper sulphate. But it was, of course, too late. Nor was it much consolation to learn that autoinhibition soon beset the phytoplankton itself, as it produced in the course of its own metabolism substances toxic to itself, so that its exponential growth, once the source of so much anger and anguish, came finally to a standstill.

Considered in isolation, of course, this particular fishkill should be cause for no more than a moment's reflection. As a matter of fact (like most things), it's all just as well, and the next time I see her, I'm going to tell her:

—Ivory, I'm going to say, it's all just as well.

And she, of course (particularly if she's still "depressed"), will say to me:

—For you, maybe, she will say. Maybe it's all just as well for you.

And I, of course (exasperated, no doubt, but certainly not angry—that's the point), will be thinking: Who else? For whom else? I will be thinking.

—Is this the man, I said (attempting, as I renewed my more-or-less impassioned disputation, to elaborate further), with whom you are constrained to exchange abdominal spasms, tit for tat?

Naturally, she was amused, but finally she said:

—Is it too much to ask, she said, that the man I love should carry me off and allow me to carry his child? Is it too much to ask, she said, that just once I needn't feel the anguish of knowing that what he has deposited inside me will just lie dormant there and become stagnant, as if the heat and compression of my own loins were boiling and fuming it clean and killing it? Haven't I a right, she said, to ask for something more?

—Birth control, I said (venturing for the first time to impugn directly Burly Bill's character), is just nature's way of eliminating inferior species like Burly Bill. And I say this, I added, without fear of violent retribution.

Again, she was amused, but she said:

—Someday, she said (as if the admonition issued from the anguish of personal experience), you shall find him beating on your face and pulling out your hair, too.

For Ivory believes that life is like a series of bores and pistons: she believes that the piston of her opportunity to bear Burly Bill's moist little babes has nearly reached the tunnel's end of the bore which represents life's gift of this opportunity to her, as if the swelling compression of the piston, bearing ever closer to that hypothetical mouth of the bore, were the cause of all her anxiety about Burly Bill's unwillingness to "carry her off." Naturally, I should have told her as much, and in fact I did say:

—Ivory, I said, I know what you're going through.

But I knew, too, that the abstract precision of my image and reasoning would escape her, and so I was forced to say:

—But you would not understand, I said, if I tried to explain it as I myself understand it.

And, of course, all she could say was:

—All I understand, she said, is that the man I love will not carry me off and allow me to carry his child.

But I also knew that, at this moment as at no other, she was vulnerable, and so I said to her:

—Someday, I said, in accord with the most unadorned instincts of the Pyles mentality, as if issuing from a brain laid bare inside a depilated, flayed, and boneless skull, he will drag you off to his cave in the woods, and there the two of you shall be happy, subsisting in perfect, mutual dependency.

—But he suffers, too, she said. I know that he, too, must have anxieties. He, too, she said, must get depressed.

—He suffers, I said (gambling that perhaps simple crudity would awaken her), from nothing that cathartic mixtures of phenolphthalein cannot relieve.

But she did not pause to be amused, and what she said was:

—And he thinks, too, she continued, of my suffering. I know that he must think of my anxieties, too. In our suffering and anxiety, she said, we are mutually dependent and think alike.

But (and, admittedly, this, too, came as no surprise) she was not amused, and even I realized that the rationale and poetics of crudity should not be allowed to fall like so much suffocating phlegm upon so anguished a soul as hers, and so I further explained myself by saying:

—Ivory, I said, you must learn to make room. You must learn to make room for the marvelous powers of your anxieties to renew themselves. Your life, I said, must ultimately become like an automotive dealership—always prepared to discount and move out your older anxieties in order to make room for the newer models. Only then, I said, will depression have any genuine meaning. My own life, I added, has become a life like that.

But she was not amused. In fact, she said:

—I am not amused. But I am, she said, guilty—guilty that we are mocking the man I love because he has the misfortune to suffer from a malady which, after all, cathartic mixtures of phenolphthalein can easily relieve.

When all of this is over, then, it will probably be left for me to say:

—Of course, it's all just as well for me, Ivory, I will say. Because my lesson, Ivory, I will say, was long ago brought home to me like the stifling recollection of some unintelligent—and perhaps striking—deed of one's childhood which one remembers suddenly as one is about to consummate some long overdue mature achievement, so that the very thought seems almost to suffocate or prickle like the unexpected—but nonetheless embarrassing—discharge of some ancient and petty debt.

And so (despite that peculiar disquietude which normally accompanies any instance of self-reflection on my part) I persisted in telling her the parable of the old widow and the pruning paint. I even brought myself to tell her (as if, however, merely in passing) how the old widow suffered from severe angina pectoris and thus spoke in healthless paroxysms that seemed to a mere child (like myself) like telltale decrescendos in the freshest of air.

—It was not, I began (struggling to find the profoundest framework in which to cast my telling of the parable), because I genuinely needed the money. Nor was it because, I continued, I had, after all, borne the responsibility of mowing her lawn the preceding year. And it was not, I concluded, because he—the other one—virtually owned the rights to every other goddamned lawn in the whole goddamned neighborhood. Nor was it because his little brother, I felt constrained to add, was in the habit of calling me names and running away before I could pummel the shit out of him. No, I said, because even I got genuinely depressed over this. Yes, I said, even I—genuinely depressed.

She evinced suitable (though demure) surprise, but said nothing, and so I continued:

—Does it not seem obvious, I said, that there was an issue here —an issue which it was, after all, my right to raise?

Should I apologize, I thought, for the level of abstraction to which I have raised this mere parable?

But instead, what I said was this:

—So I questioned his right, I said. What else but his right in the matter, I said, should I have been expected to question? Naturally, it was the responsibility of the old anginal widow herself, I said, to have devoted even her last hopeless breath to the final dispensation. But she failed for one reason or another, I said, to do so, and I found myself with no recourse (however radical) other than securing a can of pruning paint and spraying with that black, inspissate substance the license plate on the old green car that once her husband had driven and in which her daughter-in-law, the pale, spindly hairdresser, still drove her.

Naturally, I felt constrained to explain further, and so I said to her:

—My reasoning in the matter, I said, was this: for even if one cannot remove the pruning paint from the finish of the car itself —which, of course, one cannot—it would still be possible to exercise one's legal right to drive the car. But obviously, I explained, one cannot legally operate the same car when the license plate is smothered in pruning paint, so that the expense, I said, is thus necessary rather than voluntary. And that, I concluded, is, of course, the point.

Naturally, though she was perhaps amused, she said nothing, and again I felt myself constrained to say:

—You can see, I said, how genuinely depressed I was to have

stooped so low in the defense of what (even so) were my rights in the matter. But the violence inherent in the issue, I said, revolves around the fact that, three days later, I find myself facing the hairdresser and her husband, the little, prickly barber, who stand before me and my father the haberdasher and, I said (amplifying myself now in simile), like so many ashen, pellagrous judges at an inquisition, utterly oblivious to my depression, accuse me.

Should I stop, I thought again, and defend (however abstract) my concept of my own right in this issue?

But again, what I said instead was this:

—For the upshot of the entire issue, I said, is that I am condemned for the summer's duration to manicure the lawn of the old anginal widow. Condemned, I repeated, to contemplate the sweat that would surely tumble from my brow as if it were the moistest and healthiest cells of my own scalp—my own scalp, I repeated, growing so rapidly, I said, that the mere flesh of my skull could no longer hold it in place, puddling at my feet, and dampening the very spirits of the soil itself. And that, I concluded (as if by way of moral), was the last time in my admittedly brief life that I got genuinely angry.

And since there was in her eyes that questioning look which I, of course, knew so well, I added:

—But I did not ultimately find myself responsible, I said, for mowing the lawn of the old anginal widow. Because the hairdresser and the barber, I explained, soon deposited the old lady in a home, where, of course, she ultimately wheezed out her breathless days. And afterward, I said, they opened a combination beauty parlor and barber shop in her house—all of which, I explained, is just as well, because one does not, of course, have to manicure a parking lot.

Not surprisingly, it was not long after what she herself likes to refer to as this "parabolic session" that Ivory finally got around to the famous "moment" (as she liked to say) of love among the lichens, as if my assault upon her admittedly confused sensibilities no longer left her enough room for any other rhetorical maneuver.

Ronald S. Librach   127

"Little lichen," she began (as if by way of epigraph):

> "Little lichen, fondly clinging
> In the wild wood to the tree,
> Covering all unseemly places,
> Hiding all thy tender graces,
> Ever dwelling in the shade,
> Never seeing sunny glade."

—The lichen in question, she said, grew not on trees, but, as is the wont of the genus *parmelia caperata,* on the vaulted roofs of rock above our heads. Nor can you imagine, she said, in the depths of a soul which is, after all, at times stonelike, the anguish which I feel each time I find myself thinking of that moment. For he was like an angel to me on the night before the fish died, and the time, she said, was ripe on that night as on no other. We went into the cave beneath the cliffs, she began, where you can see the *lecanora* tumbling down the mountain sides in the wind as if the rock itself were shedding, and then we lay together in the cave, she went on, with the *parmelia* languishing above our heads. And as he lay atop me, I, of course, could see the *parmelia* on the cave's roof, she said, so that the wrinkled, wavy mats made it seem as if the cave were breathing around us like some vast vital organ in which we, perhaps, were but an alien growth. And the fibrils, she said, of the *parmelia* made it seem to me that we were inside the huge mountain's skull and the fibrils were the roots of the mountain's scalp growing away from us and into the night, and when I started to come, she explained, I imagined that I could reach out my hands to those roots and pull on them and draw myself off the earthen ground so that my body could, as was its wont, wrench and writhe freely in space despite the weight of his body atop me. But when he came inside me, she added, it was as if it burst right through my loins and filled up my veins so thickly that I thought I would actually suffocate from within.

—Is that, I said, all there was to it?

—What else, she said, does a girl have a right to expect out of her one short moment?

For Ivory believes, too, that life is like a neglected tuber: she believes that her life with Burly Bill Pyles is like some kind of gourd that has been allowed to grow too long on the vine, so that now its growth is a mere bloating and the moment at which it is to burst is thus inevitable. And this, of course, is the key to her notion of her debt: for she believes that now she owes him those last moments which, because it was she who allowed the tuber of their relationship to distend beyond the last possible moment of reprieve, were forced upon him by her becoming his inamorata and the woman who desires to bear his moist little babes.

Maria Katzenbach

Excerpt from
THE GRAB

"The Prayers"

The mother gives each daughter a part of her name, and during her life each daughter takes her name for her own until three separate names grow from one name. The mother gives to each daughter a part of her face, and during her life she watches her own features transforming in the three separate faces, the faces of her daughters gradually changing into the faces of three other women who no longer resemble the mother. And to each daughter the mother gives a part of her mind, and during her life she sees the threads of her own intellect unravel into three separate strands as each daughter holds onto hers, not as a gift from the mother, but as her own refined cord.

But the mother, during her life, gave no daughter a part of her soul. Her body must give up living, as it is now, before her soul is taken away. When she is dead the daughters will fight for possession of the mother's soul.

"Damn the sun," she curses. "Damn four o'clock," when the sun hits the window of her bedroom shooting the reflections into her eyes. Motion is pain. She reaches her skinny arms, the wrinkled flesh hanging like loose skeins of unwound wool, to the swollen leg. Then, holding her breath, she shifts her weight which is not the weight of a body, and turns the weightless sheath wrapped in layers of white nylon and organdy. One of the feather pillows now presses against her neck. She tries to sit up, but a flash of pain in her abdomen stops her. Her head drops down. The pain tightens its knot across her belly.

"A prayer," she begins, "is not a prayer when it asks for something. This is not a prayer. This is fact. I wish to die and I am already dead." She is talking to her God and her disease. As she continues to pray in her precise language of final business and tied-up ends, the sun turns the colorless bedroom to gold. Around her body, no longer a body but what surgeons had not scooped out, the spaces of the bedroom grow. Flat brocades are thrown into relief, the dull blooms ornament. Yellowed threads burn to ochre as the words of the old woman fall into the sun's falling, as the prayer shines obliquely on the walls, and the sound of her voice comes down over her limbs, over the inert arms of the chaise. The stiff posts of the bed listen, alerted to the last recitation.

She holds up her hands and begins to pray.

> My hands, my mothers,
> for generations they have been that way
> weaving stories out of time
> weaving life in the loom of the dead.
> The sherry is poured at four.
> The family gathers. The hands hold the glass
> beyond the shade on the porch,
> beyond generations buried under the shadows.
> The men are courted by circles the women
> make in the air with their hands, their mothers,
> holding the glass in the light
> for the daughters to see,
> fingering the stems, fingering the long-stemmed
> words of the story.

There are no stories left. There is no time for stories. There is

only the passing in and out of generation in the rooms. There
is only the invasion of the inherited house.

> The relatives have told their stories.
> My husband's story has been told,
> the story of twenty bedridden years,
> of pills, shots, hospital rooms,
> the dead story of medicine prescribed and taken.
> My story is not my story.
> My story is the inventory that has been made.
> It is typed, it is on the desk.
> My story is the property accounted for.
> The jewelry has been divided.
> I have watched three pairs of hands
> handle the rings, try on the pearls, covet the stones.
> The plants have been watered.
> The latch on the gate is fixed.
> My mind is still fresh. My diary closed.

Her hands fall to her lap. On the table beside the chaise is the
shut diary, and next to the diary is her Bible. She looks at the
Bible, reaches to pick it up, then lets her arm drop again. "I don't
need these words," she thinks. Then she looks at the diary and
thinks, "That is closed. It will stay closed. I wish to die and I am
already dead. A diary is for the others, living."

> She is born, it begins.
> On this day my second daughter was born.
> Where is the first?
> Where is the first not-me part of me?
> On this day my third daughter was born.
> Is it the end?
> Dry, womb, dry up illiterate vessel,
> and wait for the babies to learn speech.
> Animals are born. Humans speak.
> "In the beginning was the Word . . ."

She gave that word up over forty years ago. Then the doctor

said that the growth in her uterus was not malignant. He said that there was a good chance that it would become malignant in the future. So remove the uterus. Remove the growth. Remove the word "life."

But cells are cunning. Take out the nest and they migrate to another place. They wait forty years, gathering their forces, programing their nuclei for the attack in timed intervals at designated areas. Then they sprout tumors in all the full, round places on her body, mocking her female form. Her breast, her cheek, her hip, and now the cells are attacking her origins, penetrating into the vital regions around her womb, digging into the sterile walls, and soon, she knows, feels, can tell from the signals of pain, the growing army will sneak up the pathways and burrow into her heart.

Motion is pain.
The motion of generations is pain.
My brain will burst.
The snakes in the dome curling into themselves
Alive, hissing the last recitation,
will leave one sin squirming.
"Mother," my daughters will ask,
"Mother, if you could have done anything differently,
what would it have been?" Fools.
They do not know what they ask.
Animals are born. Human beings are born
to ask, Would you love me?

I would have given birth to human beings
Who from the beginning could speak and think.
But that is unnatural birth.
The natural birth is the birth
of blubbering spineless animals
who crawl and cry and sleep,
who wet the nurse's arm,
who poke their fingers in the mush,
and lie in their cradles
wobbling like junket in a dish.

Maria Katzenbach

Children are not made in the image of God.
They are made in the image of the animal.
They are made in the image the man and woman
have of the animal flesh.
The parent civilizes the offspring.
When they learn to speak
They learn sin.

I have accounted for all my sins
but one. The coils in my brain
and the tubes of my womb
will form into the lips of their mouths,
And with their voices they will divide
into three separate women bodies
from the one motherbody.
My sin is that I am one
My sin is that I hate the motherbody
who grows into two, who bears one
Individual dying body.
In the female glands the disease spreads,
The glands expand only to be
removed by the surgeon's scalpel.
I wish to die
I am already dead.

The sun glows red, round like a perfect cell. The room encloses
the sun in its central opening of the window in the wall. She looks
at the pinkly glowing sides, looks at the pink tips of her fingers,
and suddenly, her bitterness overwhelms her. She wants to take
back the confession. She is afraid that the disease has heard, that
God has heard. Always her body, always her body lies between
her and God. The woman cannot escape her body. Her body is
made to repeat itself, to fill and to empty. The surgery for the
cancer digs trenches, but the pits fill with her sin. Sin is filling the
pits in the body with hate.

You and the disease feed the hatred of my body.
You and the disease fill and empty the void

of the motherbody.
I have believed in the I am
I have believed in the Father
and cursed the I am not of the motherbody.
O Merciful Father
Kill me
whom you have already killed.

As the sun disappears and the reflections vanish, her mind
cools. Time, the narrow time of the day, comes back to her. She
has not eaten. The food that she puts into her mouth only comes
back up. She is wearing the nightgown and robe she slept in. The
organdy is crushed. She brushed her cloud of hair this morning,
and now the wisps have settled around her head. The textures of
the room, the material of her life, are rough. The pattern of the
bedcover becomes a face, a face she does not know, a face she
will speak to once, and then expire. The face will be her shroud
when she lies on the deathbed finally emptied of words.

She lifts her pale arms into the mixed light and dark of twilight.
She fingers an organdy sleeve delicately, as one would stroke the
feathers of a bird to calm the bird, to detain the flight.

To depart.
To shed the awkward articulation
of imperfect flesh, to discard
the long stemmed meanings, to toss away
the names, faces, minds,
to flee from the trinity
of daughters I have made.

I see three faces in the one face
Of the portrait hanging on my skull.
The portrait I see is as old as my skull.
One face was painted in 1885,
the year I was born. At every birth
the portrait was repainted.
I remember the dates of their births,
but I do not know how old my daughters are.

Maria Katzenbach

The subtractions and additions of their lives
is not the time that I know.
I am to escape
all subtractions and additions of my body
To depart
To leave for the perfect, zero heaven.

Downstairs in the hall hangs her portrait painted when she was forty-four. The portrait does not resemble the old woman lying upstairs in the bedroom. The portrait looks exactly like her youngest daughter. The painting is hers. The painting is her eldest daughter's who is her namesake. The painting is her second daughter's who finds meaning in the gift.

She looks over at the face on the bedcover. Will it speak? Will it decide for her this last decision? She wants only to be rid of images, of all references to her physical existence. If only the portrait would disappear when she disappears, if only generations did not have to reflect the past in their future.

But she is forgetting something, something important. She is forgetting that the portrait has already been given away. But to which one of the three? And how did the decision come to be made? Events fade out of her mind as her intellect spins itself out into the ancient, vacant light.

"Wishing it is gone, it is gone."
The face on the bedcover says.
"These laws of time do not apply to you.
Have you not noticed your weightlessness?
Have you not noticed the missing flesh,
the absent word? The gravity of generations,
the mass of pain moving through time,
Has been transformed in your body.
Give it up, give up to the missing word.
Depart."

The walls of the room deepen to scarlet deepen to purple and finally slink into black shadow. Who are you? She turns her eyes toward the face that will be her shroud, but the movement is imperceptible, the face gone. [Who, my soul, Who?] As her sense of motion drains from her head, escaping through her fingertips, her face becomes white. She is numb. Her hand is invisible in the shadow of the room. Only her white sleeve, only the layers of her white robe are visible in the dark. Around her head framing the porcelain skull her fragile hair stills the air. All is still in the room. Only the faint sound of the leaves breathing in the night air can be heard through the window. The folds of the features of her face glisten like china. Where am I? I am in the room and now I am the room. Through one thin layer of organdy she can discern the strand of her arm; through the white threads of stuff, through the dark threads of flesh-in-shadow she sees the one thread of bone. The layers of white billow around her useless legs, around her body like a soft nest of feathers. Motion is flight.

Suddenly a pain in her chest explodes. Particles of light escape from her eyes. Her head opens, and out of it fly small white discs, snakes' teeth. Now, pure spirit, snow, cool, dry snow falling, descending down from the sky into the cup of her mind, past her eyes, as the vision is purified, past her throat as the words are bleached, into her heart; she freezes. The organdy turns to ice. Then slowly she begins to rise as the ice-organdy splinters into feathery icicles, into the stiff wings of her ascent.

As she rises she hears a voice speaking through the snow, the muffled, hoarse voice of the old mother who lived.

Who will receive it?
Who will receive the portrait?
"It is already given.
It is given to the one you loved,
Afraid to admit it, afraid of the softness,
Afraid of the joy of her head on your breast."
[You, cruel Mother.]

She floats, hovering like the moon in the dark bedroom, she floats, suspension of spirit suspended; then, slowly, she ascends into the black, open zero, an ice-cold, blue lipped Angel.

Maria Katzenbach   137

Susu Jeffrey

SHELLSON, EVEGO, AND I

"Do you believe in God?"

He has a pasty face—white, the same color all over, eyelids—not even the nostrils are pink—pock-marked, zit scars from indented adolescent blemishes. He's over thirty. His brown hair is neatly combed with cream or grease with an almost perfect part, and he wears conservative, fashionable in a subtle way, expensive clothes, and he won't answer my question. Today must be his brown day: brown lightly plaided suit, tan shirt, and an embellished tie, tan and rust with brown. The tip of his tongue is faded red when it pushes out upon his lower lip and gets bitten by his upper teeth. He stays that way, biting his tongue until it curls back in his mouth. His lips are narrow and long and his teeth don't show. I don't know what color his teeth are. I don't know what kind of car he drives.

I would like to ask him what kind of car he drives. However, that would be an irrelevant question. Particularly since he has not answered my first question. If he would answer my first question I would probably not ask him any more questions. It would not matter what kind of a car he drives.

His phone buzzes. His phone is tan, his desk is brown. A yellow legal pad is on a green blotter next to a number two schoolbus-yellow pencil.

He says, "Yes."

How unpleasant. Very businesslike. What about "no" or "maybe." Maybe "yes" is the answer to my question. I smile. He raises his eyebrows. "Yes" I believe in God? Well, *yes* isn't enough, because the question carries an automatic why, unstated politely. People who answer yes always say why. It's the evangelistic urge. It spills all over them and instead of explaining why, they try to make a convert. Those are the new believers. Older ones get dreamy and pause. They take their time to choose their words and come out with a verbal pause, and "I'll tell you why." They talk about how they believed unquestioningly at first. Then they tell how they doubted. And started believing again —the reasonable, omnipotent higher force, the creative source, pre-Darwin . . .

New converts speak much faster. Immediately they launch into Biblical quotes to *prove* apriori the existence of God. *He* this and *He* that, they say excitedly. Their words beat on me like surf on the pilings. Steadily, methodically, they roll in and slush and inundate my steadfast ear. I have calluses like barnacles on my steadfast ear. My ear is warped from the believers on shore. So I took the boat out.

I smile. His brown eyes glance quickly at the smile. He thinks I am trying to listen to the conversation cupped into his ear. I am not. I am not interested in his conversation. Only whether he believes in God.

Actually most people don't need to tell *why*. Their yes, no, I think so, or I don't know is telling enough. I have asked over 300 people and it's just about all repetition. Specifically I've asked 306 people. Brownie makes the sixth after 300. Somehow I think one of the 300s will have a provocative answer. The best answer so far was from an eight-year-old boy. He said yes, because he saw Him once. I asked him when and where and he said yesterday out over the ocean and it made him feel warm.

I was at the beach yesterday too and I didn't see God. The kid gave me a shell. It was a gray oyster shell with calcified crud and shredded green slime on it. I gave him a sand dollar and told him it was a religious symbol. He broke it open and the white doves came out—five.

Susu Jeffrey

I write down what everybody tells me about God. I name and date them. That kid with the shell's doves is Shellson, July 21. So far there are 88 yeses, 63 nos, exactly 100 I don't knows, and 55 I think so's. Many of the I think so's seem like I hope so, but I'm afraid not. I forget the exact number. I used to keep percentages too, but it became too much of a game. The old God game score, ladies and gentlemen, is Heaven such-and-such to Nada's whatever. Howard Cosell could do it justice. I bet Howard Cosell believes. The simples always do. The older thinkers either doubt or definitely believe. The younger thinkers are agnostics. The young thinkers are atheists. Uneducated women of any age always believe. Kids and oldies have the best answers. After the initial 100 interviews, I concentrated on those categories of people.

The best no answer came from a thirty-five-year-old female magazine editor on vacation; she is number 67. She said she was an atheist since it can never be known—standard agnostic answer—but then she said she was not going to waste her time on unanswerables because reality is the dominion of man/woman and she appreciates her limitations. Furthermore she said she didn't care about God, but she was interested in herself and other people. It is the most unselfish egoistic answer I've ever heard. Blatant, positive. I dubbed her Evego. That was during spring, near Easter, April-something. It wasn't *what* she said, it was *how*—that she was so at ease with the question. People often contract when I ask them. Like Brownie. That's why I stopped asking that age category and specialize on kids and oldies.

I suppose now it was a mistake to ask him. He just stared at me. He asked me a whole line of questions, my name, my address, my age, my parents, my reasons for being out in the boat. I told him my name was Sally Lindsey, which it is not and told him I lived at 3308-A South Ocean Boulevard, which is abbreviated S.O.B. I don't. I told him my parents live in St. Louis—I've never been to St. Louis—but that they were on vacation in their cabin in Wisconsin, which was true, I think. That's where they usually are in August. I told him I am twenty-two, which is true, and I know they don't believe that because I look seventeen or eighteen. He did not see the gold metal around my neck on

140   INTRO 7

the gold chain. It is a saint's medallion. It is my favorite saint. I had it made. I couldn't find a St. Nicholas medal anywhere. The spirit of giving.

That's as far as I'd come. To St. Nick, the jolly old Xmas gift elf from the upper pole. He's someone to believe in. He is both concrete and ethereal. He is international, traditional, contemporary and he was recently defrocked by the Pope, which makes him more universal. He has his standards, but he's very forgiving. I've never met a kid who got a lump of coal, and I think more people believe in Santa Claus than God. Of course it could be an existential flaw.

I accept that as possibility but as merely a contingent, not decidedly probable. "What are we going to do with you?" Brownie asks me.

He put the phone down about the time I rethought Evego. I could reflect his brown eyes on me, on my hair, on the blanket, that's all I let him see. I determined not to be interrupted in my considerations. "What time is it?" I ask him.

He says, "Why?"

Now isn't that a bitch? What time is it is a perfectly reasonable question. Not that it matters. Not that I can do anything about it. If I were outside I could tell what time it is. Beach time is very specific. Three hours before sunset the gulls come in. The tourists are still out on the beach getting burned. Their kids are tired and hungry and they just lie out there and bake. They make their kids get out of the water. They tell them to build sand castles by their blankets. In the dry sand. The surfers are out then. They materialize from the bars and jobs and fishing and getting high to see what the onshore wind shift is doing with the surf. Bronze gods with golden tangled hair always upset tourists. They think their kids are going to get cracked on the head by washouts. They don't have any faith. Funny, they say they believe, but they don't have any faith. I have faith, but I don't know if I believe. I think I'm in better shape. I look like the picture of health. My nose is peeling, my shoulders are freckled, and I have drip-dry hair.

But that could be deceiving and Brownie knows it and I know he knows it. Brownie is getting boring. I am boring him. It's mutual.

I get up to leave.

"Where are you going?" he demands. This is not a question. It verges on a threat, and threats are always made out of fear.

I pause. This answer is important. This answer is very important. I stop in mid-step; my back is to Brownie. I sense the importance of this question because St. Nicholas is touching the cleavage between my breasts and that means I'm breathing deeply. I am going to use control. I am either going to breathe in and out until the red blotches on my neck go away and I can decide on an answer to comfort Brownie and the boys, or I am going to hyperventilate. I hear my mind checking off selected answers. They've heard them all before. Okay I'll be very specific and honest. No, I know. I'll phrase it like a question.

"I think I ought to get that boat back, don't you?"

"The boat has been returned."

I do not believe the boat has been returned. It did not have any Coast Guard numbers on it. Too small. It's just a rowboat. A gray rowboat. It belongs to the hotel. But it's not a guest boat. It's not even a fishing boat, because it's too small for the ocean. They could use it on the intracoastal, but it's too old. Hotel people have to have a bar on board and this is just a two-man miniature wooden whaler without an outboard. Sturdy, I appreciate sturdy boats. That's why I chose it. A nobody boat. But for people. Really a nice boat. Last night when I was scared in the swells one oar kept banging on the side of the boat. Finally the rhythm of it taught me to breathe with it. It went bang on the port side and ga-tum in the oarlock. And I inhale bang, ga-tum, bang, ga-tum, bang, ga-tum—exhale two-three. To sleep.

Sunrise was quiet. Florida sunrises are. It's almost like waiting for faith. First the sky lightens. There is a cloud cover far out, past the Gulf Stream. Generally it doesn't burn off till nine o'clock. The rays of the sun this morning broke through, between cover layers, and stretched—a transparent, luminous fan from low heaven to the upper horizon where the earth meets the sky. And there was a green goldfinch with me. They live at sea. I was surprised to find them even twenty miles out on other trips. If there is no boat or buoy they spread their wings and float, prey to fish though, so this finch was glad to be with me in Ole

Gray. I had my hands behind my back for a pillow and I was staring straight into the red ball. It spun like a yo-yo in the "sleeper" trick, whirling and inching against gravity and the gray seas. The sun sweetened the sea, from grouse gray to green. The goldfinch settled on my elbow. Never in my life has a wild bird touched me. I acknowledge that as my pantheistic baptismal touch. That advances me to a par with the cave men. Unless it was a transcendental experience. I wonder really if I have come that far already. Either that or Kant was a supernatural intellectualizer. Perhaps it doesn't matter, but it would be nice to know.

I held that position from the first moment of daybreak to sun change, from red to yellow. When the sun works to dilute the cloud cover it burns itself into a change of character. Nine o'clock and all is yellow. I was hungry. The waves drenched my French bread when my nearly dry bikini washed overboard. I stood up on the seat and clapped for the porpoises, it's their alert—jaw snapping—sounds like clapping. I obviously don't speak porpoise. They didn't want the bread, but they kept me company until I covered up under the blue beach towel for a siesta.

If a boat came by and notified the Coast Guard, that must have been when it happened. Sure. I don't blame them. I would have done it myself. It was one of the best sleeps of my life. I wish there had been a dream, one that I remember, but there wasn't, so I made one up. I became a man o' war, washed by the waves but still with a will of my own. A small blue bubble. Hanging down, poison tentacles, blind, clean. Unconsciously happy.

Then the Coast Guard boat ran out. I saw them coming, but what could I do? I pretended. I guess they never found a naked possum five miles out before. I let them help me up. What a solicitous blanket they offered after they looked. I jumped. It seems Coast Guarders don't like to get wet. Their lifesaving, what a misnomer. Sunburned—kindly gestures feel like abrasions. Their hands stuck to me. I knew one of them but he didn't recognize me without clothes. He hangs out at the Anchor Club. Wears a silver St. Christopher medal; he played captain today. They strapped me onto a stretcher. My hands were strapped down. He didn't care. He just swore at the seamen when they tried to gaff Ole Gray. And drove around in circles until I thought I would throw up.

I breathed then. I closed my eyes and listened for last night's bang, ga-tum. I couldn't hear it, so I moved my head to it. Bounce, side-side. Bounce, side-side. I kept it up. No more the will-less man o' war even being towed. Like a bait mullet. Like a stinking dead lure, nodding at the end of the line. I didn't care. Con-tro-ling, brea-thing. I thought about my soul. I wanted to think about God but I realize I didn't know how yet. My soul is something I understand. It becomes most obvious when I'm hungry. That is because I am forced to listen to my body then. My body insists on being heard until I counter with control. I breathed. I refused to open my eyes and I listened to my breathing. I had to blow my nose so it wasn't hard to hear my breathing above the motors.

Then somebody held my forehead down. Not a word. Just hands. I screamed. It might have been a yell. It sounded deeper than a scream. I had a headache from then on.

It's dull unless I move hard. That's why I can stop so quickly when Brownie, his thrust-parry, asks, "Where are you going?" Headaches make one aware of movement. I am most sensitive now. I can feel the itchiness of the blanket in the middle of my back. I would throw it down except that I'm cold. Also I don't like to make a spectacle of myself.

What makes me mad is that these people are making a spectacle of me.

"You're making a spectacle of me." I didn't mean to say that necessarily. But now I'm glad I did. If there is a God, surely He would not condone this kind of business. People dragging me around, strapping me down, interrogating me. I would never consider doing that to anyone. I am not above that, because I am human and that implies a certain greed over the will of others. But I am beyond that. That is the second most comforting thought I have had today. Since the pantheistic experience. I am not seeking the kind of power to force others to act the way I want them to.

I open the door and walk into the patrolman. He looks scared. Before, he looked as though he wanted lunch. Maybe he ate.

He is the kind of person who believes in God from habit. He likes authoritarianism. He likes definitions and absolutes. He doesn't disagree with people who make more money than he does. He steers me back to Brownie. Untouchable at arm's length. "The address don't check and the hotel isn't going to file."

Brownie must nod now. Nod let me go or nod to him? While I wait to know he unhands me; I am to him a sandbag-bottomed dummy. Brownie asks me if I want to sit down. I need to be tight. I shake, no.

I would like to lie. In a damp sand blanket. My eyelids close and I listen to the headache pound. I shall not open until it's clear.

It is happening now. I scream, I scream. I can't feel my soul any more. I am like sand in a timer, upside-down and running out. The hunger in the soul disintegrates. Headache, residue. No sticky salt scales, no itching blanket. It's all going out. Fast but it feels gradual. Sliding away, even the prickly pinches on my face. Less burning too. I cannot stop it, it's peaceful draining. At the end I can start again. A revelation in a heartbeat. Transcendence? No, that sounds down. Metamorphosis? Yes. I try to scream God, but it comes out a vowel.

Gary Gay

TROMBONE HOLIDAY

Clendon's principal unlocked the front door of the high school auditorium and held it open for us to go inside. It felt colder in there than it had sitting in the bus out front. You could see your breath. I looked up at the ceiling expecting to see icicles and thought about going back out to the bus. I would have, if the heaters hadn't been on. You could hear them cracking and popping down front. That's where everyone headed, down front to be by the heaters. Not me. I wanted on the back row. I lugged my trombone case all the way over to the last chair by the wall, as far away from the auditorium entrance as you could get without going down front where everyone headed. I sat down and brushed snow off my trombone case with the back of my glove.

I sat there with my eyes closed and tried to go over "Trombone Holiday" in my mind. It wouldn't work. I opened the case and took out my trombone. I attached the mouthpiece and raised the trombone to my lips. I sat there with my eyes closed. Not playing, understand. Just mentally going over "Trombone Holiday," moving the slide during the hardest parts. With the heaters cracking and all the contestants swarming into the auditorium, I could hardly concentrate. I was determined to go all the way through, though. Just one more time before we had to get up there and do it for real.

I was pretty near the end when all of a sudden my trombone wouldn't budge. I opened my eyes and saw *this guy* had hold of the slide. He stood there grinning and staring at me through glasses so thick that you felt sorry for him. I wondered if he'd just walked up and grabbed the slide or if he'd stood there awhile first. I got the feeling he'd been there the whole time. The thought of him standing there and watching irritated me, but I smiled at him.

"'Trombone Holiday'?" he said.

That kind of jarred me. You know, it was like having a stranger walk up and tell me I'm a Sagittarius. Then I decided I probably had been sort of humming under my breath. I mean, I must've been.

"Huh?"

"You were playing 'Trombone Holiday,'" he said. This time it was more of an accusation—like he was Perry Mason and I was trying to hide some deep, dark secret.

"Yeah, right," I said, still trying to figure him out.

"Where you from?"

I told him Arlis and asked where he was from.

He didn't say. All he said was, "You guys are out of your mind."

He turned and made his way between the rows of seats. I saw he was carrying a French horn. That meant he was in somebody's brass sextet. I watched him walk down the aisle. He was little— maybe five-foot-five—and he held his head up and shoulders back. *Too* up and *too* back. Reminded me of a rooster. He walked all the way down front, between the stage and the first row. A lot of guys wearing Spiller band jackets were congregating down there. Like they were taking the place over, I thought.

I kept telling myself I wasn't nervous, but when the rest of the Arlis brass sextet and I filed up there onto the stage, I was trembling like a tuning fork. Things like hitting B-flats and missing thirty-secondths weren't worrying me. Hell, no. I kept telling myself this contest would be a success for me if I could just get through the next minutes without *dropping* my trombone. And what got me—this really got me—I was *sweating*. Under my arms I was soaked. Somebody could have seen if they looked. And it was a good thing I had "Trombone Holiday" memorized, because sweat kept trickling down into my eyes. I didn't wipe it away. I was afraid to. Mr. Baker said the judges take everything into consideration, not just how you play your instruments.

I didn't really do that badly. Not after we got started. And I know I finished strong. Mr. Baker told me later that I did an exceptional job. I didn't, but it wasn't *too* bad.

Later we were sitting there—all the brass sextets in the district. A lot of other guys were in there, too; the place was cram-packed. But the brass sextets had just finished competing. Pretty soon a judge walked up onto the stage with a yellow slip of paper in her hand.

She wadded up the paper and spoke into the mike: "Winner, Spiller High School for their excellent rendition of 'Beautiful Dreamer.'"

The Spiller sextet was sitting right in front of us, so you had to read the judge's lips to hear anything she said after "Spiller." Their tuba player jumped out of his seat and yelled, "HOORAY!" They all shook hands and started patting each other on the back and even hugging—which, I guess, is what we would have done. Their band director stood up and clapped for them. We clapped, too. Everyone in the auditorium clapped. That's when the rooster turned around and looked at me, while I was clapping for him and the other five members of the Spiller sextet. He was grinning and through his glasses his eyes looked as big as fifty-cent pieces.

"'Trombone Holiday,'" he said. He shook his head and laughed.

I didn't say anything. I didn't know what to say. I'll tell you one thing, though. That *guy* didn't know how close he came to getting a trombone case up side the head.

After the contest we ate at the Derrick Cafe. We weren't supposed to eat, because Arlis isn't that far from Clendon. What I mean is, the school wouldn't pay for it; we had to bring our own lunch money.

Lonnie Warren, Joe Bob Barnett, and I sat in a booth at the back, near the jukebox. They had it too hot in there, and Lonnie and Joe Bob took their coats off. I was about to burn up, but I was afraid to take mine off. I asked Joe Bob to order me a chicken-fried steak and went to the men's room.

When I got in there, I took off my coat and held my arm up in front of the mirror. I smoke so much that I was afraid all that sweating might've left nicotine stains on my white shirt. But it didn't. I held my coat and combed my hair. The door to the men's room swung open and seven or eight Spiller guys poured in. Taking the place over, I thought, like they had the Clendon High auditorium.

The tuba player was the one who pushed the door open. He was carrying a coat hanger with his street clothes on it. Right behind him was the rooster. He carried a coat hanger with clothes on it, too. You don't wear your band uniform to the contest, but you can't just dress any way you want to. All the boys wear black slacks with white shirts. Arlis is only forty-three miles from Clendon, so I put my slacks and shirt on at home and wore them. A lot of people bring theirs hung-up, though. Spiller is way on the other side of Arlis, nearly a hundred miles from Clendon.

When I saw who it was coming into the men's room, I didn't look any more. Just parted my hair and slicked it down as fast as I could.

One of them started humming. When I realized *what* he was humming, I knew it was rooster. He hummed about four lines of "Trombone Holiday" and went right on into "Taps." They all got a big bang out of that. I felt the back of my neck turn red. I'd heard all that crap I wanted to hear. I slipped the comb into my hip pocket and started to leave. Only I didn't. Even though I was fixing to leave anyway, I stayed in my tracks. They weren't going to *run* me out of there. Only I didn't want to just stand there. I had already put the comb in my pocket; it'd be squirrelly to get it out again. And I couldn't just stand there and look at myself in the mirror.

I didn't think about *what* I was doing when I took all the change out of my pocket. You know, I was just *doing*. I hadn't looked at that machine good when I first walked into the men's room. Not at the way it worked. Just read the things people had written on it. You know, like, "This chewing gum tastes like rubber." All of a sudden I was worried after I took a quarter out of my palm and put it into the slot. Worried that I wouldn't be able to work the thing. I twisted the knob as if I'd done it a thousand times, though. The machine made a clanging noise, and this little packet fell into the opening at the bottom. That's when I first realized *what* I was doing, when I actually saw the little packet and realized that all the rustling around and talking behind me had stopped. I took the packet, slipped it into my hip pocket with the comb, and popped another quarter in the slot. I twisted the knob, and the machine clanged. I took that one out and left with it in my fist. Didn't *run*, either. Just strolled out of there as though I was Errol Flynn.

Sarah B. Davenport

ALL OF US AND NONE OF YOU

Uncle Lee

Uncle Lee spends all his mornings at Miss Mitchells' house. She sells liquor by the bottle and glass. Uncle Lee always buys a bottle of Seagram's Gin and drinks the first drink at Miss Mitchells'. Then he brings the bottle home and sits at the kitchen table, drinking the rest. Often as he drinks, he reads the morning paper, looking for a quotable quote or a paragraph worth reciting. Uncle Lee has a good memory. When he finds something he likes, he reads it, a line at a time, repeating the line over and over until he's learned it. The completion of his lesson always coincides with the emptying of his bottle. He usually takes a nap in the afternoon. In the evening, he eats dinner with us, smiling and carrying on a halfway intelligent conversation with my oldest brother, Frank.

Yesterday as we came to dinner, Frank asked Mom, "You got any furniture polish?" "I think so. What you want it for?" asked Mom. "To clean my blackjack," answered Frank. Uncle Lee said, "Yeah, I bet it's in bad shape Frank. All them nappy Afro heads don't do nothing but scratch up a good blackjack."

Before Mom brought the food to the kitchen table, she brought Uncle Lee a cup of strong, black coffee. Uncle Lee stood up next to the refrigerator and sipped the coffee, holding the cup with his little finger sticking straight out. He then flipped his long tongue across his top lip, around the sides and across his bottom lip. He cleared his throat; one long grunt, and two short.

He put his right hand into the front of his shirt and began to recite the Budweiser Beer label slogan.

Mom nodded her head at every other word and moaned in a singsong hum. Next, Uncle Lee spoke the words to "The Star Spangled Banner." He exaggerated his voice, emphasizing each word and spitting on almost all of them.

When Uncle Lee had finished "The Star Spangled Banner," there was cheerful silence: Mom was silently cheering Uncle Lee, and the rest of us were cheering the silence.

Uncle Lee always finishes by reciting the Baptist Church Creed. And Mom really moans on that. She moans-sings "Lord, Lord, Lord, hum-m-m," and raises to a higher key on each "Lord."

And that is our prelude to dinner every night. We have it instead of a Grace because my brother Bubba says he's an atheist, my brother Frank says he's a killer-cop, and my Uncle Lee knows he's an alcoholic.

Uncle Lee is a failure. So he drinks. He is a serious alcoholic. But, until last night, I had never seen him be a staggering drunk. Usually somewhere between a half and a whole bottle of Seagram's Gin, he excuses himself, goes to the bathroom, and puts his fingers down his throat, and brings up what he had swallowed. This way, so he told me, the liquor doesn't have time to affect his body.

After dinner, Mom gives Uncle Lee the other half of his daily allowance and he goes back to Miss Mitchells'. At eleven-twenty, he's in bed, after taking a quick bath and saying his prayers on his knees. Mom says he oughta spend the rest of his life on his knees asking forgiveness for his useless life. He says she likes to pick on him, but she's really glad he's not a responsible person. If he was, then Mom wouldn't be in charge of his government disability check. He gets it as a result of "battle fatigue" from World War II. Mom says for him not to blame it on the war, because he wasn't too bright when he went in there.

Uncle Lee always wears a plaid short sleeve shirt and in the winter he wears a v-neck sweater over it. He never wears a tie.

Mom nearly had a fit when the one time Uncle Lee wanted to go to church with us, he was determined to wear his regular clothes. Mom said maybe the Lord just wanted us to come to church and not bother with how good we looked, but she cared and that was that. Uncle Lee never decided to go again.

Sometimes Uncle Lee takes a few minutes from his nap to talk to me. Once, he came to the park and brought Cokes and a big bag of Fritos. He told me I shouldn't be sitting in the park alone because I am built older than a fourteen-year-old usually is and that could be dangerous.

I wish I could help Uncle Lee. He's so down on life. He always says the dollar has gone the way of good women. He says that because he had some bad experiences with women. When he came back from the war, no woman wanted him, except for his money. He had saved some, and when that was gone, the women went too. Mom says he went from bad to worse until she took control and made him live with us. Uncle Lee was glad to move in. He can't hold a regular job, because he gets shaking fits. Sometimes he sits for hours at a time staring at a wall and not saying a word. Mom says his drinking doesn't help him any. But Uncle Lee still drinks. I guess it's the only thing left that he can do and do well. He sure doesn't fail a bottle of Seagram's Gin.

Brother Bubba

My brother Bubba is a fool. When I look at him, I pray that there is no such thing as reincarnation. He's always picking on me. Every day I have a reason to ask "Why me, Lord," over some dumb thing Bubba has teased me about.

Bubba has absolutely no personality. He's just like every other cornerhanging black nineteen-year-old in this entire city. If you saw him in a crowd, you probably couldn't pick him out from the rest of that anonymous-looking group. And Bubba probably wouldn't see you either. He's always hiding behind his dirtybeige floppy crocheted hat that almost covers his face. He's the type of person who always looks dirty and sloppy—even when he's dressed up. And he wears the most peculiar color combinations. Two different types of plaid.

Sarah B. Davenport

I'm always surprised when he comes out of his room halfway clean because his room is a hodgepodge of nastiness. Mom sent me in there one day to straighten up. I got lost, finally found his bed and started to make it. Bubba came in and said, "Don't worry about making it up, Sugar, I'm gonna get back in it tonight."

Bubba is so cool, he makes me nauseous. He thinks women were created for his amusement. And the poor girls have been brainwashed by him to think so too. They gather around him like flies. Maybe I can't see his appeal because I've been looking at him for fourteen years and I see him as a sister.

But I do know those sickening girls are worrisome, calling up all the time, day or night. Mom has had to remove the receiver at eleven on the weekends in order to get some sleep. They should know that Bubba is still in the streets until early the next morning.

Bubba doesn't walk—he pimps. And he swings his right arm back and forth as he pimps. He reminds me of a long-armed ape. And he never calls me by my right name. In the last year, I have been Baby, Mama, Sweet Thing, Doll, and Shorty Girl. He calls everybody Sugar now. Mom says she wishes she had gone to church that Sunday morning he was created. When she says that, Bubba throws his arms around her neck and says, "But, Sugar, look what you gave the world." And Mom hides her smile from him and says, "Go on, child, with your nonsense."

Bubba works at the Metropolitan Tobacco Company. He makes four dollars an hour. He loves it because he thrives in filth. He says you gotta be a nasty nigger to work there. Some of the things he tells me (when Mom's not around) are insane. Everybody there seems to be going with everybody else's women. Fights go on almost everyday there. Once, a woman threw a foreman out the window in a fight. Bubba loves it. He is into all the action there, even selling black market cigarettes. He has a girl friend on each of the three floors. They have been known to battle over him. Bubba stands beside the fights and referees. I say let the best woman lose. Mom says she's given up on thinking he will straighten up. She says she's gonna stop worrying about him and just keep him insured, so she can bury him nice. That is, if the women leave enough of his body intact for a decent funeral.

Brother Frank

Frank, the nut, is a cop. I'm sure they accepted him because of the Equal Opportunity Employment Clause. He's an intellectual with no class. He is absolutely dedicated to one thought—that he's a cop. He is thrilled by his importance. I guess that's good, because no one else in the house is thrilled by it, except maybe Mom when he brings money home.

When Frank is off duty, he plays his two-way radio up loud and we all have to listen to police calls. He even brought Mom a police band radio for when he's not there. He's got her a code sheet and she knows them by heart. If he has to leave in a hurry, Mom'll say, "Your brother has gone on a two-five (or whatever)." He makes me sick with his police talk. He never really tells anything secret, but he can sure worry us to death with unimportant information.

Frank has been a policeman for three years. He joined when he was twenty-one, and I feel as though I went through every day of his career with him. I could probably become a policewoman with no training at all (except for traffic directions). He left for the force the day after that sergeant came around looking for a token black from my neighborhood. I don't know how he managed to stay in this length of time. There doesn't seem to be a rule that he hasn't broken or changed a little. He carries a .38 police special gun, a blackjack, and a flashlight. He has never used anything other than the flashlight. That has dents all around the top, where he used it to beat suspects' heads. I asked him why he doesn't use his blackjack instead, and he went into his police talk, using some long words and elaborate phrasing until I just tuned him out and made a poem in my head.

Mom cooks big meals for us, and she insists that Frank eat well. I don't know whether she is afraid each meal is his last and wants him to go on a full stomach, or whether she sees it as her duty before God. It must be her duty, because Frank doesn't work dangerously hard. All he does is ride around in his police car looking for heads to bust. He and his partner, Elbert James, claim they are the best of Richmond's Finest. That's the motto of the police department—"Richmond's Finest." I haven't been introduced to any of the other force men, but I do know they can't possibly be the best. If they are, this city is in bad shape.

Frank and Bert are always spending their time at our house. On duty and off. They park the car in front and sit around drinking liquor with Uncle Lee until a call comes through for them. Once, they passed by the house as they patroled, and called to me. When I went to the car, Bert handed me a half empty can of Pepsi-Cola and told me to tell Uncle Lee to fill it up with liquor. I refused, of course, and Uncle Lee came out with a mayonnaise jar full of gin to give them.

They must have a guardian angel watching over them, because they never get caught at anything.

Frank knows Mom likes to hear his car number three-eight-five being paged. She follows his movements throughout his duty. Frank doesn't mind her knowing where he is most of the time. He knows she is proud to have a policeman as a son. He just doesn't want her to follow him. When Frank bought her the radio about a year ago, she heard his car being paged to a fire at a Southside hat factory. She borrowed Bubba's car and went to the scene of the fire. She shoved for twenty minutes until she got into a position directly in front of Frank. She then proceeded to tell everyone around her, "He's my son the policeman." But that one time cured her of following Frank. She couldn't stand the crowd of people ignoring, shoving, and thereby disrespecting her son.

Frank drives their police car most of the time, because he says Bert is too impulsive. I'd call it neurotic. Once, when Bert was driving around eleven-thirty at night, he decided he would drive to Petersburg, about thirty miles away. Frank had been sleeping, and when he awoke, Bert was just leaving the turnpike and entering the city. Frank was furious. He asked Bert what he thought he was doing, and suppose they had gotten a call? Bert gave his usual dense answer, "Man, I just felt like it."

So now, Frank drives most of the time. Bert sleeps with his feet across Frank's legs, interfering with the brake pedal. I sure hope Bert's wife has him insured.

Mom

Mom used to sing with the Inspirational Gospel Singers. They traveled through North Carolina, South Carolina, Virginia, and Washington for about two years, until the sponsor and lead singer got pregnant by the piano player and left to go with him to his home in Maryland to see about suing his wife for a divorce. Somehow, the other four women couldn't make it without her, so they split up, and Mom came back here to live. Mom is still singing the "Songs of Zion," and I wish she'd stop. I don't know how she ever got in that group, because she sure can't hold a key now. Maybe she didn't have to audition. I don't know. All I know is, if I sing with her in unison, and then I switch to alto, Mom'll leave her part and come right down and sing in unison with me again. So mostly I leave her with her police radio. Except when we're fixing dinner. I sing with her then so she won't notice she's doing most of the work.

Mom is in a good mood most of the time. Except when she's meditating. Then she demands peace and quiet for her "harmony with God." She meditates a lot, which gives me a chance to do some writing. She sits in her chair by the living room window and reads the Bible. Then she starts to hum. She gets real loud at times. Bubba always leaves the house when he sees her get the Bible. Uncle Lee drinks his gin and hums along with her. I asked her why she doesn't go to the church's Wednesday night prayer service instead. She says the church is only a building and our house is a building too.

Mom is only forty-two, but she acts seventy. She has put aside everything man does except eating and sleeping. She won't even think about a man. She said she's tired and wants to rest from care. I guess she's talking about my daddy. He left home six years ago. I think her humming got to him too. Mom says that Bubba is just like Daddy. She says they're two of a kind—except for one thing; Bubba seems to be holding onto his job. She says Daddy changed jobs like the seasons change. She said he was always getting mad and cursing at his employers. She said that she told him to either leave or to prepare to meet his maker. I think she would have killed him too. And then, she would have meditated all night long, called the cops, and listened for the call on her police radio.

Mom has absolutely no appeal. She's been wearing her hair in the same fashion since as far back as I can remember. She combs it all the way back, almost flat on her head and has one tiny row of curls on the bottom strands. If she ever discovers make-up, it'll probably be televised as a Special Bulletin. She has a large mole on the right side of her nose that looks alive. I never told her that I used to be scared of it when I was small.

Mom's dresses have never touched a part of her except her shoulders and arms. And they're all longer than her knees. She wears a silk undershirt in the summer and a cotton one in the winter. She doesn't like panty hose and I think she's the last person in Richmond wearing garters. I sure hope that the virus that she caught that made her the way she is doesn't strike me.

Daddy and God

I didn't tell anyone that Daddy was coming home for a visit. He wrote me a week before he came last night. I just thought it was another letter of reasons why he couldn't send the money I had asked him for. It was mailed from Philadelphia, the third address in six months. I guess Daddy will never settle down.

I thought it best that I didn't tell anyone. I was afraid of a scene and I would have to write Daddy not to come, because everyone in this house sure knows how to throw a scene. So I prepared for his visit alone. I stayed after school for three days, typing copies of my best poetry for Daddy. I missed him. He used to make me laugh and buy me gifts. I could talk to him. He had time. It didn't matter that the time he had for me was because he was always out of a job. He was there. He was love and care.

I had hoped he would come early before anyone else was home. But Daddy came at dinnertime. He looked run-down and tired. He came to the kitchen door. Frank went to the door and I thought he was finally going to use his blackjack (his flashlight was in the car).

Daddy said hello to Frank. Frank said nothing, he just stood there staring at Daddy. Finally he moved out of the way so Daddy could come in. I ran to Daddy and gave him a big hug and kiss. Uncle Lee shook his hand and told him to take a seat at the table and have something to eat. Daddy smiled slightly at Mom, holding his head down. Mom ignored him. I sat back down, holding my breath. Bubba came in from using the telephone and went into his "Hey, baby," act and forced Daddy's hand into the current soul handshake.

Uncle Lee asked Mom if she was going to greet Daddy. Mom said "Forgive me, Lord," and began eating. Uncle Lee shook his head and went to the cabinet for a plate for Daddy.

I wanted to tell Daddy all the things I had held inside for the six years he'd been away. But I was afraid. I had to live in this house when he went away again. So I let Bubba talk about his worthless friends and his women. Everyone else was silent except Uncle Lee, who occasionally told Bubba to hold it down a little. Bubba tends to get carried away sometimes.

Mom and I did the dishes afterward. The others went into the living room. Mom still wasn't talking. I started to sing, but Mom didn't join in. I started to cry. I begged Mom to be nice to Daddy, just this once. Mom said nothing, but she sighed heavily, so I knew she might be agreeing.

I hurried into the living room when Mom asked me to. I had broken a plate and she knew I was too excited to do dishes. Daddy was sitting in Mom's chair by the window, looking out onto the street. I could hear children playing games outside. Bubba was using an Afro pick on his huge "fro." I don't know why, because he just messes it back up with his hat. Frank was standing in the middle of the room, swinging his blackjack to and fro. Uncle Lee was drinking gin and picking his nose.

I sat, facing Daddy, on the arm of the sofa. Daddy looked at me and smiled shyly. I didn't ask him what he had been doing, only how he was. He said fine and asked how I was. I began to tell him about the things I was doing in school and with my friends. The sound of my voice was punctuated by the sounds of Frank's blackjack striking the coffee table and by Bubba's voice as he talked to one of his women on the phone.

I stopped talking when Frank grabbed Daddy by the shoulder, turning him around to face the room. He said, "Look here, man, what do you want? What did you come back for, nigger? You ain't staying here no more!"

Daddy looked up at Frank standing in his perfectly pressed police uniform. Daddy didn't say anything for a long while. Then he said, "I came to see my family." Frank told Daddy that he hadn't been too concerned about his family when he left home six years ago. Then Daddy said he wasn't going to argue with Frank. He just wanted to talk to me a little more, then he would leave. Frank wasn't satisfied. Daddy's explanation wasn't good enough for Richmond's Finest. Frank told Daddy that if he didn't leave right away, he'd take Daddy in.

Mom came out of the kitchen, and I ran to her, begging her to ask Frank to leave Daddy alone. Mom walked over to Daddy and asked him to remove his body from her chair. She sat in her chair with her Bible and began to hum.

Without a word to anyone, Daddy hung his head and left the house.

Mom still has her God, Bubba his women, Frank his job, and Uncle Lee his liquor. I have poetry when I can find peace and quiet.

I wonder what Daddy has? I never hear from him any more.

W. H. Battershell

COLD SHE MOVES AMID THE LAMBENT BLAZE

A Collage with Nasturtiums

There are those who say nasturtiums (*Tropaeolus majus*) give off light at dusk and again just before the sun rises. Charles Darwin's grandfather, Erasmus Darwin, mentions this phenomenon in his work *Botanic Garden*. His lines dealing with the nasturtium or "Tropaeo," as he calls "her," using the Latin name, read as follows:

> O'er her fair form the electric lus-
> tre plays,
> And cold she moves amid the lambent
> blaze.

> (*Pennyworth's Garden Book*)

May 10, 1923

Dear Mary,
   This is not much of a letter honey but we want you to know we are coming to visit you for a few days so you can lay in a few things. Your pa wont stay he will bring me over and stay a night

or so then come back for me in about a weak. We got to get out of the house before Natalie and her husband just drive your pa out of his mind fussing over Aunt Alice's money. Pa says if we leave maybe they will so we will see. Your Aunt Natalie just got back from Paris a couple months ago and heres the war over five years. She wasnt a nurse all that time we know and Lord only knows what she done over there she didnt get no money from us. Now she cant wait to get her share of Aunt Alice's and your pa is throughly disgusted and I dont blame him. And she has pestered that poor sick boy of the preachers just terrible everybody talks about it. I wonder will he live to see fall. Hes up in that cuppalo on top of the preachers house, you remember, trees all around it and open on all sides to the fresh air. Poor Mrs. King got it fixed up real nice.

Now honey dont put yourself out none we be there Monday sometime

your loving ma

(excuse misstakes)

May 17, 1923

I am Eddie King and I am very important. Always start that way, Natalie says.

The doctor says I can write a little in the morning and again in the afternoon if I don't get too tired. Perhaps he'll let me brush up on French with Swede's textbook.

Oh, I shall leave this miserable one-horse town some fine, fine day and I'll find that little restaurant, Natalie. Till then, Athensville, dead somewhere in the womb of Illinois.

This is Wednesday afternoon. Mr. Travis just drove in and came over here, madder than hell, as he might put it. I hear him in the kitchen now, questioning my mother. Natalie and her husband both are gone, he says. There are some flowers on his porch and someone has dug up part of his back yard.

Natalie's husband did the digging. I saw him down there, just before dark Monday night.

As I fell asleep I could hear the spade slipping into the earth.

"Rimby's Greenhouse."

"This Harry Travis. What's all this crap on my back porch?"

"Why, them's nasturtium plants, Harry. You better get 'em set out if they ain't. Your sister Natalie ordered those day before yesterday."

"She did?"

"Nineteen dollars seventy-five cents' worth. Paid cash for 'em. Give Davey a twenty-dollar bill."

"All paid for, huh?"

"You just check with her there, Harry."

"Can't do that, she's gone. Me and Emily left Monday afternoon and these damn flowers all over the porch and half the back yard dug up and nobody home. I found your bill with the flowers and I just want to know what's goin' on."

"I see . . . Well, Davey delivered them flowers early Tuesday morning, she called the order in Monday, about four-thirty Monday afternoon, after you left, I guess. Anyway, Davey took it over Tuesday morning, couldn't raise nobody. Told me he found the twenty dollars in a envelope on the porch. Had a note in it said leave the plants on the porch and not wake her up and keep the change, which he done. Davey said the place was all dug up in the yard ready then and not a sign of life nowheres. He done what the note said. . . . Harry?"

"Yeah, I'm here. I'm thinkin'."

"Listen, Harry, this is Thursday and them plants has been sittin' there for two days."

"Oh, I started on 'em. Out there last night till after dark. 'Bout three-fourths done."

You will be glad you planted nasturtiums, especially if other flowers are near, for they attract aphids and other pests which will prefer them to roses and other show flowers.

(*Pennyworth*)

"Well, Preacher?"

"You're planting nasturtiums, Brother Travis? A noble flower. God is generous. He takes your Aunt Alice and gives beauty."

"They're gonna die, too, if they don't get set out, but I'm about done now. Natalie spends nineteen dollars and seventy-five cents on these fool flowers, then goes off and leaves 'em. I was out here last night till after dark. Some of 'em dead already, I think."

"My son is going to die, Brother Travis, and I can't tell him. And I must praise the Lord. They watch my every action and search my every word to know if I praise the Lord."

"Well, your wife told Emily—Sunday, I guess it was—what the doctor said. Now, we're here, Preacher, right next door, and you remember that. Emily'll be back in a couple days and we wanta help anyway we can. I wanta tell you I'm sorry if Natalie went and bothered him too much. Told her to stay home."

"Don't look up that way. He might see us look up and guess that we're talking about him. Only twenty years old and got no strength, just tired all the time, but he sits up every morning for a spell. Wasted, Brother Travis, wasted . . . Doctor says he must go back to Norberry's as soon as we can get him in."

"It's too bad, Preacher. I wish we—"

"I walk up town and they all look at me. Now it's your turn, that's what they're saying. We've been through it and now it's come to you. . . . That's not very good ground, Brother Travis, and your flowers don't look very healthy."

"Nasturtiums don't like rich ground. The richer the soil, the fewer the blooms."

"It was all right for Natalie to talk to Eddie. It seemed to brighten him a little. She knew a world he'd never dreamed of."

"And I'm sorry she ever knew it, Preacher. It ruined her, comin' home here a degenerate, chasing every man she sees. Maybe that Charlie's her husband, maybe he ain't. Some former jailbird from Peoria, if you ask me, come down here to help her cause trouble over poor Aunt Alice's will. Why, they live up there in a hotel. That ain't no good. She ain't fit to live, Preacher. That's honest to God the way I feel."

May 19, 1923

I am Eddie King. I am unique.

Make it a journal of thoughts and impressions, she said, not a diary of events. Nobody else can think like you, not another soul can have the same impressions. The sad thing is you live in a dead little town with dead little people who never knew about being special. They probably think it's sinful to think that way about themselves. Can you tell me one among them who really tries to develop his differences, his own way of seeing? If any of them do, they do it secretly, afraid they'll be criticized. Don't you live in that kind of darkness.

I am better today. If I sit up straight, I can see the nasturtiums, all in place now, and all looking as weak as I feel.

She said she would plant them for me.

Les fleurs dans le jardin. Swede remembers far more French than I do, and we were in the same class at Illinois College.

I miss you, Natalie.

ATHENSVILLE RECORD
LOCAL NEWS ITEMS

Claudine Du Bois
Neighborhood Correspondent

Mrs. Harry Travis returned home Sunday after a week's visit with her daughter and husband, Mr. and Mrs. Russell Crain, in Winchester. Harry and Emily were over there week before last to attend the funeral of Miss Alice Gardner, Mr. Travis's aunt. Miss Gardner was the last surviving member of the famous Gardner family, founders of the city of Winchester.

Edward Lee King, oldest son of the Rev. and Mrs. Kenilworth King, will be entering Norberry's Sanitarium again soon for test and treatment. Eddie has been living up in the trees with the hoot owls this summer in the cupola room on the Methodist Parsonage. We wish you the best, Eddie, and we want you to hurry back.

Mr. and Mrs. Charles Hill, who have been visiting her brother and wife, Mr. and Mrs. Harry Travis, have departed. Natalie has been in Paris ever since the Kaiser gave up. Did you find Athensville anything like Paris, Natalie?

May 29, 1923

The great Eddie Hill again.

I can't write every day. I lie here most of the time and stare into the trees, deep into the trees. I see places the sun never finds —cool, mysterious places, dark with green. Tiny people live in there, too ghostly for sex, so they are the same ones who have lived there from the beginning. On cloudy days I see them clearly drifting along the black curling limbs. They come out to look at me. Hello, I never have sex either. See how thin I am, how fragile —a sunken, sexless skeleton. They don't answer.

Fifteen adjectives. Hell. Un paragraph pauvre. I can't even think of the French word for paragraph. Swede is so much better—yet he's the one they expelled.

Natalie has been gone two weeks. The nasturtiums look fine. Should be blooming soon.

> The nasturtium is a strong, sturdy plant, a good one for a child to grow in his first garden. You will find it nearly always successful, regardless of treatment. Its only reason to exist seems to be that of producing seeds and reproducing itself.
>
> (*Pennyworth*)

"Hello? Hello, Central?"

"Yes, this is Central."

"Central, I want to call the Royal Hotel in Peoria and talk to Mrs. Charlie Hill."

"This is Emily, ain't it?"

"Ye-es. Emily Travis number 273. Is that you, Gladys?"

"Well, it better be. Now you just hang up and wait for a little bit. I'll call you back when I get 'em."

> ("You talk to her, Harry."
>
> "I won't talk to either one."
>
> "I know something's wrong, something's wrong."
>
> "Yes, she's my baby sister and she's lost. She's ruined herself. It's good that Ma ain't here."
>
> "Well, you ought to do the talkin', not me."

"Just tell her she won't get a cent of Aunt Alice's money till she gets her ass back down here to sign them papers."

"There's Gladys.")

"Hello?"

"Here's your call, Emily. Went right through."

"Hello?"

"Royal Hotel."

"Hello? Is this here the Royal Hotel in Peoria?"

"That's right. Can I help you?"

"Well, I want to talk to Mrs. Charlie Hill."

"One moment, please. That's, uh . . . that's Room 507. That's *Mister* Charlie Hill."

"All right."

("They're ringing the room now. You talk, Harry. She's your sister."

"I don't want to.")

"Hello."

"Hello? Is this you, Charlie?"

"Yeah. Who's this?"

"This here's Natalie's sister-in-law. You know, Mrs. Harry Travis in Athensville."

"Ah. A call from the end of the world."

"What's that?"

"What's wrong, Mrs. Travis?"

"Why, I want to talk to Natalie. Is she there with you?"

"Mrs. Travis, your sister-in-law was never really with me. Didn't she tell you about our disagreement?"

"Ain't she there?"

"No."

"Well, she ain't here either! . . . We left you both here over three weeks ago and drove to Winchester to see our daughter Mary. Harry came back first and nobody was here."

"Well now, you listen. You two drove away and then she went clear off the beam about some kid that got sick and she ordered a mess of flowers. She said I had to dig up a place in the back yard so she could plant 'em, and we had a big fight. I was mad enough to kill her, just kill her right there. Well, I went out and dug awhile so I could calm down and I never went back in. I just got in the car, and it was after dark then, and came back up here and I never saw her again. Your sister-in-law is sick, Mrs. Travis. *She is sick.*"

"Hello? Hello? . . . Why, he went and hung up on me. Hung up on a long-distance call. . . . She ain't up there, Harry."

Its botanical name, *tropaeolum,* comes from the Greek word *tropaion,* which probably meant a pile of weapons put up where the enemy turned and retreated. Later it meant a "trophy", a symbol of victory. So the nasturtium is a "trophy plant", with clean green leaves shaped like shields and golden flowers shaped like helmets. It is associated with victory, and in the language of flowers it stands for patriotism.

(*Pennyworth*)

June 30, 1923

I am Eddie King. Je suis something nouveau in the universe.

Always start with a reminder that you are special. That is my armor in Athensville. Put it at the top of every sheet. You'll feel better, you'll see better, and you'll write better. It's one of the things they said, those happy people in the little restaurant, somewhere in Paris.

I wish I might live to see that restaurant. I wish you and I could go there, Natalie.

Natalie, Natalie, the nasturtiums are blooming. And I'm leaving in three more days. I keep looking for the light you say hangs over them, but I can't sit up every day.

Simple things in common places.

You see, I remember.

June 30, 1923

Dear Mary,

Honey I am worried sick. Your Aunt Natalie has just disappeared clean off the face of the earth. Wasn't neither one of them here when your pa and I came back and I stood it just as long as I could so I called Mr. Good for Nothing Hill called clear up to

Peoria on the telephone and he says she ain't there. He went and dug up half of our backyard for some nasturtium plants and they was wilting away on the back porch and your pa Mr. Easy Touch himself went ahead and set them out thats $19.75 worth and we could have sent them back. Sick all winter and he goes out there and works till after dark in that damp ground. They are blooming now and they sure are a sight. Well I dont know about your Aunt Natalie I dont know where she went to. Your pa says dont worry but I do.

Now can you get me a appointment with Dr. Barrow over there Ive just got to get my glasses changed and that will be another six dollars. Last night just before it got dark it looked to me like a kind of cloudy light over them nasturtiums just hanging there and I couldnt blink it away. I went in and washed these things he give me three years ago and when I looked out it was still there kinda ghosty like.

Your loving ma

P.S. Your pa looked over my shoulder just now and says what if he killed her we left them here alone and he dug up that place for the flowers now theyre blooming going to hide everything. They are just gorgous but my Lord what if she's under them.

THIS WEEK IN YOUR GARDEN

By Claudine Du Bois
Horticultural Consultant

Flower lovers, flower lovers, there is a sight in this town that beats anything I've seen in seventeen years of writing this column for the *Athensville Record*. You must walk by Mrs. Harry Travis's house and stop to look at her nasturtiums.

Mrs. Rev. King told me about them at church Sunday and I went right down there. It is a riot of color.

Emily is real stingy with information. I asked her what in the world she used for fertilizer.

"Oh, please don't ask me that," she said.

You keep your secret, Emily, but you can't keep all that color to yourself.

"Will you do me a favor, Swede?"
"Anytime."
"I go back to the sanatorium tomorrow, and if I die—"
"Shit."
"Well, look at me."
"What's the favor?"
"You'll think I'm crazy."
"I always have, all through grade school, all through high school, and two years of college."
"Take these notebooks, see, all six of them and get rid of them."
"OK."
"Nobody knows I've got them. My ma thinks I'm writing in this one all the time—just lousy poems—and I do now and then. It's all right for them to find this one, but not these. They'd feel terrible about some of the things I wrote. Don't you look at them, either. I could outdrink you once, but I never could write like you."
"I'll burn 'em."
"No, wait. Just hide them someplace. Someplace safe—not at your house and not in your desk at the newspaper office. Then give them to Natalie when she comes back."
"You're really stuck on her. She's old enough to be your mother, but she's got class, real class."
"No, that's not it, dammit. . . . I don't want to explain, I'm too tired."
"Well, I'll find a place. . . . Now, I'm leaving. You watch those nurses up there. I'll send you a free copy of the *Record* now and then—when I have a good story in it."
"Yeah. Yeah."

July 10, 1923

I am Eddie King. I can't write any more. I haven't even got a journal any more. I just think or maybe dream what I want to say.
"What did they say, those happy people in the Paris restaurant? What can you remember, Natalie?"

"I remember how wine made them glow. They turned into a garden, and all of them, even the ugly, fat woman who talked all the time—all of them were beautiful. When I was with them I didn't always understand, but the dark was gone and I was warm and beautiful too. Write about the things you'd miss the most, one shouted, if you should slip into the dark tomorrow. Write about the simple things, the big young man said. Like wine? Yes! Like bread? Yes! And trees? And tools? Yes! And bed? Yes!! The simple things let light through."

I am Eddie King. I am translucent.

Father in Heaven, if it be thy will to take this boy, my oldest son, so be it. Give us the strength we need, dear Father, to face whate'er may come. This is a willful child, Father, one who has rejected his father's teachings and one who has listened to a strange and worldly woman.

I pray that Thou wilt remember his youth, his illness which now must carry him off. Prepare him, Lord. Comfort him and strengthen him and oh, dear Father, ease his suffering. Forgive me, Lord, where I have failed and give me greater wisdom in bringing his younger brother close to Thee.

Oh God, dear God, be with his mother.

Be with us all, our Father, and help me to stand and praise Thee.

In the name of Him, the Light of Life, Who died for us. Amen.

July 24, 1923

Dear Mr. Travis:

Mr. Charles Hill, your brother-in-law, has asked for my services in the case of Mrs. Charles Hill, your sister, who has, as you know, been missing for several weeks.

I am sure that you and your wife are as anxious to shed some light on this matter as my client. Your sister's prolonged silence is most peculiar, and my client now suspects foul play.

Mr. Hill and I will motor down to Athensville on Friday of

next week, August 3. I am most anxious to view the situation from there and to ask you and Mrs. Travis a few questions.

Respectfully yours,

Abraham Hunnicutt
Private Investigator

I am Eddie. I'm Eddie. I can't write.

She said I don't have to look all over the world for experience if I learn to write about the simple things. I can live all my life in the darkness of a little town if I can learn to see. A writer's eyes are torches; when he sees into a dark corner he lights it up. No one else can see exactly what he sees, what I can see—I'm Eddie—and most people can't see anything at all until a writer sees it first. Je vois.

Look, Eddie, look. See, Eddie, see.

It's not the first-grade primer, Eddie, it's the reason you're alive.

The Paris restaurant, Eddie, it's just down the street.

My fingers burn to write and I can't even sit up.

"Come in, Harry, come in. Have a seat."

"Hello, E.A. I'll have to talk to you. I need a lawyer's advice."

"Yes, yes. I'll shut the door here. What's wrong, Harry? You look worried."

"Well, I'll just show you this letter. Read this here letter come this morning from Peoria. Some jack-leg private investigator up there."

"My God, Harry, is Natalie still missing?"

"E.A., you know I'm a reasonable man. Maybe I didn't get all the education in the world, but I don't have crazy pipe dreams and I don't make crazy statements, but I think Natalie is dead. Dead and buried, not missing! Now, I think she's buried under a patch of flowers in my back yard and I think her husband killed her and buried her there."

"I'm a sonofabitch. Harry, you mean that?"

"Got nothing but a hunch. No proof. Now he's acomin' down here with his private detective. He knows Aunt Alice left that money in the Winchester bank. He knows I get it all if Natalie dies. He thinks he can come in on it. And I believe he thinks he can bring that damn detective down here and make everybody think *I* killed her."

"Well, he—"

"*He* killed her, I know he killed her, when Emily and me went to Winchester last May and left them alone in the house. He dug up that patch of ground for some fool flowers Natalie bought, and I never knew him to do a lick of work before that. And that's when he buried her, then he left and I come home and set all them plants out right on top of my own sister. That's awful to think about!"

"All right, Harry. What you want me to do?"

"I want to get a warrant for his arrest and have it ready when he gets here Friday."

"We can do that."

"Then dig them damn flowers right in front of him."

August 5, 1923

Dear Eddie,

I want you to have a little more information about yesterday's remarkable events than you'll get from Claudine, crime reporter for the *Athensville Record*, that outstanding example of fearless journalism. There will be an abject apology in here somewhere, too.

Even the weather was crazy yesterday—a chilly rolling fog on the fourth of August! Plenty of us turned out for the showdown at Harry Travis' place, fog or no fog, and we were all there by 8 A.M.—all the dignitaries, including Officer Heavy Reese, the mayor, the coroner, and me, your stalwart reporter, who lost this story to Claudine, dammit. We had to squint to see each other. The first ones I picked out were One Eye Anderson, gravedigger first class, and his runny-nosed son.

Ah, would that you could have seen that fateful tableau. I glanced up at your room, wishing for you, but your ma has pulled all the curtains down. But surely you can visualize this: Harry Travis, quivering in jowl, dewlap, and belly, and Charlie Hill,

W. H. Battershell

dark, sleek, and greasy, standing there stiff with greed, pointing at each other, accusing one another of murder, a very confused Heavy Reese behind Harry and a seedy private detective behind Charlie. Caption: "Officer, arrest that man!" A tense moment!

On the left up against the Travis house, all the women in the neighborhood formed a line, unanimously expressing concern and disapproval, the two favorite emotions of housewives when they get together. Your mother and Mrs. Travis were side by side, weeping softly. I caught a glimpse of our own Claudine Du Bois—big teeth, big adam's apple, big elbows, big feet, everything big but what should be; my father says her chest is flatter than a privvy door.

The crowd, fifty or sixty by now, restless because the fog wouldn't go away, kept moving and muttering, some condemning, some philosophizing, a Greek chorus desperately in need of organization.

And then, the piercing voice of Tiresias, Lawyer E. A. Thorpe —Elwood the Plump, I call him, and my father, who always has to fill in initials, refers to him as Elephant Ass—a piercing voice which almost dispelled the fog rang out and reached us every one:

"We have no corpse! We make no arrests until we do! I command these men to dig!"

It was the place for a mighty cheer, yet the crowd fell silent and began oozing forward through the fog.

"Stand back!" ordered Elwood the Plump.

So they fell to, One Eye and his boy, on the nasturtiums. Yellow, red, and orange fell through the mist, and the crowd, pressing forward once more, began trampling them.

One Eye's boy yelled, "I've hit something! You dig, Pa!" And he threw his spade against the barn, where it hit with a clang that ran a chill through us all.

One Eye took over and was pulling at what he'd found when in the awful silence we heard a door slam behind us on an invisible automobile. A thick, unnatural voice grunted, "Get the hell back where you belong, ya two-bit whore."

We turned, we peered, we listened, and out of the whiteness a stumbling wraith came at us, getting more real with every step until there emerged the scarlet woman herself. I swear the fog began to swirl and burn away before her. There, my friend, wavered your dream woman, pissy-assed drunk, one eye black and the other behind her falling hair, her dress ripped, one stocking down around her ankle. A mess, man, a mess.

Yet she made it the greatest moment of all.

Picking up a golden bloom and steadying herself against a tree, she yelled at us between sobs:

"What's going on here? . . . I paid twenty goddam dollars for these nas—, for these nas—, for these flowers! . . . Get out! Get out, you—children of darkness!"

And then she threw up.

Women screamed, men dissolved in the fog, and One Eye's boy, they say, is still running—but I won't go on, for now I've got to tell you what One Eye dug up was your notebooks, wrapped in heavy oilcloth the way I'd put them there to await the return of Natalie. Well, your pa took them, and I don't know what to do. I'm sorry, old pal. When I get up the nerve I'll tell him and Natalie what you said.

Sincerely,

Swede

I am Eddie King. I am dying.

Waiter, garçon? Oh help me help me, sweet garçon.

At your service, sir. A votre something.

Do you see those happy people over there, all red and gold and yellow? Do you see the light around them?

Yes, I mean oui, monsieur.

How can I join them can you take me there is it far?

C'est très simple, monsieur just through this bottle.

But it must be dark in there how can I see?

Ah, monsieur, avec these—what are they, ah, monsieur—flowers called nastorchums hold them before you ah you see we are almost there—but monsieur, monsieur, ah but you are dying, monsieur.

Quelle pity!

W. H. Battershell   *175*

POETRY CORNER

By Claudine Du Bois
Literary Editor

To all my readers out there: Here is a poem I have just written to the memory of Eddie King, who showed so much promise. I felt that I just had to write something, and where this came from I don't know.

I know a lovely garden gay
Where red and yellow dance all day.
Nasturtiums there so full of light,
They must be summer's grandest sight.
Come, dear friends, and take this flower;
Hold it close and light this hour.

II SYMPOSIUM "WHICH ONES ARE THE ENEMY?": OR, BOOK REVIEWING IN AMERICA

Collective power in literary politics means, first, the capacity to make a work of writing, or group of writers, far more popular than it, or they, would otherwise be. In addition, it means the capacity to thwart, rather than merely criticize, the claims and careers of professional antagonists. Collective literary power is thus based not just upon friendship and comradely backslapping, but also upon interpersonal organization, institutional leverage, and effective action.

from *The End of Intelligent Writing*
by Richard Kostelanetz

Where, then, did that leave the literary establishment? Well, it left it in the hands of clerks like me: technicians, middlemen, disc jockeys, vending machines of opinions. A service class, really, too busy with our own

*careers to do much permanent damage to literature—
all we decided, after all, is which books would get a
little more publicity than they deserved each season
—but full of beans.*

from "Do Chickens Have Lips?"
by JOHN LEONARD
(The New York *Times Book Review,*
September 29, 1974)

EDITOR'S NOTE

Nobody seems to be very happy about book reviewing these days, not even the people who do it regularly for fun and profit. For this "Symposium" we asked a number of people, with somewhat different points of view, to say whatever they wanted to and felt like about the subject. That they end up saying at least some of the same things, without co-ordination or collusion, indicates that the parameters of the problem are fairly clear and known. That alone may be the beginning of something.

The cast, in order of appearance, includes:

CHARLES P. CORN, a Senior Editor at Atheneum, formerly with Houghton Mifflin.

GENE LYONS, a young and highly regarded critic, based in Little Rock, who regularly reviews new books for a variety of publications.

DAVID R. SLAVITT, who since 1961 has had published four collections of poetry, two volumes of translations (Virgil), and ten novels; during 1958–65 he was an associate editor at *Newsweek* and often reviewed books for that magazine; by the time *Intro 7* appears, Doubleday will have published his new and selected poems—*Vital Signs*.

WILLIAM PEDEN, novelist (*Twilight at Monticello*), short-story writer (*Night in Funland*), scholar, editor, teacher, and a regular reviewer of books, for a very wide range of publications, for more than thirty years.

I wanted to include something from a passionate pessimist, my friend R. V. Cassill. He was overwhelmed with obligations, but consented to a brief phone interview.

Garrett: Can you think of anything that would help the book reviewing situation?

Cassill: A number of public beheadings might be a beginning.

Garrett: What about the new crowd, the replacements, would they be better or worse?

Cassill: Worse, oh yes, worse than ever. It always gets worse.

Charles P. Corn

1.

The question is disturbingly familiar, perplexing to author and publisher alike. When raised it cuts to the heart of the matter of successful publication. What chances does a writer of a serious book have of seeing it reviewed adequately and intelligently? Publishers are troubled by the dilemma daily and out of necessity have adopted an attitude of enlightened pessimism. Publication date approaches for the writer, the days darken, the creative impulse withers into its cave, as he waits to see how his book will be received.

There are a number of considerations. The very first practical one is that there are not enough publications to review the staggering number of books published. Publishers and booksellers alike control their inventory by means of the most elaborate system of computers, while the number of possibilities for review attention can be run off in a few seconds on an abacus. Moreover when a book is selected to be reviewed, there is always the question of how it will be treated. Not so much whether it will be given a positive or negative notice because, after all, a review is a responsible judgment. Rather, whether the reviewer will follow what L. E. Sissman has referred to as the "set of commandments and a rigid protocol" inherent in the discipline. Reviews and reviewing, then, are exclusive: to some degree, by virtue of their quality but more so because of their elitism by default.

The state of the printed word is one that has everyone concerned: from the gargantuan New York publisher who performs his periodic house cleaning of staff to the writer alone with his typewriter in a garret. Newspaper demises and consolidations have become standard over the country, and we all shiver over the curious spectacle of magazines with millions of subscribers that become such economic liabilities that they must close down. It is all the more discouraging when one considers that the most vulnerable publications have been those of exceedingly small circulations while possessing the highest intellectual content.

One might add that the reviews and little magazines in America have traditionally been as shortlived as their enthusiastic purposes have been varied—from Washington Irving's *Salmagundi*, which celebrated a new urbanity in early-nineteenth-century New York, to the varied and eclectic list in our own time. One takes some comfort in the teachings of literary history—that the review is perennially young and like the novel absolutely refuses to die. In our time the review's place in the mercurial world of letters is unique and indispensable, for it is a platform for dialogue in our time of compulsive public affairs, reaffirming a commitment to what Eliot called the highest standards of thought and expression. And certainly an integral part of this dialogue has been the reviewing and criticism of books.

But what has *happened* to those magazines whose main concern has been books? Within the memory of living readers there were once in our country two dozen or so commercially successful magazines with primarily intellectual appeal, but where are they now? That list, now yellowed and tattered, was distinguished by diversity, and some names are more familiar than others: *Scribner's Magazine, The Century*, and certainly *The Bookman*, which devoted itself to reviews, criticism, interviews, news—entirely about books. But to most of us those publications, now literary historical abstractions, might have occurred during the Renaissance. Of those two dozen, only two magazines with circulations substantial enough to qualify them as commercial publications remain: *The Atlantic* and *Harper's*. But, alas, they no longer pay much attention to books but instead are engaged in a frenzied preoccupation with topical subjects, mostly politics and sex. Of the newer publications, *The New York Review of Books*, which recently celebrated its tenth anniversary, is noteworthy. Though the high quality of the writing can hardly be disputed, the trend is unmistakably toward the inclusion of articles not remotely related to books.

So what attention can you reasonably expect your first novel to receive beyond your home-town newspaper? Will your debut be regional, national, or will it go unnoticed?

Publishers must work with the knowledge that the fate of a book, insofar as reviews are concerned, rests initially at least in a very few hands. He is also aware of the American tradition of faddism, and exploits it by attempting to build for a book a groundswell of critical approval so that it will be widely discussed. A cumulative process. Certainly around publication date the publisher looks hopefully to the New York *Times Book Review*. As one of the two publications subscribed to by virtually every bookstore in the country (the other being *Publishers Weekly*, the book-trade news weekly), not to mention the number of persons who receive the magazine as a Sunday supplement, the *Times*'s power is awesome and legendary. *Playboy* in a brief sketch several months ago described its editor as perhaps the most powerful individual in publishing, an appraisal that may be more accurate than not when one considers these factors: the volume of books published and the rigid process of selectivity on the part of the *Times* with respect to its limited space, the qualifications (or lack of) of the reviewer who has been selected for a book, and the magazine's vast circulation.

How ambivalent is the publisher's attitude toward the *Times*, which consumes his books as fuel as much by neglect as by attention? Of course the ideal reciprocal benefit is that a book is given a place in the world of letters beyond its own inherent reach, and the exhilaration one feels is rare when a book he has worked hard to publish successfully is chosen and praised, one selected out of many other game afoot. But almost as often the publisher is shocked and angry, surprised in his corner like a prizefighter before the bell when the book he has sponsored is ignored or given to an inept literary hangman. His responses are invariably exchanged among other publishers, and they too echo his shrieks of derision and hoots at the telltale mannerisms and *hubris* of reviewers whose predictability is by now familiar to everyone. There is in the nature of the work of publishers with authors

Charles P. Corn   *183*

something of the worshipful irreverence of squires toward great knights, something of their pride in reflected glory. The publisher breathlessly awaits the signal of a reviewer at which moment the reading public will, like the crowd in Barrault's *Children of Paradise,* break into cheers or catcalls.

It should not be surprising, then, that to publishers (and probably everyone else) reviews and reviewing is a subject cast in *chiaroscuro.* Reviews are either favorable or unfavorable, informative in dealing with the book's subject matter or irresponsible in its use as a springboard for the reviewer's own prejudices. And so it follows that reviewers stand either in the light or shadow. They are either decent, exceedingly intelligent men of high noble purpose who are aware of the moral imperatives of book reviewing, or gadflies and dilettantes, convinced by their own tireless, cloudy, and discordant rhetoric. There are other frustrations as well. Often the most intelligent reviews appear in the magazines and newspapers with the smallest circulations. And as for timing, it is not unusual for a book to be reviewed in a literary quarterly a year after the bookseller has exercised his option to return his merchandise to the publisher's warehouse.

But it is mainly the *Times* that engages our attention over morning coffee. By virtue of its circulation, its whim becomes holy writ—affecting the fate of a book profoundly. The *Times Book Review* editor, who by reputation is a driving, versatile man, has established an editorial policy and follows its dictates. For all I know, he doesn't relish his power, though I would suspect that he does, as most people would. If he is a man of impartiality and complete dedication to task and its implications, and I have no reason to doubt that he is, then he is good for the book business. God knows, it is hell to encounter his opposite: book review editors and reviewers across the country who are so governed by whim, peevishness, or simple lack of imagination that they will break any rule and ignore any precedent of responsible book reviewing. More often than not, books that are reviewed in America are chosen for news or human-interest appeal rather than for their quality as books. Reviewing controlled by such men is chaos itself. So when I place the *Times,* as the apotheosis of book reviewing in America, under my own professional scrutiny, as everyone in publishing is bound to do, I find that its staff probably does as well as any could, given the idiosyncrasies and limitations that any staff is bound to possess and the number of divergencies that must be reconciled. But, alas, that is not enough for you and me and them: for writers, publishers, and readers. For bibliophiles who want to see culture properly served and the book business thrive.

Our reading needs are far too diverse for us to be so overwhelmingly dependent upon a single magazine to impart to us critical understanding. I do not believe that the necessary alternative should be in the guise of another review published in New York City. Not that the *Times* shouldn't be competed with: quite the contrary. But the site for the games must be carefully selected. The presence of the *Times* with its powerful editorial platform has perpetuated the myth that New York City is the domicile of the "literary establishment" or some such nonsense. Writers do live in New York, but writers live everywhere else, too. There are no salons here. Paradoxically, whatever professional literary mantle New York has, it doesn't wear very gracefully or comfortably, contrary to what many might think. And nowhere was that mantle's weight more keenly felt than at the National Book Awards held at Lincoln Center in the spring of 1974 where the audience was treated to a streaker and later to a witless monologue by a stand-up comic who had been retained by a fiction co-winner's publisher to accept the award on behalf of the author, who is a recluse. My colleague, a Texan, remarked as we pushed our way outside with the flow of the crowd: "The Country and Western Music Awards are done with more style." New York is a fine place to live and work, but he who is tired of it is not necessarily tired of life.

We live in a generous culture, perhaps the most generous on earth. Such generosity has not always assumed the form of both private and public subsidies of the arts, but that situation fortunately is changing. At risk of choosing prophecy over effectiveness, I would suggest the following. An independent foundation could do worse for culture than to announce with optimism, enthusiasm, and self-assurance the first issue of a weekly book review to be brought before American readers. Its form would be that of a tabloid, a supplement for every Sunday newspaper in the country that would subscribe to it. Initially, it might be a free subscription, but it would encourage advertising from publishers as well as bookstores so that eventually the review might be financially feasible for all concerned. A unique feature of this review would be the unconventionality of its structure and administration of its editorial board, or rather boards, because there would be several regional ones in addition to a central office. While books of an obvious national interest and sales potential would be reviewed in pages distributed from all editorial rooms, the remainder of the review would be regional in the sense that its contents would be determined by the regional editor who would see to it that a local writer's debut doesn't have to be so dismally anticlimactic after all. The spirit of interaction in the service of a higher purpose would be made real, while no one's privacy would be invaded. Reading after all is one of the few remaining private occupations. In a real sense, culture would be well served by such a responsible alternative whose opening statement of editorial purpose might well recall St. Augustine: "The truth is neither mine nor his nor another's: but belongs to us all whom Thou callest to partake of it, warning us terribly not to account it private to ourselves, lest we be deprived of it."

Gene Lyons

2.

While every subject pertinent to the literary arts is blessed with more than its share of cant, bombast, and sheer humbug, few areas attract so much misdirected passion as book reviewing. Because more books are published than even the most conscientious reader could keep track of, let alone read, we all depend upon reviews more than we would like to. Or so we say. As someone who is at least a part-time reviewer for two provincial newspapers (the *Arkansas Gazette* most frequently and the New York *Times* whenever they ask), I find that most literate people spend a good deal more time reading reviews than they do on new works of fiction or poetry in hardcover editions. And so do you.

Why is it important to make this point? Because most people who are involved in the fabrication end of the Quality Lit. Biz. (i.e., writers) will tell you that the whole reviewing trade is permeated by a cozy back-scratching or -stabbing venality that puts it on a moral par with such pastimes as pimping or running for public office in the state of New Jersey. In any case it is no matter, a writer will once in a while tell you knowingly, since book reviews have little or no effect upon book sales anyway. So why then does every writer I know consume organs like the New York *Times Book Review* with all the runic zeal of a savage rummaging about in the entrails of a slaughtered chicken? And why do they devote what ordinary mortals would consider astonishing amounts of time discussing who said what about whom, where, with how much justice, and for what hidden motives? Is it all, as saith the preacher, vanity? Partly it is.

And yet such behavior is not at all unreasonable. Book reviews in the prestige places do make a difference in the sales, sometimes an enormous difference. Equally tangibly, they help to establish the reputation of a serious writer, without which nothing. It is true that short of hiring a hit man there is nothing the *Times, Commentary, New York Review, Atlantic, Harper's,* or even *Newsweek* could do to prevent Harold Robbins from selling a million copies, since his books, like those of the other big canned porn kings, are marketed and distributed as relentlessly as vaginal deodorant sprays. But for the Alison Lurie, the Tom McGuane, the Harry Crews, the Alan Lelchuk, the Michael Mewshaw, or the William Harrison, that is to say for the serious writer who needs the ancillary benefits of the Lit. Biz., i.e., the cushy writer-in-residence job, the grant, the fellowship, the slightly better advance, the modest paperback sale, not to mention the recognition that allows him psychologically to continue writing, the review is of inestimable importance. Since *Intro* is sponsoring this symposium, perhaps it is not necessary to go on about the centrality of reviews, but one does hear so much nonsense.

Now then. As consumers of reviews, we are often inwardly divided. When we think about them as writers we can be half-convinced of the following half-truths: that reviewing is a contemptible activity; that it is pursued largely by vendetta-inspired literary plotters in New York City (an attitude which often becomes tied up with the pettier forms of anti-Semitism); and that for those reasons it leaves the best writers of our time to wallow in ignominious poverty and obscurity until their works are discovered by more even-tempered and contemplative readers than the journalistic hack. I understand that Richard Kostelanetz has recently devoted an entire book to this theme (*The End of Intelligent Writing,* Sheed and Ward, $12.95).

Not surprisingly this particular line of twaddle is shared not only by writers who would like to be better read and more famous, but by literature professors, most of whom do not read contemporary work lest they be victimized into wasting time on what is not "first rate." Mention to the average scholar that you have spent the weekend curled up with *The War Between the Tates* or *Ninety-two in the Shade* and your reward will be a numb stare, as if you had confessed a passion for "Columbo" or drag racing, and a "From the reviews I shouldn't have thought. . . ." The real reason for this, of course, is that most Ph.D.s know and care less about fiction or poetry than Your Old Man and are terrified mostly that they will be caught going ape over something posterity judges to be second-rate.

A further irony, to give you the second half of the inward division I spoke of earlier, is that posterity is generally correct. Most writers at any given time *are* second-rate by the standards that the ages have set, and as *readers* of reviews our most frequent complaint is that we have been had—conned into laying out almost as much money as it would have cost instead to take in *Last Tango in Paris* and have a couple of beers afterward (pizza and babysitters not included); for a novel with obvious flaws. (The relentless overpraising of movies is another subject entirely.)

That most writers at any given time are not of Parnassian eminence is the reason that George Garrett's students invariably discover, in an assignment he is fond of giving them, that when they read the literary periodicals of bygone decades they find authors being touted as geniuses who are now either totally forgotten or regarded as figures of fun. But how could it be otherwise? A weekly book review, of which there used to be more than one in this country, has to print at least fifty-two front-page reviews every year. When was the last year you can think of that fifty-two American novels were published that have survived even ten years of posterity? Quick now—1964. Can you name even a dozen? And if there had been, who would have read them?

So true is this observation that the most difficult thing for a halfway honest and competent reviewer to do is to adjust his sights downward in order to perceive the real merits in most of the books he chooses or is assigned. It takes some practice to achieve and sustain a balanced level of judgment which is fair to the writer and reader, especially in the limited space necessity allows. I have often wished I could take back, for example, some of the mean things I said about Alan Lelchuk's *American Mischief*, which in retrospect I realize to have been one of the best first novels of 1973, in spite of some of the irritating things that are in it, an injustice I can repay only if his second novel bears equal promise. But then my review was in the *Arkansas Gazette,* which compared to the pounding Lelchuk took elsewhere is of no consequence whatever.

Even more significant, I think, is the fact that there is hardly an important American writer of this century who was unknown and poorly reviewed during those years when he was doing his best work. Faulkner is often cited in this context. But Faulkner (examine the record) was not so obscure as we sometimes pretend. And by his early fifties, let us recall, he had won the Nobel Prize, which is doing pretty good for an old boy who chose for his own reasons to remain in a place where most people read the newspapers with the help of their finger and thought all writers were Communists. It is no doubt true that one can achieve a kind of temporary celebrity by hanging around New York pandering to the great, but not for long unless one can deliver the goods. It has been my impression that far more writers are destroyed than are created by high-powered literary logrolling in and around Metropolis. If he had not been praised so generously by Philip Roth, do you think Lelchuk would have gotten it as he did? And if you think that kind of abuse is fun, think about it for a while. So unless you have a brass-plated ego and the aggressive instincts of a timber wolf it might be best to stay out of it. A major league curveball can be a terrifying thing.

One reason that somebody you never heard of, writing in Little Rock, Arkansas, for Christ's sake, speaks with such assurance is that besides reading and reviewing a lot of books I recently had the enlightening experience of serving as one of two readers in fiction for the National Endowment for the Arts Literary Grant Program. There I had the honor of reading 353 entries from all around the country of published fiction writers who were seeking the Endowment's five-thousand-dollar grant. Allow me to summarize my findings from those activities briefly: the best-known "serious" writers in America are also the best writers in America. This is not to say that either the money or the fame are distributed exactly or even remotely in proportion to quality and consistency. We are, after all, talking about America here. But quite in defiance of it all, cliques, logic, publishers, agents, even capitalism itself, the best writers still surface, find their way into the hands of reviewers, and are made known to the literate world. Considering how small that literate world is when it comes to new hardcover editions of serious work, one might even say that the American system of doing things, in all its amorphous and suffocating genius, is financing a kind of public *samizdat* for quality writers, of whom I believe there are more now working (especially when considered in proportion to readers) than at any time in recorded history.

Take your pick of overpraised novelists who set your teeth on edge. Mine are John Updike and Joyce Carol Oates. Had I encountered more than a tiny handful of applicants to the NEA who matched either of them in style, in vision, or in over-all fictive quality, I should have cabled Washington at my own expense to recommend the prize. But I did not. Or choose the writer you know best whom you believe to have been unfairly ignored by the reviewing media. First, how ignored is he or she? No fair picking somebody like Wright Morris. We are talking reviews here, not the justice of the gods or sales. Now, having selected a novelist or poet who qualifies, evaluate as honestly as you can the real stature of his work against Saul Bellow, Philip Roth, William Styron, John Barth, Robert Lowell, John Ashberry, John Updike, Joyce Carol Oates. There now, do you see how silly you have been?

Better to see writing as the art form that it is supposed to be. Sooner or later, if you do as well as you hope to do in your work, the reviewers, over a period of time and with numerous exceptions, digressions, and manifest outrages, will catch up with you. If it is financial security you seek, you are in the wrong line of work. More people do better playing professional football than writing real books in this country.

Having said all this I should add that I think it a shame that a few periodicals in New York City should have so concentrated an effect. But that is not their fault, it is ours out here in the boondocks. Book reviews died and book pages wallow in schlock because no one cares about them. For what I am paid by the *Arkansas Gazette* for my reviews it would be more sensible to work nights at the Seven-Eleven. Of course the university likes it if I publish things. I get free books and get paid to read them.

And every once in a while the New York *Times* sends a telegram, or I get a nice note from a writer I have reviewed, or an offer to write something else. You see, *they* are worried about this New York thing themselves.

So, if you want better book reviews, by God, write them. Visit your friendly city newspaper and explain what you want to do. Being cynics, they will want to see work before they commit themselves. Don't expect much money, and above all do not expect tidal waves of response, either from the resident journalists or from the public at large. Be sure you send two copies of your review to the publisher. You will be surprised at how forthcoming they will be if you have any kind of newspaper or magazine connection at all. *Publishers Weekly* will let you know what is coming out far enough in advance to write for copies. A decent bookstore can help you out that way too. If the newspaper isn't buying, emulate the folks at *Books: A New Orleans Review* and organize your own. That is the only way it will ever be done.

David R. Slavitt

3.

Take dentists. They are figures of fun, being neither fish nor fowl, intellectually trained but working with their hands, odd-smelling figures who intrude themselves regularly into our lives and mouths, telling us boring stories of their camping trips to which we submit, unable to reply because of the hardware and weaponry cluttering our mandibles, or lecturing yet again about the dreadful specter of plaque. Even these vulgar vaudevillians stick together, have a minimal decency, give one another professional courtesy. Doctors are notorious for it, treating each other for free, unwilling to testify in malpractice suits against a colleague, loyal and fraternal. Even college professors have a minimal sense of confraternity, and will come together to fight against the more blatant violations of academic freedom threatened by the tycoons and politicos on the boards of trustees, regents, overseers or *Übermenschen*, or by invidious administrators. But reviewers?

But then there is, in fact, no such animal. Who wants to grow up to be a reviewer? Can we imagine such a creature? Not even those peculiar birds in molecular biology or geophysics, with their unfashionable briefcases and their bizarre haberdashery could suffice. Any young man or woman who claimed—or admitted to —such an ambition would have been, would still be an intellectual and moral monster, a thalidomide deformity. And yet there are reviews, and must be reviewers. Who are they? Cincinnati, putting down their plows to take up, for the nonce, slender fowling pieces. Reviewing is a parergon, after all. Without rules, without ethics, without the slightest shadow of the dream of civility other kinds of intellectual labor like to draw about themselves. Quiet academics, tender poets, kindly husbands and fathers, decent sportsmen on the tennis court or the golf course, given a book, a typewriter, a deadline, and the promise of a few (miserably few) dollars, turn vicious, imagine themselves powerful, delight to flex the thews of influence, and in a slashing attack upon shoddiness, foolishness, inaccuracy, and infelicity cut up . . . whom? Some other poor son-of-a-bitch who has put in two years of work on a book. A writer. A fellow intellectual or artist.

Sad, funny, painful, but true. And the trouble is that the reviewer feels good doing it. He has struck a blow for good taste, for responsible historiography, for better writing or clearer thinking. Some such will-of-the-wisp.

Don't get me wrong. I am religious also, believe in these gods as much as the next parishioner. I have even performed, from time to time, such ritual sacrifices of my fellow creatures' offspring. But we ought to admit what we are doing when we review —if only because it helps to bear the pain when we are reviewed, or when we should have been but aren't.

The difficulty is that the audience is gone. Or maybe never was there in the first place. But when 20,000 copies of a book is enough to put it on the best-seller list, and when most of the books on the list are rotten, it seems plausible enough to say that there's no audience. Not for fiction, nor certainly for poetry. And the unreading public is a great torment. But the relation between writer and public is indirect, controlled at various points by keepers of the sluice-gates. Sixty or seventy publishing companies stand between author and gentle reader. The writer must get the manuscript published. And then? And then, pray, watch and wait, and look at the New York *Times Book Review,* and *Time,* and *Newsweek,* and maybe *The New York Review of Books.* A couple of provincial papers, maybe. The *Los Angeles Times,* and the Chicago papers. *Book World*'s last wraith in Washington at the *Post.* And that is bloody *it.* So the seventy rivulets and streams confluesce into the merest handful of commercially significant reviewing media. Or two, really. The New York *Times* and the *others.*

A calm, reasonable man might suppose one of two things.

Either the public is irretrievably stupid, or it is being misled and manipulated by these curious organs. In neither case, however, is it true that writer X is deprived of his share of money and praise by the unfair and unreasonable appetite of the public for, or attention of the reviewers to, the books of writers Y or Z. This is where the dentists make us writers look like fools and savages. They understand that the world is divided up into dentists and patients, know the difference between a tooth and a drill. If, in the enviable simplicity of this arrangement, they sometimes bore us (oh, pain!), God bless them and keep them all smiling like Steinways.

A sane writer—if the conjunction of that adjective and noun is not a self-contradiction—might be moved to action. He could plant bombs in all the suburban railway stations and blow up the middle class, meting out to the public precisely what it deserves. Or, at a slightly more sophisticated and lucent moment, he might put out contracts on John Leonard, Robert Silvers, the guys at *Time* and *Newsweek* . . . the whole crew. Twenty grand, and he could strike an unambiguous blow for good taste, discrimination, fairness, decency.

If it were only that simple. It isn't actually a bad idea, and might be helpful. But the problem is that the space crunch of reviewing is cruel, more cruel than the specific and general densities of the editors of the various book sections and pages. And the worst insult is silence. When I was a kid, working at *Newsweek* and filling in during the summers as a book reviewer, there would be a mountain of books each week, of which maybe eight would be reviewed. I mean reviews of eight would be written. Of the eight, perhaps four or five would actually appear in print in the magazine. Not that it was such a big deal to have your book reviewed, and to have the review appear. At least in the "Movies" section there was an assumption that the magazine's readers might, in some number, go to the movies, might experience at firsthand the film under discussion. One could, therefore, talk seriously about films sometimes. The notion that governed the book page—never stated explicitly, but it didn't have to be—was that the review was a substitute for the experience of the book, in itself a kind of instant-book. Just add water and it tastes like fresh-perked. Oh sure, now and then some enthusiasm comes through, some reader likes something. Or some editor decides that a writer is hot, is news. Then, maybe, you have a cover story. But that decision is always an excuse to look away from the book and at the writer, a swap of the hard job of reading for the easy business of celebrity watching. The writer as paraclete to his art . . . and not even contracts on these desperadoes can change that.

What you have, *messieurs-dames*, is an ecology of scarcity. Novelist, poet, historian, biographer, gentle creatures all, grazing animals, ruminants really, have run out of grass. No fodder, no *moeder*, orphans. And a few have turned to carnivorousness for dietary supplement. By reviewing. Not that the $150.00 or $50.00 or $15.00 (yes, yes, from the Boston *Globe* last year) is going to buy a lot of food for wife and kiddies, but the herd will be thinned. And the process of thinning must be good for us all, because there are too many books, too many writers, and not enough bookstores and not enough readers.

When lemmings do it, they all go together. The practitioners of what we call, in hideous inaccuracy, the "humanities" are all standing at the cliffside, picking on one another and trying to push over those of their own kind, in the name of excellence, in the name of Art.

William Peden

4.

A PEEVISH, ILL-MANNERED LETTER TO A LADY BOOK REVIEWER*

My dear Miss Kelly:

Every published author I've ever known, from comparative beginners to semi-professionals like myself to established major figures including a couple of Nobel Prize and National Book Award winners, has his own favorite horror story about newspaper reviews of his work. My own is your review, published in the Memphis *Commercial Appeal,* of a collection of my stories entitled *Night in Funland.*

I certainly respect your right to dislike my stories, or anybody's stories. I do, though, question—and am indeed upset by—the generalizations that constitute the major part of your brief review. To wit: that my stories are "poignant, because of the waste of talent on thoroughly unlikable and unambitious characters" and that they are "monotonous" and "dreary" because I am "engrossed in the recitation of the entirely mediocre cast and scenes, in the reeking atmosphere of experiences that cannot by any means, accommodate themselves to art." I really don't believe that that "reeking atmosphere" exists in my stories, or that I have depicted a "lost society whose only resources lie in bedroom dawdlings." This, though, is merely my opinion as opposed to yours, so let's call that a standoff. But when you nail down your highly contro-

* Identified only as Sally Kelly, Porkin, Arkansas.

versial Bible-belt generalizations with the following, I really have to holler.

"Proof," you say, "of the author's self-indulgence appears in the story 'Requiem'; 'she closed her eyes and looked absently at the ceiling.'"

My goodness, Miss Kelly. Did you read the story? First of all, you have the wrong title. *And* the wrong sex. *And* you've omitted one little one-syllable word that makes a great deal of difference, and made up a couple of your own. The actual sentence which you misquote is from the story "Wherefore Art Thou, Romeo?" (p. 19), not from "Requiem," and it reads:

"he *half* [italics mine] closed his eyes and studied the ceiling."

My goodness, Miss Kelly!

Sincerely,
William Peden

P.S. The title of the collection is *Night in Funland,* not *A Night in Funland.*

III POETRY

My dear fellow Poets,
Those of us who remain
Are still hungry.

Those who don't
Were delicious.

—*The Awards Banquet* by REED DURBIN

INTRODUCTORY COMMENTS

Here are poems, by poets who mean to write well and work at it and turn good lines. There's joy in the experience of those lines, and that would be enough if that were all. But there's also a good deal to be learned, for those who can abide a didactic moment.

The poets are concerned with precisely the same problems and possibilities that have always concerned poets; they write about death, sex, awe, and ambition—which is to say that they write about our lives.

They know better than to take either their subjects or themselves too seriously, through which sole redeeming grace the world comes to forgive a poet for being that.

There are still the running colors of surrealism, curiously the least successful and most influential of literary movements.

There is a terrible energy, just in harness.

The poets see the world with the ironic vision that has always made good poems ring true, the abiding realization that all human statements contain their own contradictions and that all human acts contain the seeds of their own defeat.

It would be good if we could say that these are the poets of the next decades, the poets whose works we will be reading in journals and anthologies and their own books. But it's a rough life, writing, and that's not the way of it. What we can say without hoking it up is that among the poets in this collection are some we will come to know well and believe in. We can say that whatever is going to happen, some of it starts here.

That matters. If we have to lose part of ourselves on the way to wherever we're going, and it seems that we might, it's good to remember that we can afford to give up everything but beginnings.

—MILLER WILLIAMS

ORANGE SUNSHINE

In spring at Jim's
Children's theater
I listen to his gypsy wife
strum her guitar

I hold my breath
at the lines where death
is approaching
the evening fire
walking in quietly
as a vagabond
who has wandered the
earth so long he
comes from nowhere

II

he sings our songs
until I sleep
and Jim's wife
like some old lady
who makes roses
out of coat hangers
and crepe paper
sighs like a rose

I breathe again
without thinking anything
and pull from a
brown-sacked bottle of beer
the music is so beautiful
and I am braver as death
approaches like a fluorescent hum
I never noticed until now the guitar
collects the parings of my erratic faith
and weaves around my hair the knowledge
of the mole in his tunnel
seeking the sunwarmed loam
that warms and worries
him with dreams of light
as things worried Plato

So I burrow
silent in my dark place until I hear death
like a subway door
closing and Jim's wife
gives a sigh and shrugs
and starts a whispery song

III

and my heart's perpetual hunger
is fed with soft weeping
for the spirit's lack
of history

IV

worn with our enemy's agony
we look into his eye
like looking into a well
and on his face

feel the warm spring wind
fluff the dead
dove's feathers like a boy's
fine hair

                    —WES ZEIGLER

THE COMING OF THE DROUGHT

In candescent July weather
scarecrows roam the brown
fields around Concordia
searching for flesh
to set against
the melting sun. With
each breath of prairie wind
you feel them come
closer, straw bodies
rustling, crackling
like insistent grassfire
at the edge of vision.
Stalking the east
quarter, you glimpse their
sundrenched rags
flagging in rows of sundown,
and the sky becomes faded
as the eroded name
on your gray mailbox.

—JEFF WORLEY

POEM

Those who live with Ice
shall find their places
as the poets of Michigan
and their poems shall last
until winter is over
and laughter bends its creaking bones.

The Ice shall carry you
in his shabby cart
all through the year
until summer
when you shall hide, quaking,
beneath it,
fearing to trust the sun,
believing Ice's lies.

The Ice shall bridge
your brows
so that all your visions
will bear his footprint.

—DEBRA WIITALA

I DREAM A THREE FOLD DREAM

There are no complications. (I can stand
on one foot for hours) (and love you
from any position). But the woman

you live with pulls you to her and enfolds
your heart. Beside myself, I totter;
I pretend not to see you reach to include
me. We are all friends.

Last night, in a field, was it
nasturtium? Her favorite flower, my tongue
tapped messages inside your clothes. I had you
open.

I walk three paces behind
to the parking lot. I wait for you to slow
and you do take my arm and from behind,
trace assurance to my elbow.

                    —Georgette Cerrutti Wickstrom

SOMEDAY

Someday,
I'll take you with me,
And we'll stop our work and go.
We'll saunter on down
To the Club CaCa del Toro.
    and
        ROSY AREOLA
      and the
Lower French Eastside Range Riders
    featuring
        Peaches LaMore
              (on the maracas)
Will play our favorite song.
And you'll remember.

—David Lloyd Whited

FOR CLEOPATRA, WHOSE NAME
SHOULD NOT BE IN A POEM
BECAUSE OF THE
ASSOCIATIONS

But it's not your fault Mother ran off with the American,
and and what had you to do with being the first born?
An old method: name the baby for the disowning grandmother
and she will forgive. With her Greek legacy and a Southern
      accent,
you practice forgiving alone.

How many times have you listened to: "It's not really your
      name!"
or explained, No, it's not Cleo.
Taking and discarding names from father, stepfather,
and two husbands, you still haven't found a surname
to match. Grandmother knew. Arranging love for you
she beckoned the young man from Athens. Promising dark eyes
in great-grandsons, he came. Was it your American half
rebelling, affirming the freedom of your winter skin?
Or the fear of becoming Greek too soon?

In Montana, I dedicated a poem to you,
and ten poets sitting around a table shook their heads, no!
The name suggests too much.
Consider Shaw, Shakespeare, the legends, Britannica.

If you must dedicate, use the initial,
or omit the name competely.

My dear "C," my sister,
I strike surnames and each month send a letter east to Cleopatra.
With violet ink on yellow paper, you transcribe
Louisiana syllables. The mirrors need cleaning, you write.
Your hands fly like frightened chickens, scratching
at your hair, to mask your face.

Remember the night you woke, hearing Greek music
and crept downstairs to watch Grandfather
pacing folk dances on the rug. Seeing you peering from the
    shadows,
he motioned you closer and guided you in his steps.
Tonight, after reading this, stand alone in your house
and recall those steps. I will stand by you,
my arm on your shoulder, and we will dance.

—KATHY WEST

THE OCCUPANT
for *B.H.*

1.

The neighbors think you away
visiting, or gone. They talk
of your mother, how after her
death you retired, and for weeks
burned a house full of lights,
how one by one you slowly turned
them off. One cuts the yard;
another keeps sacks of mail
mostly addressed occupant,
and a month of newspapers
from October '72. None guess
that for these seventeen months you've sat
barefoot before the television
in the easiest of chairs.

2.

The boy could not be seen when he
pried open the window and crawled
headfirst inside. There on the table
a black loaf of bread, a newspaper,
the leftover odds and ends of breakfast.
He listens for a moment.

The clock hands refuse to move.
When no one comes the search begins.
Crossing in front of the unmade bed
and dry aquarium he stuffs his pockets
with whatever coins can be found.
In the living room a television sits.
There he finds you staring blank
at the screen, and runs.

3.

The television is empty of news.
Your eyes cold as glass, and still
you sit staring. You've refused
for more than a year to open the door,
to answer even the most impatient
knock. The last neighbor left
when your mother died, and you
expect no one. The dust gathers
in layers where she once cleaned.
Dishes go unwashed. At night
even the lamp by your chair
remains dark, your eyes faded
to small dots. When the boy
who found you ran, you could not tell
how tired you were of such comfort.

—RICHARD WEAVER

SENSUALITY

Suddenly it was all as clear as
a tear shed for no reason

a tangle of strings can't tell
where one leaves off, the other begins

a pot of noodles: suck at either
end of the same one, face to face

beribboned eels in a slough

—GRETCHEN VAN HORNE

THE BIG M

The last Sunday of vacation my father decided
It would do us all good to drive down and inspect the new bridge
That jumps the river from Memphis to Arkansas. Right away
It was a good idea to everybody until downtown and lost
Under the very suspension of The Big M itself, tangled in barricades
Of new streets that twirl us away to circular confusion onto
NSEW
Ramps we count on from the start to bring us back
To try all over again, which we do, our Sunday spirit not bought
That conveniently, not yet, at least.
We cannot find our way to the big bridge shadowing us, as we
stop
Each time for new bearings on the thing we want, arranging ourselves
With new hope for one more shot, a magic approach that will
Break the spell.
The first ramp carries us in slow circle all the way to touching
Distance, a lane away, and not enough. Another delivers us from
left
To right of The Big M, and back under until we have seen it all.
Our last try in faith, that nearly sends us home, we remember
worst
Of all; we drive a ramp to the brink of double-deception, a giant
high-dive

To the wild blue yonder, grasping its deficient truth at the last
      minute
Only, but still in time to brake down, reverse, realign, call it a
      day.
We shift down to terms of safe domesticity, Sunday night dinner,
      and
Reconcile air castle adventure to be read about in newspapers.
We gather our senses to decloud, untangle toward earthward our
      mistake,
And puzzle in blind, unreasonable accuracy into the chute chan-
      neling us
As simple magic onto the promised Big M itself.

—DAVID TILLINGHAST

LAKES

I long for the continence of high lakes.
Their stillness is of unknown winters;
no easy snow or ice and insensible wind; simply
a chill and quiet.

It will be impossible to call
even a sound from me.
My eyes will reflect only
the sheeted water.
Silence will settle in me and grow—
widen at my heart and ribs; filling
all organs, all cavities, strengthening.

There will be no need
while holding the deep
caught lakes
in the flat of my easeful palm.

—FRANCES THRONSON

THE POUCH

When you stand it in the dark,
It slouches with the full weight
Of the vanished—this cowskin slick
With shine; this satchel of old weathers:
Stomach sagging, ruined with grief.

Last survivor of the Indian Wars:
Bag-of-Breath; its true, maiden name.
There is fringe stitcht to the collar;
Around its throat, a string of beads.
The mouth is a trough
Thieves come to empty in the moonlight.

What remains when they are gone,
Is what has always been there—the wrinkled
Spirit; the pouch of all lost things:
Needle, rope, fire-flecked sheet, the spoon
With our dead brothers' medicine still in it.

—THOM SWISS

DISTANCE, LOST

Apprenticed, in the absence
of alternatives,
              to an ever-childhood
of learning, to ivy tangles, darkening
against green lit panes, to small windows
and roof tops,
there is one thought, only;
that, being
              that a pigeon lights
to church spire, wings, gleaming open.
And there is sun.
And there is sky.

Childhood, spent
in my father's study, and now my own,
forever;
              with so much distance lost,
I have traveled, little.
Connections, extensions, distance,
lost; I have traveled,
little.

Even in the oldest universities,
traditions persist.
                    Stone buildings
stand centuries, where students,

in their way of following,
pass forever;
pass forever.
                And as a sundial,
grown of flowers, the carillon
sings time, world over,
sings time, in sweet measured
caligraphy, sings time,
ages, falling.

And I am home.
I am home.

—Elizabeth Spence

SAVING THE ELECTRICITY

We've got to tape up the outlets,
before it all seeps away.
The rooms are just full of it.
The cat's fur's alive, and she's howling to get out.

So much is loose in our bedroom
we can't sleep.
We're restless, on and off, all night.
We turn and turn, and the blankets snap.
We reach out—only to hurt each other.
I put my tongue to his—
to a battery, testing.

We've got to stop this.
We've got to save our electricity.
If we can't seal it off,
at least we should try to soak it up somehow.
Think of Franklin.
He must have been on to something
when he advised: "Take an old woman for a mistress."
Imagine now: an old woman in every room
storing it all up.

If we can't end all this
there'll be nothing left
but to get down

and pray for one good way
to connect, to set alive
the fine wires of pubic hair
or to be left alone in the dark,
cold and worn out,
picking the last pennies out of the eyes of fuses.

—MERRY SPEECE

THE RECEIPT

I think the reason that
I fell in love with my first girlfriend
was because she pointed out to me
how much Mississippi John Hurt's accent
sounded like Renoir's crippled hands.
There were probably other reasons,
like her red hair or
the way her pointed eyeteeth made her look
like a cat when she smiled.
Still I'm sure it was her argument
that finally won me over
because to this day
whenever I talk to anyone with red hair
I never know what to do with my twisty hands
and my mouth sings some old man's blues.

—DAVID SHEVIN

SPANISH HOTEL

The room was hot and small.
The Mediterranean roared.
A baby cried,
and a cement wall outside the window
was the thing we wrote of most
in our letter home.

—Sam Schnieders

DRIVING HOME FROM CONEY ISLAND

The fog began gathering
just after we left the park.

Asleep now in the back seat,
the calm children do not hear

the tires hissing beneath them,
the fog spreading past their sleep

like threads of cotton candy.
Always I get the feeling

of something lost, something left
behind, when leaving the park.

Somehow it wants to remain
there, throbbing with its own life.

Driving home I discover
again that there's no meaning

in anything I once did.
And the magical funnel

of the car's probing headlights
glides through the ponderous fog

like an ice-cream cone floating
in a clouded mudpuddle

beside the freak's yellow tent.

—Clifford Saunders

STORM WATCH

clouds gather
like judges with burning brows
their hands rumble in
dark pockets.

lightening, a giant's
eye slit open,
white with anger.

grass shivers in
early wind.
the world
waits like a
mother bowed before
the lion,
children at her side.

—Clare Rossini

READING MY TAROT
for Cynthia

The matter at hand is the emperor overthrown,
but the matter is clouded, for the emperor
has abdicated his throne. He calls out
from his tower, "See, there is no one to oppose.
Leave me alone." He rattles his keys in my face.
"They open nothing, nothing but doors. Go home."

I sharpen my sword. I am the new influence on
the matter, the grinning sword that cuts through
the path of smiles with its own slicing song.
I want to talk to the emperor alone, but the emperor
has flown. I sit in the vacant throne.

I am crossed by the bound man, by the blind woman;
the deaf and mute who ignore what the blindfolds
conceal, who consider existence preferable
in any suit, while I demand my own deck.
I want to shuffle myself.

The cards will settle the outcome, but this hand
will turn up the pentacled queen, who sets
her dark body in the earth, and then bursts
out of seed, out of shells, out of rock.
Her arms unfold in the sun. She can never be plucked.

Her lap ripens with fruit. She holds the stars
in her hoops and sings her song into the earth,

> "I give without miracle,
> I take without force.
> I plant the red mare,
> I harvest with the white horse."

—Karen Robert

OPEN CLOSE

Looking for a poem
  I look at my hands,
reptilian,
   innocent,
   doers, performers,
but suddenly covered
  with cold drops of rain.
Today, as foretold in my dreams,
   Bela Lugosi defeats Bogie,
    while the history of rock and roll plays on,
disturbing my sleep with mother
whose gently closed eyes
   sound of Offenbach.
And though I can continue,
  I find I am not one for journals,
   much too indifferent,
   much too personal.

                    —RALPH REMIS

POEM FOR MY FATHER,
SHOE FACTORY WORKER
FOR 43 YEARS

You taught me shoes:
soles stitched to uppers,
edges trimmed.

My shoes were always wrong.
Canvas, or cemented leather
made for shine.

Father, I am sorry about shoes.
When I see them, feetless behind glass,
I hate them.

—ROBERT EMIL RAPPOLD

POEM

The man who would kill my child
Would kill my child
And words that would sink deep come up
Shallow frantic echoes.

In the bleached room, sterile
Hands that will scrape me out
Turn over themselves under water
And whispers crawl down my legs.

The woman who would kill her child
Would kill her child
And the air smells like fur
That won't be shaken dry.

—SUSAN PIPPIN

FOR GENEVIEVE APOLLONIA

Daughter, daughter
A thousand ways I call you

Before now
I called you

All-night parties in Berkeley
Girls who carried tattered copies of *The Prophet*
Bleak bus rides from Terra Linda to San Francisco.
  Sitting next to comptometers, file clerks
Bus rides, ah, yes
The Chinese man in Wyoming—my purse intelligently between us
They pyramid, these moments.
Somehow, I only guess the way.
And in the middle of the night
Resting between feedings and cigarettes
I remember. I remember well
Their plaid jackets. Their hands on my knee.
And what I know now is that I can't let you cry.

—Suzan Magdalena Hill Pieprzyk

SHORT WALK TO THE INTERSTATE

I

It was a case of
finding yourself half-
way across a room,
surprised to be there.
Caught midway between
one step and the next,
you notice that
you are not sitting
before your coffee,
smoking on the coffee
table, but are going
outside.
　　With one
thoughtless glimpse
of the drab greens
and browns and grays
grabbing at the light
that backs in the windows
of good afternoons;
one glimpse of a broom
and its muster of dust,
useless notes, spent
wooden matches and
the clotted lint that

234

just this morning
hung as a frail web
in the arch of the door;
with one glimpse, or two,
you are gone.

II

The light is making
its last impression:
searching across
Twelve O'Clock Nob
for the first of
fall's bloodletting,
lilting down Bent Mountain
as if the summer
were not sick
with the fresh air,
turning my open eye
upon the shadow
that steps with me
across the lawn.
                    I move
like a ground fire
through damp woods,
up the smell of the drive
and onto a blacktop road.
Two tan and noisy children
leave their bikes as signals
in the sun and scrabble
down the roadbank
into high waters of green
and deeper green.
Wanton, lyrical hounds
steal the beat of my footsteps
from bassnotes the semis
press from the interstate,
below me now,

running gray and tepid
to New York or New Orleans.
I am hot and cold
within the change, and leave.

III

Back by steps,
the same steps always,
down the road,
down the drive
to the yard and its
long grass, combed
by the wind, ratted
with walnuts and acorns.
Back by steps
to the stones bedded
upon stones: noises
failing into sounds,
the afternoon into
dusk, the summer into
fall.
　　The houselights
shine out now, and
you are not surprised
to be turning in.
You are not surprised
the mailbox is empty.

　　　　　　　—MICHAEL PETTIT

AWAKE IN AUGUST

I'm wakened at 3 A.M. by a buffalo
herd thundering shoulder to shoulder
across the sweaty sky. A mosquito hovers
close to my shoulder. I pull the wet sheets
over my head and lie awake.

My old friends are paranoid.
They change their names to rock
sounds which I forget. They give
nervous snorts and steal in the dead
of night to Seattle.
I can't help but be critical.
I no longer love them. I love
them. I can't remember.
Once we slept side by side
in hotels. I can't forgive them.

My wife dreams of college presidents
and Xerox machines. She dreams
of queens and leather wings
and wakes to tell me I'm clammy.
Her salty skin etches deserts
into mine.

Blinding light. I'm no Christian.
Still, I think it's a vision.

But it's headlights from a car
full of friends. My mother's
driving. She runs me down on her way
to church to pray.

                              Dogs bark.
The paper boy walks by and swears.
Buffalo grumble in the dark clouds.

                    —R. PEDERSON-NELSON

CASCADE WINTER

Slide I

Grinning by the fireplace, the old man
listens for skis. Those who ride the powder
to his door must drink his brandy,
must leave him knee-deep, shouting
his stories to the wind; a shadow, a leaf on snow.
He greets each avalanche with lectures.
In turn, they roar through his dreams.
He chats with the fire and all the dead in that room.

Slide II

The porch is long, its glass thin cracked.
They slept here last winter, after the baby,
Malamutes howling beneath the silver floor.
They watched snow filter through like insects,
settle white on the spread, and melt in the shape
of bodies. Once, his beard frosted, he woke
to the wind and touched her—long hair turning
the sheen of glacier ice, of high peaks in sun.

—RICK NEWBY

LONG DISTANCE

Mother, your voice is more distant and muted
than the sound of barking dogs at night,
coming over miles and miles of thick wire
passing over highways
stretching over fields of corn, of cows and horses
but more than miles of
yes, dear, how are things, what are you up to,
have you enough money
a woman's voice much like mine could only be half an inch
from my ear
and still the miles of wires, where birds sleep and
dew gathers
over cows and roads.

I see you though, sitting there on the edge of your
king-sized bed, he next to you perhaps already breathing
heavy with sleep
naked, as even in small motel rooms with us all on
wall-to-wall rollaways
beneath your soft silk gown where we all know your body
moves like a shadow, well preserved except for your protruding
belly, stretched out of original shape by us.

I see you holding the phone with a small hand
blue with thick veins
greasy with night cream,

inside those sheets the smell of you
of motherhood and dark secret and the small hairs there.
I'd like to touch the voice I try to hear
as it tires of things you accept now without hearing,
I feel you slip away, more and more miles
you slip away beneath those covers.

Thinking maybe that virgin tips of flower petals
remind me of you, with creamy softness, moist sweet scent
finger tips reaching into a space
for purity that does not exist, lonely once without your care
that fades with your voice.

Yet you conceal yourself in the bedcovers, safe from the fear
of me
and long before you hang up you have said nothing, heard
    nothing.

—MARY MYER

THE NURSING HOME

Pretend you are lost,
that you have never been here,

that you have never been anywhere
until now.

And as you stumble
through these rooms

full of old broken people,
pretend you are the unspoken word

that spills from the waxed lips
of the dead.

—David A. Mullon, Jr.

WINDOW SHOPPING: 510 CEDAR

Yes, if I could find you in the broken eyes
of Maggie's house, I'd tell you there are cracks:
that it's raining, that the sky raves in blue and gray,
that the roofing cannot last.

I left you in a row of lint-throated dolls
small, mad birds in a line
along the wall; the laughter
molded to their rubber tongues.

I left you in a closet
with my Maggie and with all my other
wounded things: the face that I took off
like clothes. I moved away.

But now, here: the smell of rain. Dolls
falling quietly apart. I know where you are.
Your hair moves vaguely, and ancient lint
ripples in the draft.

I look for a door. I know where you are.
The first house holds you like a seed
in wooden hands. I tell you there are cracks
and Maggie is ten years dead.

Yes, I will find you in the hard cracking:
in a corner of dolls when the house breaks open
when a door falls open.
I am waiting in the rain for a door.

—CHRISTINE McMONIGLE

MAINTENANCE

A fern grows, unrolling
at the tip of each leaf,
gentle progress in my north-lit
kitchen, in a room quiet
except for ironing, the sound
of the iron as it cuts
through starch on damp curtains.
I roll the lace slowly,
keeping the ends off the floor,
turning the tube, slowing
the time it takes. The length
of time, of cloth, the same
small movements, layers
covering gray cardboard:
this job marks time
passing, is layering time,
is seven years spent with you—
in a marriage of curtains,
in wishing for growth.

—SUSAN MATHER

TO MY MOTHER, WHO FEARS FOR ME

The rapists you planted in trees
at last Fourth of July's picnic
I never met, when I tripped
down to the beach, alone at dusk.
You said watch for their grins
behind leaves. You feared for me
their quick and violent greenness.

I wish I could tell you
That I have been quicker,
and that we did not wrestle
in the weeds (the first time)
but on cool, cotton sheets.
We surprised each other
with knife-bright cries
and afterwards, we slept
together like spoons.

—LAUREEN MAR

HIJACKER

I've seen events of violent extremes:
They come from nowhere and possess my brain.
I've had a thousand murderous daydreams.

I saw myself drive twenty white mule teams
To death out on the Oklahoma plain.
I've seen events of violent extremes.

I've been police chief for the two regimes
That wiped out all the Moslems left in Spain.
I've had a thousand murderous daydreams.

Once I was dumping bodies into streams,
All axed to pieces, in some woods in Maine.
I've seen events of violent extremes.

I shot that chinless Cardinal of Reims
For praying for a stained-glass windowpane.
I've had a thousand murderous daydreams.

I'd waited years to hear those eight fools' screams
That I killed on the New York shuttle plane.
I've seen events of violent extremes:
I've had a thousand murderous daydreams.

—James Mann

TO JERENE: MARRIAGE

This flight I *am* nervous—
Plane jumping like
A Baptist preacher around a pulpit,
I choke on my tie.

Decision ineluctable since Paris,
Yours, mine, I never got it straight,
We come naïve as hell,
Strange to this as worms to the sun.

Cerberus chortles from the abyss,
(Stare too deeply and
It looks into you)
Rattling bones of the tentative.

This is a second virginity;
A drumhead broken mocks tape.

—SWEP LOVITT

INJURIES

Awaken to the storm's passing.
The anxiety dreams fall away like leaves,
Until you pass the shadowed mirror,
See the long stitched scar. You have remembered
We can hurt you. You must consider that
As no dream. You have experienced
The broken bottle, the sidewalk,
the moment a life shifts from acting
To waiting, weighted with the fear
We can hurt you. You must consider that
Fear stops only when the impulses are severed,
The blood silent in the veins.
Each twinge until then is memory.
Recovery is not granted. You know
We can hurt you. You must consider that
Without consideration of chance:
Like the certain pull of gravity,
There is always a purpose,
Never a mistake. You cannot rage.
We can hurt you. You must consider that.

—WILLIAM LOGAN

FOR D. HALL L.P.N. WHO TOLD ME FLORENCE NIGHTINGALE WAS AN EASY MAKE

How many days, just as the day begins,
sharing a smoke over a breakfast tray,
listening to you tell about the way

you laid it to some lucky stiff. Miss Nurse-
baby, you've come along well, and i'll bet
you come on strong, with waft of bodyheat

and boob so wellracked your uniform screams.
From the heat you put out, i could explode.
For hoses to extinguish fires: praise god.

When you step out, twitching your candyass,
sugarplum hunches dance round in my head,
concocting schemes to con you into bed

or chart you—a therapeutic device—
a daily spread, strictly routine, would do:
you could have taught the Lamp Lady a trick or two.

—CARL LAUNIUS

CUBISM

Deep-eyed painter peering through black windows
Across night
            Mountain rain
Dripping blue
Cézanne thinking
Six triangles of sunlight

—Yusef Komunyakaa

PREDATORY

Not the hawk broken off in its flight
Like a shard of dusk
Above the clapboard coop

Not the hound
Padding in slash pine
Where the hare's heartbeat
Quickens
To a berry-colored blur

But this third body, this field
Sown with risk,
Pulsing between attacker and prey,
Its snares and escapes
Adjusting
To the sniff of the instant.

It is this shape
Of the space
Between the hunt and the hiding
Into which
Wile and matched wits
Tally with a cold precision

Leaving in its shadow
On the grass

One disemboweled, one fed.
It is this shape
We embrace
When we lie down together,
Astonished at how, to the touch,
We appear to each other

Almost human.

                    —Thomas Johnson

BERT'S BOTTLE

With his Evenflo bottle, he circles the rug,
lays himself down on his back.
What does he think as he bend/kicks
the rattan coffee table, fingering a pillow.
It might be mumbled around the edge
of the nipple. His mother worries about
a future smoker or worse.

At Bob's the collie dog turned quick,
lightly bounced away, Bert's bottle
like a snaggletooth sideways in its mouth.
It was, we said, the last bottle, arms folded
gave it final mutilated rites, laid it
beneath a stickwire cross, too careless.

Late in the daisy afternoon, we saw
Bert scratching in the dirt. He bared
the trophy, grabbed his sister's dress, went
skiing to the house. She turned left
sharp down a narrow hall, he shook loose, cross-eyed,
looked over the bottle back at us,
sailed into the wall
harder than a womb.

—Lucky Jacobs

254

SETUP
for Fred

At Trail's End day wipes over night
through windows where shot stars linger.
The barrel of half-sun fills with first light,
prods the caulk around my head for cracks.
I rope my stare to the photograph of a tractor
knowing this marginal morning won't last.

The jukebox whorls scratched Dave Dudley's
"six days on the road in a loco truck."
A drunk dances with a Lucky Strike. I nod.
"Hey boddy," he fumes, "whar the women gone?
Can't ride it right with no partner."
Just keep moving to the music of darkness
drawing you to the shadow's centerline.
Spin to the warps of your one decent memory.
Ripple the dust settling in the back corral.

I'll sit here forever, keeping the time
that keeps us both delaying departure.
The world's setup for our mutual excavation.
See that CAT? What we've hidden and feared
will be dug out in plain sight,
transported to the open pit. Our absence waits.

—TOMMY HUEY

DEATH OF THE CARNIVORE

i was coming down with a sore throat but
you stuffed your way in,
rutabagas.
the east coast kids all
seemed to know about you.
you were worse than spinach.
halcyon soufflé!

one night everyone was asleep in my house.
i was making rutabaga popsicles.
i don't know what they look like;
it was very dark.
i kept going anyway.
now i am sole distributor for the western hemisphere.
it's still very dark in my plant.

i grew up on milk so much my bones
bent with the extra weight.
my gums retreated.
all teeth. for meat.

my friends have turned vegetarian.
they look so healthy.
oh breast, mama milk, oh meat
piece of meat, oh ass
eggplant, i'm afraid of you for a reason.

eggplant, how long have i resisted?
people stuck you on doorsteps
to keep the kids away.
it was such a halloween
when i met your spongy interior
& felt your pulpy thighs.

in the refrigerator nothing can make you die.
your stem's had me pegged for days.
the meat's dead. now i have only you.

you will convert my body to your own
seedy impulses
& turn me into a nodule only
a knife & plate would love.

—MARCIA HASTIE

POEM

In mid-sentence
My reading was overshadowed
Again by thoughts of you.
This time an old man in an older city
You were broken and dying alone,
Thin beneath your clothes.
Your tongue dry as a bird's,
Aching to have said something,
Somewhere, to someone
Without that constant fear of smothering,
That fear of catching or of being caught,
That fear that has barred your words,
Your thoughts, your life from soaring
As you lay thin and fading
Beneath your clothes alone.

—Cecelia Hagen

THE GREAT AMERICAN SPACE DREAM

The Martians have arrived
Smiling happily
Eating television cameras
Stealing girls with long pale hair
Humming along with the top ten
Embracing cars
They are smoothing away the panic
With wide, spoon-shaped gestures.

They have arrived
Waving at crowds
Saying hello to the clocks
Talking to the street lights
Climbing trees
Falling in love with neon signs
They are throwing stars into the sky
To make the children smile.

They have arrived
Stroking the buildings like cats
Staring at the all-night diners
Sending postcards
Asking which way to the Senate
Trying on Fruit of the Loom
They are agreeing that in some ways
This strange place is a lot like home.

—C. D. GRASSI

SUPPOSE THE LIONS ALL
GET UP . . .

Somewhere men are figuring on blackboards
To win. Double numbers only are being
Multiplied in the greatest game show of them all.
The winner is not yet known, but already
The products are coming in.

Already posters are rolling out
Doubles to betray the ignorant and the uninformed,
Especially the apartment dwellers of the world—
Whoever they are. Don't you know there are always
Business deals behind everything?

Somewhere in a book-lined room
Thomas à Kempis will fall from a bottom shelf,
And a young blue-eyed boy who has known from the womb
The screaming lights of night-horrors will say
With the dustcovers of time: not bad.

It's then
That the lions will come. First, the male lion.
Then, the lioness. They will leap free from the broken
Bars of their impossible cage—right in the middle
Of the greatest show on earth. And

It's then
That the indifferent children of the earth
Will find themselves in a new condition. Walking
Among lions on the loose, they will be afraid
To move. And their hands will be in grave danger.

For it will not work on that day,
Children, to try to pet the lions. You can't say
Nice kitty then. Because 4 A.M. forever
Is on the way, and Bing Crosby won't be able
To help a thing.

Already, I see it.
Looking down from the trapeze of a dream,
I realize I am out of reach—and probably safe.
But still I'm shaking. Every muscle
In my body is tensed

For you. If I could just get inside of you,
I could help you. For I think I've got the exact
Right moves. But I'm up here and you're down there—
And that's just the way it is. The only thing
I can do is try to tell you.

—PAULA GOFF

HOMEFIRES

Once
again
we wrote home to mom
that the hot water wasn't
running and
lo,
she responded with that's a fine
how do you do

girls don't like sweat
all that much
but know no better
than to twist
like a sugar bun
around the finger
licking it

afterwards

we gathered at the railway
to see them leave,
their banners shambles
their once-solid minds broken
like a marriage vow

we cried in our soup that day
and the milk from our udders ran dry.

—John Gery

PORCH

Think of the terror   how it is so tangled
around us, we most of the time don't
let on about it at all   and of

the beauty   mist on the morning salt
marsh   midnight dance of fiddler crabs
the brown and white tufted hawk divebombing

swordgrass at midday   how, raveling
any beauty out, the loosening threads lead
to   are interwoven with   the terror we at most

hardly and briefly can bear   there
in the corner   battered, torn by moths the porch-
light frenzied   a thousand-stranded web sags out

of form   look   on the lawn below   the cat's
grace subdues the field mouse's skittering
panic   and beyond   into the dry marsh stalks

from a wheeling glide   the hawk swoops out of
sight   rises   chases a moment a swifter, lighter
bird   Sandpiper, whose *sweet-sweet* stings the salt air.

—DANIEL FOGEL

RIMBAUD

The local poets have scrubbed your face
and picked your head to kill the woodlice,
and you have become a priest
in search of a cassock.
They will stop to give you a name,
whatever would serve the cause, a chair
at the club; and ask only a place,
a small footnote to be remembered.
There, below the street they wave to you
like scarves, and you, as clean as you are
will cut the silk from each and every wrist.
You will show them your hand,
strips of linen or flesh.
You will be photographed, and framed.

You sit for days in front of this wide street,
your paper, and quills. Your pockets are
filled with poems and bits of sawdust.
Near the window an old woman threads a needle.
A soldier coughs in his hat . . .
It was all so different months before
with the gunfire from Sedan, the horses
and cannon, the women watching the graves
along the road. And you, you walked for miles
counting the heads, the bard,

the schoolboy they fed
at fifteen who left the town alone.
Who left a note, and flowers to amaze the dead.

—MICHAEL FLORENCE

THE MARKET AT LIMOGES

Fishmonger

Comes from La Rochelle loaded with herring,
cod and tuna, oysters from Soulac,
the catch of de Puisaye's boats, my nephew
who is sixteen. To lend my trade dignity,
I say to him I close the nets, Reykjavik
to Porto, I am scythe to the perpetual crop.
My fingernails are kelp. I allow Stephen
fifteen francs to buy dinner for Triscot's daughter,
pale and deaf since her brother was drowned
in a squall off Jutland.

Chemiste

Usury is no part of pharmacy, urban rumors.
I heal arthritis with quinine and the book
of Revelations. Gentlemen from the provinces
come to me, bent across their belts after a quart
of Pernod. They drink to make the market a monastery.
To mend their faith in medicine, I tell them
I store a gram of each powder and acid in a tin
and on each twenty-eighth day deposit my medicines
on moss near Dijon, potent with an oath to the soil,
Quasi modo geniti infantes . . .
My wife asks why my lips smell of Pernod
and why I carry the green bottle in my apron.
I draw pictures of pork on my palm

and hum the Gregorian Introit for the feast
of the Assumption.

Prostitute

There are no closets or brass bedposts,
my dresses are unembroidered. I refuse
costume or cosmetic.
There are no mirrors or colored lights,
but his design and my own attract. Faces are kept
in hatboxes. Twice there were complaints of lice,
claimed I brought them to the mattress in my hair,
that we were born with them in our ears, eggs hatched
on our mother's legs at the ninth month,
as all else about me, another lie from the imaginations
of men. A mortician from Aubusson offered me
twenty francs to crouch under a goat.
Men here believe sex is different for me
because I am a Jew.

Concierge

My tenants compose histories on my bidets.
Only the tourists can find history here. The Italian,
Tiretti, rents rooms farthest from the street
and pays local girls to be naked and pose
though I've never seen him with paints or canvases.
On the fourth floor is Struerman. Every April he comes
to buy porcelain but spends mornings at the Loire
killing birds he ties to prams at noon. Guillaume says
the quail population has declined by half since Struerman came.
Guillaume owns dogs. Above my room is the bridal suite,
Fresh water, new sheets, mirrors, a balcony and a thin floor.
The bed has been replaced six times in the past year.
Once I found two men there.
Across from my room is Willett. English. He reads
History and uncovers relics for our priest.
He shows no interest in the hotel, rather converses
with dead popes and Charlemagne. He turns his back to me
when I say, There is no decade or period but our own.

Vagrant

My cousin Adrien died of lead under his nails
from paint he spread on Mabille's fence in Argentat.
Ten days after, fence and household were two candles—
a cow should not be tied so near to kerosene.
Goats graze the kitchen, all charcoal, seeded with dung.
Two weeks in November I warmed a barn in Rochechouart
where for eight francs and use of a quilt
I rubbed varnish from picture frames and an oak chest,
preserved them with oil and beeswax: closets of collection.
"Our Lady of the thousand acres, Our Lady of the poached field,
Our Lady of the twelve-stepped winecellar . . ."
All bondage. I would have Charles I's chamber pot
planted with radishes. In Limoges, tourists pay me
to recite odes to Burgundy, Pinot Noir and barley.
I paste labels on my chin and forehead, dance with Mme. Poule's
pekingese. A profitable art, vagrancy innocent as a goat.

Street sweeper

(for Deena Metzer)

To Danielle, her uncle is collector-of-the-useless
who catalogues receipts. Though I don't deny
pails of fish heads, eggshell and tobacco tins
or my broom thick with tar, there is payment
for my concern—which is not the city's:
June 12 I found a watch wrapped in a copy
of *Le Soir*. I've no idea how a Viennese watch
should find its way to me by the French press,
Unless the Austrian who had me dust his lapels
went stiff with guilt after he stole it on the train
from Paris . . . the wages of guilt is generosity.
The watchmaker's stamp has the same initials
as the gentleman from Salzburg.
I remember them as well in green leather on his wallet.

—JON-STEPHEN FINK

POEM

a proposition, my
   lady, to drink
from small bowls and let
morning come as
   undone as
your hair.

     —THOMAS FAGAN

INSOMNIAC'S TALE

After so many
hours my hands twitch
restless and whisper
from their sleep of
other lives. They
hiss like cinders.
So I listen.

Outside night
trains labor
above the poor
neighborhoods
in Wichita. Moan
moan. Cats drop
furtively
like tin leaves onto
the long moonlit backs
of sidewalks.

I imagine that
nightwatchmen in
all parts of town
are suddenly startled
and lose their place.
But turn again
to thrum the veined
pages of their ears.

The night hums.
Through the city's
thin voices the
distance stands up
like a nail. Traffic
lights tick go
but nothing moves.

Turning turning
from a past life
clandestine
I squint through
sleep's illuminated
apartments where
speech descends
like tiny fires
crackling.

        —DAN DYER

DU VILAIN ASNIER

THE VILLAGER AND HIS TWO ASSES

(Thirteenth-century French anonymous)

Il avint ja a Montpellier
C'un vilein estoit costumier
De fiens chargier et amasser

A .II. asnes terre fumer.

.I. jor ot ses asnes chargiez;

Maintenant ne s'est atargiez:

El borc entra, ses asnes maine,

Devant lui chaçoit a grant
  paine,
Souvent li estuet dire: "Hez!"
Tant a fait que il est entrez

Devant la rue as espiciers.

Li vallet batent les mortiers,

Et quant il les espices sent,
Qui li donast .C. mars d'argent

Ne marchast il avant .I. pas,

Once there lived in Montpellier
A villager who every day
Gathered dung which he
  wrapped in packs
And bore on two fine asses'
  backs.
One day, as soon as he had
  loaded
His asses with manure, he
  goaded
Them into town with much to
  do.
He shouted, "Git up! Move
  along!"
So loudly that before too long
They reached the spice retail-
  ers' quarter.
Apprentices were beating mor-
  tars,
And when he smelled the fra-
  grant spice
A world of gold could not entice
The man to take one step
  ahead.
He fell, and lay there looking
  dead.

Ainz chiet pasmez isnelepas,

Autresi com se il fust morz.
Iluec fu granz li desconforz

Des genz qui dient: "Dieus,
merci!
Vez de cest home qu'est morz
ci!"
Et ne sevent dire por quoi.

Et li asne esturent tuit quoi

En mi la rue volentiers,

Quar l'asne n'est pas costumiers
D'aler se l'en nel semonoit.
.I. preudome qu'iluec estoit
Qui en la rue avoit este,

Cele part vient, s'a demande

As genz que entor lui veoit:

"Seignor," fait il, "se nul voloit
A faire garir cest preudom,

Gel gariroie por du son."

Maintenant le dit .I. borgois:
"Garissiez le tot demenois;
.Xx. sous avrez de mes deniers."

Et cil respont: "Mout
volantiers!"
Dont prent la forche qu'il
portoit,

The people there then felt a
great
Uneasiness at the man's fate
And murmured, "For the love
of Pete,
Look at that dead man in our
street."
Not one could tell another why.

The asses meanwhile were
standing by
In the middle of the road, for
such
Is an ass's nature. It won't
budge
Unless it feels its master's goad.
A man who was standing up
the road
Had seen the driver have his
stroke.
He sauntered down the street
and spoke
To those who stood around the
man.
"Sirs," he said, "if no one can
Or wants to cure this man, I
will
For what he gives me when he's
well."
To this a citizen replied,
"Cure this man, and I'll provide
Twenty sous from my own
pocket!"
The other answered, "Thanks,
I'll take it."
At that he took the driver's fork

A quoi il ses asnes chaçoit:

Du fien a pris une palee,

Si li a au nes aportee.

Quant cil sent du fiens la flairor,

Et perdi des herbes l'odor,

Les elz oevre, s'est sus sailliz,

Et dist que il est toz gariz;

Mout en est liez et joie en a,
Et dit par iluec ne vendra
Jamais, se aillors puet passer.
   Et por ce vos vueil ge mon-
   strer
Que cil fait ne sens ne mesure

Qui d'orgueil se desennature

Ne se doit nus desnaturer.

That was used to drive the
   beasts to work
And forked some dung the size
   of a rose
And brought it to the stunned
   man's nose.
The moment his nose absorbed
   the smell,
The scent of spices was dis-
   pelled.
He blinked his eyes, and up he
   sprang.
"I'm fit as a fiddle now," he
   sang.
Happy now and overjoyed,
He made a vow that he'd avoid
Forever the avenue of spices.
   The moral's clear, and my ad-
   vice is:
Though you be humble as
   manure
Stick to your nature. Pride is
   sure
To make you sick, but Nature
   cures.

—JOHN DUVAL

THE ADVENTURES OF THE PENIS
AND WONDER BOY

The penis leadeth you ass over teakettle
It maketh to knock the farthingale from the pussy
You might be sitting back reading the paper
But it knows when you're awake
It's coming to town
There you are
It backs up and hitches to you ho hum
It hauls you cross country
A shipment of bananas to Canada here

The penis roars into the motel parking lot
You see how it uses your true name to sign the register
It hastens to rip the raiment from the pussy
It maketh you to lie down with mean gestures
The ash trays hold onto their butts
The TV loses its vertical hold
The bed vibrates off its coasters across the room
Through the wall into the cafe
The children run to their milkshakes
Burners turn on—wieners butt buns
The menu shoots open and sleeps
As the new prices taped over the old ones come unglued

You'll have scrambled eggs and a morning paper please

Penis Eludes Police Flees City
Here is mild-mannered citizen drinking coffee
Nice day yes it is might rain

—REED DURBIN

PAT'S POEM

It took time—
    she couldn't even kiss
    with lips apart
and now she talks about most intimate
    measures of love
and so exotically—
    like their union of
      lingam and yoni.
She's experienced now
    and well read.
And at this moment she finds
    time to joke about it
    (No, Pat, I don't know how they do it
                  in India.)
She laughs
    but the punch line is lost in a groan.
Bouncing back, she begins
    making preparations for the debut
        the cornrows plaited neat and tight
           (like she used to be)
        lips painted technicolor red
        in celebration of the births—
           (and 'cause Doc said it was OK
              if the cameras roll)

She and the man beside her
   can epitomize home movies
   by showing posterity
                The First Home.
Thoughtful of them to face the issue
   with healthy attitudes—
Hers still so vivid:
                couldn't even kiss
                with lips apart.
She lays there now
   beneath the mountain
   made from love—
So different from the last
   time I saw her.
Who would have thought
             the child,
             the last-born daughter
       could put away her inhibitions
       and one day support
             the beautiful mound
I can remember when—
   She couldn't even kiss with her lips apart.

                          —Janice Cooke

APPALACHIAN SPRING

sunrise, and the milk cows are being herded
to the east pasture along a path
of redbud and dogwood in bloom: the cows walk like brides.
my tall husband stands at the mirror dressing himself
his starched collar turned up,
he is putting on his tie: his flowers, his lips, his skin,
are male. I watch him from the bed,
myself full and white.

—Priscilla Cane

BALBOA ISLAND

Leaning against a post, in the dark where anything can happen,
I watch a man part the white skirt of a lamp and wonder where
he is going, with the moon in fragments, the land cooling off,
everywhere the green chime of leaves. In the space between us,
he has the shoulders of my father, tall as a lover I left at a corner,
on a one-way street a year ago. Coming closer, the shadows, in-
verted triangles slip from his face exposing a mustache. Crossing
the street, he heads for the beach, the auto-ferry, the Pavilion.
Too cold for cod fishing he will sit in the bar by the window,
above the running lights of the boats and think how his girl friend
left him, pulling out of the garage without looking back, how to-
night an empty fireplace edged him out—the tide in, high winds
fifteen miles out. The bartender will tell him that just across the
channel there is a bridge, a canal which reminds one of Venice.
Looking across, the man cannot see the bridge which reminds
me of Central Park, nor that just now I've turned to go, trying to
remember his face, how it changed in the night like a sail, a hand
moving in candlelight.

—CRISS CANNADY

HIGH YELLOW

The mulatto limbering up
loosens his pink kimono
and plugs in the fan.
"Your true nigra," he tells me
"don't have nipples
as distinct as mine."

I sit like a sunbather
uneasy on the sandy sheets
of his bed,
rubbing my back against a wall
of naked musclemen
and brass thumbtacks.

—JUSTIN CALDWELL

THE WATERMELON

I am queen of picnics.
Straws balance and turn
on my plump, green body.
A duke furrows his brow,
thumps out that same stiff question.
No matter what I say
the answer is always the same.
Everybody gets a little.
At night, young boys risk rock salt
to steal me from my chamber.
My vines, helpless in the field, chant,
"Live long, Liz, live long!"
Foolish boys dip small quick fingers
inside my cool rind,
divide my red fat.
Their treasonous mouths
spit black seeds.
The regime of the future takes root.
Older boys fill me with booze,
suck me dry with royal straws.
This is the end of my reign.
The soil, my only loyal subject,
carries me away in a slow moldy coach.

—John Bush

THE MAGICIAN IN THE BOATING PARTY

He is standing in a corner
Rolling up his shadow
It is the silk handkerchief
He stuffs in his lapel pocket.

Small applause.
A red music begins.

Next, he mounts the stage
And reaching back
Picks up his footprints
Placing them one by one
In the palm of his hand—
It is a stack of flapjacks
He eats as if it were evidence.

No one is quite sure
What he is doing now,
There in the middle of the great stage—
Concentration showing all over his face.

An assistant dabs at the sweat,

But then the wind stalls
And falls straight down

Into his cupped hands,
He carries it off stage
to thunderous applause.
He has left us here,

Rows and rows of blank faces,
As if the swirling prints
Of our individual finger tips
Were a single pattern.

We leave the theater slowly
Testing the climate
As if it were bath water
For a lover.

—WILLIAM BOWIE

CODES

Through gray-green, sheer curtains,
these old walls appear dyed grass,
and when dying sun shafts splinter
on the faded, broken window panes
and haunt this tiny room with hints
of a cold winter coming, here I sit,
deciphering your summer love notes.

—MICHAEL ANDERSON

NEAR SAC CITY: PREFACE

We were killing pigeons
down in the yard
four summer kids
a knot with dogs and pups and a kitten
resting the rifle
along the pumphouse roof
squinting off the sun
slowly sighting in
while the flock circled
circled
then settled
on the spine of the big humpbacked barn

Snap
a single shot
would shock
them into upward chaos
resolved in seconds
to a patterned family
flighting in a great rounded path
over three farms
there and nearby

Zowee
skybound birds
Hey

you'll be back
except one

who had gone rolling and flapping down the roof's angle
over the edge
into the sideyard in a flurry of dislodged shingle sand
and broken feathers

Three out of four that afternoon
were only winged
but we dreamed ourselves
pioneer shots
minutemen
marine sharpshooters at such a distance
we chased them down
we four yapping kids
we black bird dogs
we pups and Janie's kitten
we
grabbed them up
walking wounded
some had lice
broke a wing or leg
so they could never fly
barely hobble
threw them into the hoglot
flap flop
chased by piglets
ha ha see how they run
finally eaten
feathers and all
by sows and sires

One bird
violet brown and scuzzy white
crapped on my hand
blood and muck
all up the sleeve of the flannel shirt

grandmother gave me for Christmas
I slung it by a wing
into the manure mud
flapping and drowning
pigs came to say hello

Up at the house
the backdoor screen opened
and shut
bang once
slap
an echo
off the bare-faced barn

My uncle
who'd ridden a tank in the war
who'd killed Nazis
who'd come home
with a funny leg
with four bullet scars
shrapnel needling his bones
came down around the machine shed
between hen house and corn crib
to the hoglot
to we eight

we kids and dogs
we pups
we kittens
while the last bird
struggled in the wallow
and a pig munched its wing and head

My uncle
without his cane
I wondered how
stopped and stood
finally said

we don't do that
in this country

The Starkey boys
Steve and Sonny
went on back home
Janie cried and wet her pants
my uncle
took her hand
went away from the yard
between corn crib and hen house
around the machine shed
to the house
I went too
later
put my bolt-action .22
behind the washroom door
and didn't use it again
until winter

—VerKuilen B. Ager

ROWBOAT

It is night & an opening window
I beg the hour or the lake
as a pond. It follows
the silence. A car backfires
& I am no longer asleep.

A man enters my room.
He is looking for a famous book.
There are many fingers
in the drawer, a light hand
on my forehead. I tell him:

She has the fever.

He begins a calypso song.
My wife takes off her socks
to listen. Years before,
at the alley of the beach,
she remembers. I grow dizzy.

Then they are alone. He
puts all the jewelry in a paper bag.
They undress again & again.

He instills her with a slender
& vacuous magic. Flowers are

brought in by a stranger.
I follow him in the room.
We all thank him as he leaves.

I hide with the solitary droppings.
The bed rustles,
rests.
We had forgotten the squeakings.
It is in the nature of things.

Then the rain.

—HOWARD AARON

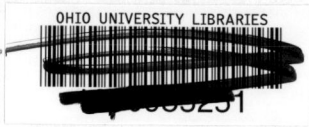